Terri

At the Interface

Volume 45
A volume in the *At the Interface* project
'Perspectives on Evil and Human Wickedness'

Probing the Boundaries

Territories of Evil

Edited by

Nancy Billias

Amsterdam - New York, NY 2008

The paper on which this book is printed meets the requirements of "ISO 9706:1994, Information and documentation - Paper for documents - Requirements for permanence".

ISBN: 978-90-420-2369-7

Printed in the Netherlands

Contents

Welcome to *At the Interface/Probing the Boundaries*

By sharing insights and perspectives that are both inter-disciplinary and multi-disciplinary, *ATI/PTB* publications are designed to be both exploratory examinations of particular areas and issues, and rigorous inquiries into specific subjects. Books published in the series are enabling resources which will encourage sustained and creative dialogue, and become the future resource for further inquiries and research.

Territories of Evil is a volume which belongs to the research project *Perspectives on Evil and Human Wickedness* (www.wickedness.net). This wide ranging project seeks to explore issues connected with evil, suffering, pain and the consequences of human actions. It recognises that even the language of 'evil' is a problem, and attempts to find ways of beginning to make sense of human wickedness.

Key themes that are central to the project include:

- the language of evil
- the nature and sources of evil and human wickedness
- moral intuitions about dreadful crimes
- psychopathic behaviour; is a person mad or bad?
- choice, responsibility, and diminished responsibility
- social and cultural reactions to evil and human wickedness
- the portrayal of evil and human wickedness in the media and popular culture
- suffering in literature and film
- individual acts of evil, group violence, holocaust and genocide; obligations of bystanders
- terrorism, war, ethnic cleansing
- the search for meaning and sense in evil and human wickedness
- the nature and tasks of theodicy
- religious understandings of evil and human wickedness
- postmodern approaches to evil and human wickedness
- ecocriticism, evil and suffering
- evil and the use/abuse of technology; evil in cyberspace

Dr Robert Fisher
Inter-Disciplinary.Net
www.inter-disciplinary.net

Introduction: Considering Evil

Nancy Billias

1. First Impressions

The conference which took place in Salzburg in March 2006 was my first experience with the Interdisciplinary.net conference project on evil. As a philosopher, I have studied the "problem" of evil for several years; as a psychotherapist and social worker, I had experienced evil firsthand in the damaged lives of children and families for twenty years before that. I have stood between a wife and her husband as she made the decision to return, yet again, to a situation of physical abuse that somehow they both called love. I have cooked dinner with a paedophile, content in the knowledge that as long as he was in my home, he was not out on a playground looking at little boys. I have listened to a 10-year-old sex offender recount with no affect - certainly not remorse - why what he did to his little sister was no worse than cheating on a spelling test. I have sat at the bedside of a woman weeping over the death of her newborn, and listened to her litany of denial, heart-sick sorrow, and impotent promises to kick the addiction that led to the baby's death. I wondered what new insights on evil this conference might afford me.

As it turned out, the conference was quite disturbing on many levels. Each day the snowy silhouette of picture-postcard Salzburg stood in stark contrast to the intense exploration of human wickedness that filled the conference rooms. A truly interdisciplinary group (including nurses, psychologists, philosophers, professors of literature, history, computer studies, and all sorts of social science) presented papers on the Holocaust, terrorism, all forms of abuse, virtual and actual violence, and depravity in a variety of media, from film to literature to animé to the Internet. We talked about villains and victims, dictators and anti-heroes. The group experienced its own small encounters with evil even before the conference began: several would-be participants were unable to obtain travel visas from their governments. During the conference, evil continued to manifest: a passport and wallet were stolen; miscommunication and misunderstandings broke out between participants; people felt overlooked, offended, attacked. Yet the gathering was lively, collegial, engaging, sometimes even light-hearted. Each day I was more and more unsure of what I thought. The conference left me with more questions than answers; for a philosopher, this is an extremely satisfying outcome.

The chapters in this volume will give the reader some idea of the flavour of that gathering. Each of the chapters winds around the same theme: the awareness and recognition of the force of evil as a matter of urgency, as a point of desperate importance in the world today.

One paper which does not appear in the present volume is particularly emblematic of the spirit of the event, in that it represents a deeply-felt reflection from the border between the personal and the professional. This paper came from the main organizer of the event, Rob Fisher, who is the driving force behind Interdisciplinary.net. In one sense, listening and speaking from that borderland is one of the primary messages of the conference: evil is not only an abstract concept to be analyzed intellectually, but a concrete reality that we all experience and wrestle with on an ongoing basis; to truly understand evil we must always approach it from both angles: the intellective and the phenomenological. This same assertion resounds through each of the chapters in this volume. In his paper, Fisher issued a call to conference participants and to all who come into contact with the topic, to broaden both our understanding of the notion of evil and our responses to it. The Salzburg conference was infused with the spirit of that call.

In his essay "Let Evil Be Evil," Fisher urges us first to move beyond the traditional notion of evil as merely a matter of human ill-will, and rather to understand the tragedy of loss as a manifestation of evil. To humans, who are congenitally programmed to try to make sense of what we encounter, the rupture of loss is experienced as a wound, as a question that admits of no answer. This, Fisher maintains, is the essence of evil: the palpable presence of absence, ineluctable consciousness of the void. His argument stems from his own reflections on the death of his child. What he observed in those around him concerning this event was a tendency, almost a compulsion, to diminish the experience of loss, to attempt to compartmentalize it, to name it, to categorize it, as a means of taming the wild, boundless madness that might otherwise overtake the world of sense. In responding to the evil of that loss, Fisher heard the sound of the void - and the ensuing flurry of people trying in vain to slam the windows to keep it out, by attempting to sugar-coat the agonizing pain, rationalize the irrational, or justify the inconceivable.

Instead, Fisher exhorts us to consider evil as it really is, insofar as we can bear to do so. This, he says, is the only truly moral response to evil: Open your eyes to all its ugly, disgusting, heart-rending reality. Let it live within you, be with it, give it time and space for reflection. Only when we are ready to encounter evil in such a way will we become able to withstand it, to fight against it, and to deal with it as a truth. That way lies real hope for the future of meaning. It was this attitude which made the Salzburg conference so exciting and impactful.

2. Towards New Conceptions of and New Responses to Evil

The first chapter in this volume presents a rather new way of understanding and thinking about, perhaps even making sense of evil. Psychologists Christopher Burrell and John Rempel devised a series of experiments to understand people's emotional responses to evil. What is it about certain actions that engenders consciousness of evil? Is the sense of evil simply another name for fear, disgust, or some combination of the two? Burris and Rempel offer the hypothesis that people identify what they encounter as evil if it appears to them to be intentionally and undeservedly harmful. That is, persons experience evil when a harmful action is intended which is not justified by any prior action on the part of the person acted upon. Thus, in the traditional nursery rhyme Miss Muffett ran away when she saw the spider because she perceived some potential harm that the spider intended to inflict on her, though she herself was just sitting there innocently minding her curds and whey. The authors designed and carried out a thought experiment to confirm and clarify their hypothesis.

But why, Burris and Rempel asked, did Miss Muffett run away? Is the fight/flight instinct really so one-dimensional? Their subsequent research focused on refining the range of possible responses to a perception of evil. They identified four dominant attitudes, and their article explores the nature, risks, and benefits of each. It also highlights the often helix-like nature of exploring evil: as the researchers began to look more closely at how people respond to what they perceive as evil, they also began to see how the different types of response themselves become models which affect the perception of evil.

A similarly helix-like movement can be observed threading through the third chapter. In "How Civilians Became Targets," William Myers examines how changes in language can result in shifting understandings of moral acceptability and responsibility. As advances in military technology make it increasingly possible to divorce humans from the actual act of killing an enemy, the concept of being personally responsible for the death of that enemy comes to seem an empty abstraction. Thus we have the development of such tactics - and such terms - as 'carpet bombing,' 'side effects,' and 'collateral damage' - none of which mention the possibility of actual deaths ensuing from one's action. Myers explores how the principles of Just War Theory, which attempt to provide some sort of ethical scaffolding for military thinking, have been perverted by modern theorists to allow for a fuzzy non-understanding of personal responsibility, such that, while these days, anyone can be a target, no one appears to be responsible. Myers sees this confusion as a moral catastrophe of the most urgent order, as it leads us to a lack of self-understanding on individual and societal levels.

Wayne Cristaudo's chapter, "Evil and the Loss of Intellect", provides a slightly different slant on both this theme and the subject that Fisher focused on in his address. Cristaudo sees evil as anti-rationality, a form of mindlessness that begins on the individual level and becomes exponentially malevolent as it is accepted by groups, societies, and civilizations. The devil, as Cristaudo understands it, is a force that is both within and beyond us, a force that, if we are not very careful, will ultimately enslave us. This force urges us to do what Fisher initially warned us against: to speak of things as other than they are, to avert thought of evil by calling it by other names, and so to move away from truth. The desire to protect ourselves from evil by refusing to name it becomes a perverted means of promoting evil: by hewing to lies rather than truth, by helping us to deceive ourselves, by disordering meaning. Cristaudo advises a return to a more reflective stance on the true nature of the meaning of love and belief.

Stephen Morris' essay analyzes one historical manifestation of such a stance, by examining the actions of Vaclav of Bohemia, who became known in Christian circles as Saint Wenceslas. According to Morris, three classic responses to evil developed as normative in Byzantine Christianity: fighting back, pacifism, and apparent cooperation in order to subvert. Morris examines the dual moral roles of emperor and Christian in the writings of Chrysostom and their subsequent realization by the emperor Justinian. He then outlines how in 921 Vaclav interpreted these roles and chose to fight political evil by the middle road: non-violence and self-surrender. During his life, Vaclav reinvigorated the practice of Christianity in Bohemia; by his death, he provided a model of self-sacrifice of the ruler on behalf of the nation, following the role of Christ as 'passion-bearer.'

Morris then raises questions about the moral acceptability of pacifism in the face of evil, and compares the differing perspectives of Eastern and Western Christianity on this issue. He then turns to a much more contemporary exploration of the same question, encouraging us to look in the mirror at our own responses to current political acts of aggression. As another model, he outlines the actions of several bishops of the Russian Orthodox Church in response to the actions of the Soviet regime between 1917 and 1964. He also looks at the bold preaching of the Roman Catholic bishop Konrad von Preysing as a form of non-violent and subversive *Resistenz* to the evil of Nazism. His essay ends by challenging us to reflect on the ethical nature of these varying responses.

Next, Lee Quinby examines two discourses on evil which have long shaped U.S. culture. The first emphasizes an apocalyptic sense of doom and divine decree. The second, which might seem to contradict the first, stresses human agency and social justice. In between the two spins a culture of moral confusion: rampant individualism combined with a possibly fatal case of nationalist group-think. In the context of these competing discourses, Quinby asks, how can people learn to live morally? The answer, she suggests, can be found in an aesthetic counter-tradition which underlies U.S. culture, a tradition in which ambiguity and interdependence are accentuated as foundational to a 'geopolitics of prevailing': the tradition exemplified by two quintessentially American authors, Melville and Faulkner.

But before we can look for an answer, we need to understand the genesis and impact of these discourses on the society which they have helped to frame. As Quinby points out, both perspectives share the metaphysical belief that humanity can be reduced to strict dualism: us *versus* them, winner *versus* loser, good *versus* evil, action *versus* reflection. Such absolutist essentialism does not admit of ambiguity; rather, it implies, justifies, and relies on moral certitude. It is both rooted in and dependent on a literal view of the world, which chooses a specific set of proof-texts around which to construct impassible levies - impregnable to the needs and demands of the other. Quinby sketches the rise of this worldview through U.S. history from the Puritans to the "Axis of Evil."

She then turns to Melville's portrayal in *Moby Dick* of the danger to which several of our authors have already alluded: the mindlessness of power-hungry political leaders which comes to take the place of the individual conscience as mass movements overcome our sense of personal responsibility. Quinby challenges us not to succumb to this trend, but rather to rise against it in a staunch refusal of such doom-saying. If we follow Melville's anti-hero, we will sink into the narcissistic sea with Ahab, and drown in human treachery. But to do so, Quinby asserts, would be to miss the point of Melville's scathing social critique. Rather, she says, we should follow the example of the sole survivor, Ishmael, who lives to tell the tale. Quinby ends by quoting another iconic American author, William Faulkner, who in his Nobel Prize acceptance speech urged young writers to devote themselves to encouraging others, even if their writing is inspired by nuclear fear. The poet's task, as Faulkner conceives it, is to prevail over doom-saying, and perhaps even over doom itself, by presenting alternatives, even fictive ones. So doing can effect a shift away from totalizing beliefs towards the possibility that meaning may be, at least in part, constructed through context, and thus open to change. This shift may be the first fundamental step towards a different kind of future, one that leads away from the apocalypse and towards a geopolitics not of domination, but of cooperation, away from fear and towards something like hope.

Scott Powers' essay on the 2003 novel *Windows on the World* explores one powerful literary example of Quinby's theme. Frédéric Beigbeder's compelling novel provides a post-modern framework for thinking about the events of September 11, 2001. Powers follows a series of literary analysts to unfold a contemporary and specifically post-modern understanding of evil. Prior to the Holocaust, evil was generally understood as a quality measurable on some sort of 'moral continuum' between vice and virtue. The inhumane horrors of the Holocaust went, in a perversion of Nietzsche's trenchant phrase, 'beyond good and evil.' Thus, after the Holocaust, theorists looked for a new model of understanding evil, and eventually "outlined a post-modern perspective on evil by reconsidering human tragedies as the products of multiple forces and historical conditions that exceed human agency."[1] The events of 9-11 engendered a similar sort of immeasurable horror, and similar attempts at understanding. As Powers points out, what both events attack is the notion of the individual. Both events defy attempts to posit blame on any one agent, and neither has either a specific target or victim. The evil in both is of a more absolute nature of pervasive but diffuse destruction. Rather than agent or patient, the self is understood as a vehicle for action or suffering on behalf of impersonal forces. Thus both intentions and results have a multiple, fragmentary character, well-suited to the post-modern understanding of meaning.

Powers then inquires what, if anything, a post-modern analysis may have to add to the question of evil. He sees the post-modern perspective as contributing something of significance to our understanding of the *origins* of evil. More specifically (and here his work intersects directly with the research of Burris and Rempel), he explores "how the ways in which we think and speak about evil are themselves implicated in the genesis of events that society considers evil."[2] We bring down upon ourselves the evils we imagine and portray in literature and popular media. As we envision the world, so it becomes. As the lines between virtuality and reality become ever more blurred, our understanding of morality is contorted and obscured. In a final, post-modern twist, it is left open-ended, ambiguous, uncertain. But Powers denies that such an understanding is inevitably nihilistic. Perhaps, he argues, it allows for a more accurately complex perception of evil, one that will enable us not to give up, but to go on.

Charles Nuckolls' chapter explores yet another twist on how notions of evil are portrayed, communicated, and promoted through literature. "The Uncanny and the Feminine Sublime in Japanese Political Fantasy" delves into the world of Japanese popular culture, in which traditional mythological figures are given contemporary expression, in *manga* (comic books) and *anime* (animated cartoons). Nuckolls shows compellingly how in these media the uncanny and the feminine are woven together in fantastic ways in order to explaining or upholding dominant political perspectives. He argues that comprehending this relationship is key to understanding the Japanese sense of self both on a personal and a national level, and thus to understanding Japanese ideas of agency, authenticity, and the possibility of transformation. Nuckolls' chapter provides an illuminating introduction to these popular art forms and their shaping of a national soul.

The next chapter in the volume was in fact the first paper of the conference, and opened the proceedings in a most provocative manner. Roger Davis introduces us to a very specific type of evil in the form of two rather appalling manifestations: a cannibal and an autophage. He notes that our attention is immediately captivated by one (the cannibal, for whom we have well-developed tropes), while the other is largely overlooked. On possible explanation for this, he suggests, is that we have no place to put the notion of a person who consumes his or her own flesh; this is a form of being with the self that we cannot really conceive of. Yet, Davis maintains, this act of self-destruction may well be illustrative of the overall nature of evil in contemporary society, and while shockingly real, may also be an apt metaphor for our times.

Davis outlines and analyzes the details of a case which occurred in Germany in 2001, and which has only just gone to trial in 2006. A self-designated cannibal sought (and found) a willing victim for a fatal sexual encounter, in the course of which the victim participated in the consumption of his own penis, after which he was killed and his body preserved and consumed by the cannibal. Davis explores the possible psychoanalytic meanings of this exchange for both parties.

In the course of this analysis, Davis raises several intriguing and challenging questions. We instinctively perceive such an act as evil, but in what ways is it transgressive? The cannibal was ultimately arrested. But on what charge could he be prosecuted? Cannibalism is not illegal in Germany - perhaps such a law was not previously imagined as necessary. Are such actions a form of madness? Were the cannibal and the autophage engaged in the shared psychotic bond known as a *folie-à-deux?* Is perversion essentially psychotic? And finally, what might such an action have to say about our own senses or illusions of identity? In what ways might cannibalism, and specifically auto-cannibalism, reflect or project the appetites of contemporary Western society?

Alejandro Cervantes-Carson's chapter describes another personal encounter with evil, much less grotesque but no less compelling. In 2003, Cervantes-Carson had the opportunity to interview Luis Echeverría, who had been president of Mexico during a turbulent and epochal time of unrest and upheaval, and was being prosecuted for crimes against humanity during his regime. In his chapter, Cervantes-Carson takes a phenomenological approach to narrating both the interview and his own reactions to meeting and speaking with an incarnation of political evil. He explores the ethical crises that he experienced in this process, and reflects on subjectivity, both his own and that of Echeverría. In the course of preparing for and carrying out the interview, Cervantes-Carson encountered some deeply disturbing questions. Who holds what power over the 'truth' of what is said in an interview? What is the nature of the gaze of the one being gazed upon? What ethical stance can or should one hold towards a host whom one knows to be a brutal murderer? Is it possible to meet such an other without either demonizing him or being complicit in his crimes?

Anders Johansson approaches the question of evil from a much more theoretical perspective. He sees scholarly discussion of evil as primarily problematized in one of two ways: either as a practical matter, and thus in some way measurable, and so open to minimization or even trivialization; or as ontological, and thus enshrouded in myth or mystery. Either approach, he contends, is a dangerous fallacy based on a hidden assumption. Although philosophy (at least since Heidegger) has lost its status as an ideologically pure vehicle, somehow literature is still felt to be acceptably and effectively neutral. As Powers has already shown, the post-modern, and allegedly post-metaphysical perspective in fact continues to hold on to certain metaphysical ideals; here Johansson cites the enduring notion of the inherent goodness of literature. Rejecting this presupposition, Johansson turns to the comments of Theodor Adorno on the possibility of using literature as a means towards understanding evil (encapsulated as "poetry after Auschwitz"). Following Adorno, Johansson explores the notion that literature cannot and need not be privileged as being above morality - that evil can be found in literature as readily as anywhere else. The redeeming quality of literature, if there is one, lies in its capacity for stimulating understanding, reflection, and possibly even reconciliation, in a way that philosophy is no longer able to do.

Johansson illustrates this argument with two contemporary artworks, the Austrian film *Funny Games* and the Swedish novel *Äldreomsorgen i övre Kågedalen* (*Elder Care in the Upper Valley of*

Kåge). Both are narrations of sadistic violence unredeemed by happy endings or revelations of meaning. Yet both open up avenues for deep understanding, by providing the audience an opportunity to recognize, reflect on, and ultimately reject evil. Both do this through an aesthetic appeal, which offers a wealth of images even as it strips the viewer/reader of distance, objectivity, and moral neutrality. By becoming a participant in the aesthetic event, one becomes a collaborator in the violence that is perpetrated. Thus one is no longer a bystander or even a witness, but is implicated in the action. This change of perspective, Johansson asserts, is one way in which literature can meaningfully engage in moral activity: not trivializing evil events, but rather "doing justice to the particular in its particularity."[3] This is one way of living out what Fisher described as letting evil *be* evil, and so, perhaps, coming to some sort of reconciliation with the evil in ourselves.

Confronting the evil within ourselves was very much the impetus behind my own contribution to this volume. I began my exploration of evil by attempting to hold the mirror of self-consciousness up to the concept of terrorism. I wanted to investigate an idea which to me seemed obvious: given the right circumstances, the right set of perceived threats, any one of us can become a terrorist. My inquiry into this concept went in the two directions of my main areas of expertise, psychoanalytic theory and contemporary Continental philosophy. The object relations analyst Otto Kernberg has written at length what he theorizes as the psychoanalytic origins of terrorism, rooted in the primitive paranoid process that is projected and expressed as the earliest internalization of a persecutory experience - separation from the mother. From this primary terror, Kernberg maintains, one can discern the evolution of all sorts of fear of the other, which may be expressed as prejudice, intolerance, or hatred. In this interpretation, difference is understood as a danger which must be pre-emptively annihilated, lest the self be obliterated. This existential dread is acted out by groups or individuals who feel that they have no other way to be recognized.

The struggle for recognition, however, is not thereby achieved, but rather permanently impeded. What the id desires (perfect static unity) is permanently frustrated by the reality principle (the disruptive presence of others). But the French philosopher Alain Badiou helped me to understand a new way through this impasse, with his ethical model, based on set theory of 'counting-for-one.' In Badiou's model, the other becomes necessary to my achieving full subjectivity (and in a less idealistic way than Levinas' model would suggest). Using Badiou's model as a platform for my own ethical theorizing, I propose a new location for the ethical valuation of an event: neither in agent nor patient, but rather in the phenomenological and ontological space between. This proposal, which has its own post-modern overtones, is an attempt to reintroduce the notion of interdependence and ambiguity, to clear a space for thinking into which responsible selves may yet emerge.

The theme of responsibility and thinking for the future is very much at the heart of the final two chapters. In "As Others See Us," Graeme Goldsworthy invites us into the world of professional landmine clearers. As a humanitarian activity, this would at first glance appear to be unequivocally an action on the side of good. Goldsworthy unpacks the seamy sides of this endeavour. He reveals its sketchy past, its questionable present and dubious future. Why, he asks incisively, are the same countries and corporations that produce and market landmines the same ones to profit from their defusing? How are such contracts conceived, condoned, and encouraged by governmental and non-governmental agencies alike? Why are the efforts to clear landmines not controlled and implemented by the indigenous peoples whose land the mines endanger? What happens to the supposed neutrality of NGOs who accept contracts in this supposedly humanitarian but in fact highly profitable undertaking? Do they not become complicit in the chain of dependence that keeps indigenous peoples subjugated to more technologically advanced nations? If knowledge is power, what are we to make of the flow of information that these NGOs provide, which may facilitate future military planning against those peoples? And finally, is the current structure of landmine clearance the most ethical, the least evil possible? In this field report, Goldsworthy advocates the rights of indigenous communities to take control over their own demining efforts, as a means of ending the vicious cycle of domination.

The next essay in this collection deals with another, very different manifestation of evil: heterosexual paedophilia in the U.K. Sarah Goode, a medical sociologist, explores a notion that has been suggested by several of the other contributors: the evil we see is the evil *we* want to see, the evil *we* help to construct and define, to make palatable, desirable, and marketable through popular mass media. It is *our* evil. Yet we resolutely (and almost uniformly) endeavour to promote the idea that evil is located in the other, in unclassifiable monsters utterly different from ourselves.

Goode examines the details and coverage of several recent child murders in the U.K., and explores what is included and omitted in shaping reactions to these events. She then looks at competing understandings of paedophiles and child sexual abusers. The dominant school of thought seeks to compartmentalize paedophilia as a uniquely dangerous perversion, thus splitting the world into essentialist categories, and so absolving 'normal people' of blame or guilt, and opening the way to scapegoating what is perceived as different, deviant, and depraved. This stance forecloses reflection or the possibility of reconciliation. We are able, in this interpretation, to view paedophiles as other than, less than human.

But while dominant, this viewpoint is by no means the only way of thinking about paedophilia in current parlance. The inherent extremism of this stance has naturally given rise to a comedic backlash which pokes fun at its rigidity. Beyond that, the Internet is full of sites which promote paedophilia as a normative and positive activity, as a natural expression celebrating the beauty of innocence, or as a form of sexual and political identity "akin to other oppressed sexual minorities."[4] Some endorse and encourage an almost chivalrous, and certainly romantic ideal of sexual intimacy between young girls and adults. Goode introduces us to some of these perspectives, both in a review of Internet sites and through consideration of the 2005 film *The Woodsman*. Finally, Goode settles in to a reflection on why the dominant perspective has taken the ascendancy. What are the benefits to society of this viewpoint, and what are the risks? What are the implications, practical and theoretical, of this stance? How can we move forward in such a way as to reduce evil and increase good?

The final chapter of this volume deals with the problem of innate aggression. Havi Carel examines Freud's understanding of the death drive, arguing that we should not view his position as a pessimistic message of despair but rather as a new way to formulate the 'ethics of finitude'; rather than thinking of death as a limitation, a more productive reading sees it as a limitation which can be a source of joy. All human emotion – love, hate, joy, beauty – are inextricably grounded in transience; positive experiences intimate mortality, indeed, are only what they are because the tone of finitude is bound up with them all. Recognition of this fact turns the anticipation of death into a potentially productive if not therapeutic experience as we learn to control our emotions and dominate the superego which is the cause of so much of our aggression and instinct toward violence and destruction.

Through her critical analysis, Goode and Carel trace out a number of themes that have, in fact, run through most of the essays in this collection. First, whether we are considering child sexual abuse, landmines, terrorism, cannibalism, or any other manifestation of evil, we need to be careful not to attempt to distance the concept of evil as different, as outside of ourselves, as other.

Second, we need to remain open to evil, or at least leave evil open as a question to be explored, critiqued, interrogated, reflected upon, owned. We must, ourselves, be open to new interpretations, new perspectives, new understanding. This may not be a comfortable process, it may in fact be quite disturbing. But ultimately, it may be the only way forward towards a truly ethical response.

Notes

[1] See below, p.131.
[2] See below, p.131.
[3] See below, p.180.
[4] See below, p.209.

The Devil You Think You Know: A Psychology of Evil

Christopher T. Burris and John K. Rempel

Abstract: In this chapter, we argue that evil is the label people assign to events that are characterized by three psychologically meaningful properties. Specifically, we suggest that the label of "evil" is particularly likely to be applied to events perceived to involve *harm* that is *intentional* and *unjustified*. We subsequently present a model of four dominant responses to whatever people regard as evil - ignoring, embracing, attacking, and avoiding - and we consider the risks and benefits of each. We also offer speculations on how these chronic response styles themselves may affect what is perceived as evil, and why. Finally, we suggest that the variations in people's perceptions of and responses to evil that we have identified may aid in understanding the profound disagreements that often emerge concerning nature and experience of evil.

Keywords: psychology; labelling; prototype; responses to evil

1. Introduction

An interdisciplinary dialogue on evil is both valuable and challenging. It often seems that the concept of evil varies greatly, not only from discipline to discipline, but also from person to person. In adding our psychological perspective to this dialogue, we contend that varied perspectives on evil are not only to be expected, but that such differences are inevitable. Thus, our goal in this chapter is not to bridge or integrate the differing perspectives, but rather to offer an understanding as to why such differences are bound to occur. We will attempt to do so in three steps. First, we will present our understanding of what evil is. Second, we will present a model of the basic ways in which people respond to evil, as they perceive it. Third, we will speculate regarding whether chronic tendencies to respond to evil in certain ways may, in fact, cycle back into what people perceive to be evil, and why.

Our approach to evil is *psychological*. The chief implication of this is that we make no attempt to define evil in *a priori* categorical terms as a philosopher or a theologian might. Indeed, we suggest that evil must be *perceived as "evil"* to be psychologically relevant.[1] Consequently, however valuable attempts to define evil in categorical terms may be, our focus is as much or more on "evil" - a label that people use to come to terms with specific experiences - than on evil *per se*. Stated differently, we assume that "evil" is inherently subjective - that it (like beauty) is in the eye of the beholder.[2] We assume, moreover, that "evil" is inherently contextual - that the same act may be perceived as more or less evil depending on the situation. For example, consider the following act:

"Ms. X killed two men."

We suspect that, taken by itself, Ms. X's behaviour would evoke negative reactions - perhaps even judgments of evil - from many people. Observe what happens when the identical behaviour is embedded in different contexts, however:

"Ms. X killed two men *after luring them to her apartment with promises of wild sex*."

"Ms. X killed two men *who were raping her 6-year old daughter*."

The different contexts, we suggest, pull apart judgments of the identical behaviour: we certainly suspect that Ms. X would be perceived as more evil in the former instance than in the latter one. Indeed, in the latter case, it is more likely that her victims would be judged to be evil.

Although the above thought experiment and its conclusion seem intuitively reasonable, as scientific psychologists we generally prefer a method of verification that is more systematic and empirical. That is, we strive to express our ideas in the form of testable predictions, and we design studies, collect data, and subject those data to statistical analyses that yield a probabilistic sense of the plausibility of our predictions.

Consequently, as a first empirical step toward understanding the psychology of evil, we asked approximately 200 Psychology of Evil students at the beginning of the first day of class to list whatever came to mind when they thought of "evil." These students' responses were then coded into the fewest possible meaningful categories: 1) Physical Victimization (e.g., murder, rape, war atrocities); 2) Psychological Victimization (e.g., abuse of power, coercion, betrayal); 3) Emotion (e.g., crying, fear, no hope); 4) Description/Evaluation (e.g., bad, necessary, human nature); 5) Religious Symbols (e.g., devil, 666, Adam and Eve); and 6) Secular Symbols (e.g., money, Darth Vader, black).

Looking for themes across these six categories yields four preliminary insights about what "evil" means to people. First, "evil" is seen as applicable to events involving intentional harm - broadly defined - by one or more perpetrators. Second, "evil" is associated with disapproval and/or negative emotional reactions. Third, "evil" is a salient enough part of human experience that people seek both to explain it and to represent it symbolically. Finally, although the concept of evil may have its historical origin in the religious realm, neither the experience nor the symbolic representation of "evil" is restricted to religious motifs.

Given the rather select sampling of Canadian university students (enrolled in a psychology of evil class, no less!), some specific associations to "evil" that occurred - like references to "Dr. Evil" in the *Austin Powers* films - would not necessarily be expected to occur in other samples. This factor notwithstanding, we would not necessarily expect that associations to "evil" among the broader population would differ substantially at a more global level. Indeed, a cursory examination of the contents of several recent social scientific volumes concerning evil.[3 4 5 6] reveals an almost exclusive focus on human intentions and behaviours involving harm to others. Of course, social scientists are not theologians or philosophers, so pointing out their focus on human behaviour is hardly revelatory. The interesting thing, however, is that an equation between evil and harmful human acts seems to be more or less assumed, as in a seminal volume titled *Evil: Inside Human Violence and Cruelty.*[7] Consequently, although much attention has been devoted to understanding what is often labeled as "evil," very little has been devoted to understanding the label itself - specifically, when and how it is applied.

2. Two out of Three Ain't Evil?: The Evil Prototype

One psychological approach that has proven useful in understanding when and how concept labels are applied involves the *prototype*, which can be understood as a set of characteristics - stored in memory - that most directly capture the essence of a class of objects, persons, or events, and thereby distinguish one class from another.[8] Consider the "chair" prototype, for example: Central features may include a seating area, a back (distinguishing it from a stool), proportionality (distinguishing it from a bench), and primary function (distinguishing it from a toilet). The key idea is that, as more of a prototype's central features are perceived in a novel stimulus, the more likely it is that the stimulus will be seen as belonging to the class or concept represented by the prototype. Still, one or more features can be missing without entirely negating the prototype's applicability: The seat can be removed for repair while the "chairness" of the chair remains intact, for example. Likewise, bean bag chairs have no backs proper, high chairs are as disproportionate as benches, and potty chairs serve the same primary function as do toilets. None of these, however, would be recognized as a chair with the same facility and swiftness as one that possesses all of the central features of "chairness."

The point of this discussion is simple: If evil is a concept, then there may be a prototype of evil composed of one or more central features and stored in memory. The implications of this assertion are considerable: Although the perception of evil is both subjective and contextual, it is not *random*. Rather, this analysis suggests that people may apply the label "evil" whenever enough of the central features of the evil prototype are salient in a given situation. The question, then, is: what are the central features of the evil prototype? Two likely candidates were apparent in people's spontaneous associations discussed earlier: Linking "evil" to murder, rape, betrayal, and the like suggests that both *harm* and *intent* are part of the evil prototype.[9]

Without a doubt, the co-occurrence of harm and intent may be associated with the perception of evil, even if the perpetrators are anthropomorphized mythic figures. Yet not everyone who intentionally harms is "evil." Remember Ms. X, who killed the two men who were raping her daughter: We suspect that very few people would see Ms. X as "evil" under such circumstances - in fact, some might even see her as heroic. This points to a third central feature contained in the prototype of evil: *insufficient justification.* Thus, we suggest that the label "evil" is most often applied in response to *harm* that is perceived as both *intentional* and *unjustifiable.*

We tested this characterization of the evil prototype by conducting another study. Approximately 100 first-day Psychology of Evil students read a brief story about Mr. X, who initiated sexual contact with Y. To assess the effect of harm, some read that Y contracted HIV, whereas others read that Y contracted a "painful but easily treated urinary tract infection," as a result of sexual contact with Mr. X. To assess the effect of intentionality, participants read that Mr. X either did or did not know he was infected when he initiated sexual contact with Y. To assess the effect of justifiability, some read that Y was 30 years old, whereas others read that Y was 12 years old. Thus, participants read any one of eight versions of the story, after which they rated - among other things - how evil they judged Mr. X to be on a 1 (*not at all*) to 7 (*very much*) scale.

Consistent with our conceptualization of the evil prototype, all three target variables affected judgments of evil, such that Mr. X was rated as least evil when he unknowingly transmitted the urinary infection to the 30-year-old, and as most evil when he knowingly transmitted HIV to the 12-year-old. The disparity between average ratings in these two conditions was dramatic - 1.6 in the former and 6.2 in the latter on a 7-point scale. At first glance, this disparity may seem obvious and uninteresting given the respective ages of the victims, for one might expect Mr. X to be branded as a paedophile and seen as evil without qualification when Y was only 12 years old. This did not happen, however: when harm and/or intentionality was reduced, evil ratings for Mr. X dropped considerably (up to 2 points). Likewise, although Mr. X. was given the benefit of doubt when he unwittingly infected Y with either disease, he was seen as somewhat evil (with an average rating around 4) when he knowingly transmitted the minor infection, and very evil (with an average rating of 6) when he knowingly transmitted HIV. Thus, although by no means definitive, this study provides suggestive evidence that harm, intentionality, and insufficient justification are components of the evil prototype.

With this in mind, we should note that, in any given situation, one or more aggravating factors can accentuate specific components of the evil prototype. For example, severe harm is likely associated with more extreme judgments of evil, as illustrated by the intuitive distinction between a "murderer" and a "mass murderer." The role of severity was also evident in the results of our "infection study" above, in that judgments of perpetrator evil were greater when he infected the victim with HIV versus a painful but treatable infection. Indeed, although we doubt that there is a clearly defined threshold of perceived harm beyond which the label "evil" is deemed appropriate, we have little doubt that the link between perceived severity of harm and "evil" helps account for the status of the latter as a "fine china word" that is typically brought out and used only on special occasions.

Just as perceived severity amplifies harm's contribution to judgments of evil, repetition highlights the role of intentionality. Certainly a single "evil" act has a tainting quality with respect to one's impression of another person. The tainting capacity of multiple harmful acts is much greater, however, because repetition practically eliminates the possibility that such acts were prompted by anything other than the desires of the doer. Repetition is thus diagnostic: "Evil deeds" are done by "evil people." Indeed, we suspect that the "serial" in "serial killers" helps account for why these killers are perceived by many as the very embodiment of evil. Repetition is also informative: If "evil deeds" are done by someone *because* he or she is "evil," then it is reasonable to expect that that person will do "evil deeds" in the future. In light of this, it is curious that many legal jurisdictions have now employed "habitual offender" sentencing (sometimes nicknamed "the bitch," according to one offender) testifying to repetition's impact on judgments of incorrigibility, if not evil *per se.*[10]

Compared to either harm or intent, perceptions of justifiability are often more subjective and context-dependent: If Ms. X is standing over the still, bloodied bodies of two men with an ice pick in each hand, harm and intent are rather unambiguous. The question of whether her behaviour was justified is much more open to debate, however - and this is precisely where we believe many of the disparities in judgments of evil arise. Multiple, interdependent factors likely to influence the perceived justifiability of an actor's behaviour include the observer's moral principles ("What s/he did was wrong under any circumstances"), proximity to the situation ("To what extent am I a victim, or at least close to someone who is?"), and capacity to take the actor's perspective ("S/he and I are totally different - I would *never* do something like that"), as well as the actor's perceived goals ("Why did s/he do this?"). Regardless of the specific factors that may feed into the judgment, when an act - even a harmful, intentional one - is seen as justifiable, it is unlikely to be seen as "evil." This illustrates the interdependency of the three components of the evil prototype: That is, in any given situation, the impact of any component(s) may be muted by the absence of the other(s), as our "infection study" data have already shown.

Also illustrating the point, when an act is harmful and unjustifiable but unintentional, "evil" may be a less likely label. For example, a driver engrossed in a cell phone conversation who hits and kills a pedestrian may be seen as incredibly irresponsible, even contemptible, but is not likely to be seen as evil. Young children learn and apply this principle early: "I didn't mean to…it was an accident!" really means "Yes, I may have caused indisputable harm, but my behaviour lacked intent. Therefore, please don't see me as evil!"

Finally, intent to cause unjustifiable harm may not be labelled as evil if the intended actions are ineffectual. Take the example of a scraggly canine and his relentless pursuit of a gangly, fast-moving bird. His persistence clearly indicates intention, and his seemingly limitless financial resources rule out justifications for his obsessive pursuit based on hunger. Yet, owing to his mounting, inevitable failures to catch the Roadrunner, Wile E. Coyote (reminiscent of Goethe's Mephistopheles) is certainly more of a comical figure than an evil one. Harmlessness in spite of intent and lack of justification may simply be too laughable and pathetic to be seen as "evil."

3. After the Spider Comes Along: Responses to Evil

The chief importance of the preceding analysis lies in the simple fact that "evil" is a consequential label, one that seldom evokes a neutral response. Indeed, owing to the recurring frequency with which diatribes to rally support against enemies include characterizing the enemy as evil, we might easily surmise that use of the term "evil" is seldom - if ever - intended to evoke a neutral response from the intended audience. What, then, are the possible responses to "evil" so labelled?

Although it is not our first inclination to look to nursery rhymes for great psychological truths, the saga of Miss Muffet serves as a useful starting point for describing our model of responses to evil. As a reminder, the story was:

Little Miss Muffet sat on a tuffet
Eating her curds and whey.
Along came a spider, who sat down beside her
And frightened Miss Muffet away.

For us as psychologists, the core question that emerges from this narrative is: *Why did Miss Muffet run away?* She did have other options, after all: For example, she could have simply brushed the spider aside and paid it little attention. She could have adopted it as a pet. She could have tried to drown it in whey or smash it with her bowl. But she ran. Why?

The text offers a half-answer: Miss Muffet ran because she was frightened. So let us ask another question: *Why was she frightened?* The answer lies in her perception of the spider, and of herself, in that situation: In simple terms, she perceived the spider to be a threat with which she could not cope. A different perception would have yielded a different response.

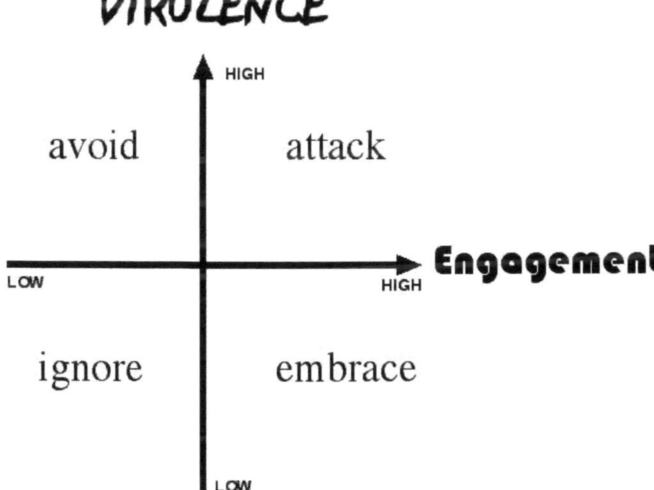

Figure 1. A two-dimensional model of responses to evil

Similarly, people's responses to whatever they label "evil" depends on the extent to which they regard evil as a destructive, threatening force, a dimension that we have termed *Virulence*, and the extent to which they judge directly confronting evil to be appropriate in light of its perceived threatening potentiality, a dimension that we have labelled *Engagement* (see Fig. 1). Crossing the two dimensions yields four distinct responses to evil: Evil may be *avoided* (high Virulence, low

Engagement), *attacked* (high Virulence, high Engagement), *embraced* (low Virulence, high Engagement), or *ignored* (low Virulence, low Engagement). We will describe these four responses in reverse order, and speculate regarding the costs and benefits associated with each.

A. The Ignore Response

Although the label "evil" is usually provocative, it does not always evoke threat or necessitate a response, and so it is simply ignored. Some who opt to ignore evil may do so because they see the concept as an antiquated religious artifact, as hopelessly subjective, or as otherwise empty and irrelevant. Others may acknowledge the viability of the concept while remaining detached from any personal implications thereof.

The extent to which such detachment is motivated, of course, is an open question. It is possible that, for those truly lacking a concept of evil, effortful disengagement is unnecessary: For example, William James wrote of "a way of feeling happy about things immediately,"[11] which he termed "involuntary healthy-mindedness." Although such equanimity could certainly have mental health benefits, we wonder how common such a disposition is. Likely more common are those for whom the dismissal or redefinition of evil serves to relieve them of personal responsibility for action - reminiscent of the U.S. government's preference for the phrase "acts of genocide" versus the word "genocide" in reference to the Rwandan massacres in the 1990s, because the former phrase did not necessitate intervention, whereas the latter did. In such instances, certainly the expedience of "letting oneself off the hook" is offset by adverse consequences for others.

B. The Embrace Response

Like ignoring, embracing is an outgrowth of the perception of evil as relatively non-threatening. Unlike ignoring, however, embracing is typified by motivation to engage evil directly. For those with a predominant embrace response, evil is less likely to be externalized - that is, seen as foreign to oneself - or regarded with dread or disgust. Instead, the attitude is more one of healthy respect: evil may be seen as a logical necessity or counterpart to the concept of good, as a source of creative tension, or as intrinsic to oneself.

On the positive side, the recognition of one's own dark side can serve as a basis for humility and an awareness of the fundamental similarity between oneself and a stigmatized other. This, in turn, can foster a capacity to empathize with, and demonstrate mercy toward, those branded as "evil." On the negative side, it is possible to become so enamoured with one's own destructive potentiality that tenderness and self-restraint are perceived as expendable. In such instances, an individual may identify more readily with "evil" than with "good" - a phenomenon evident among public Satanist groups, for example.

C. The Attack Response

Like embracing, attacking involves confronting evil directly. Among those with a predominant attack response, however, evil is not a sleeping dragon but a rampant lion - a salient, impending threat. Consequently, we would expect militaristic language and imagery to loom large among attackers: evil may be seen as a powerful enemy, but one that can be defeated if people are willing to sacrifice their own interests and band together to protect the greater good.

Consistent with this mindset, we expect that attackers would be willing executors of justice when such a response is necessitated. Unlike embracers, we suspect that attackers may be particularly likely to externalize evil - that is, to deny their own capacity for evil and instead to locate it outside of themselves. In such instances, attackers may be devoid of empathy for a designated enemy and, consequently, their zeal for justice could very easily deteriorate into vigilantism. Moreover, it is possible that the motivational underpinning for some self-designated attackers is self-elevation at the expense of others. Simply put, if one's *raison d'être* is to attack evil, one can feel like a superhero or "the chosen one" only when doing so. Thus, if an evil enemy does not exist, then one may have to be manufactured through propaganda.

D. The Avoid Response

Avoidance shares the recognition of evil's threatening potentiality that is characteristic of an attack response, and the lack of direct confrontation typical of an ignore response, but the combination of these elements means that avoidance differs from both attacking and ignoring in profound ways. That is, among those for whom avoidance is the predominant response, evil may be perceived as too powerful to attack and too menacing to ignore. How, then, is the threat of evil addressed by avoiders?

At least two strategies are possible. The first is based on the premise that avoiders and attackers of evil may co-exist symbiotically. That is, although avoiders do not necessarily see themselves as having the resources to confront evil directly, attackers do. Consequently, as avoiders shrink back in a paroxysm of dread and wish that the "evil thing" be dealt with, attackers are more than happy to comply. Thus, avoiders may readily offer up their allegiance and resources to cocksure attackers who offer the promise of eliminating the threat. In effect, to use a domestic analogy, attackers may become the "designated bug killers."

The second, complementary strategy used by avoiders to help manage the sense of threat evoked by evil is - as the term suggests - deliberate avoidance of situations, symbols, and the like that may serve as reminders of evil's threatening potentiality. This may sometimes be accompanied by attempts to fill the mental spaces with soothing distractions, but this may be more of a compulsion than a choice: In effect, avoiders may not simply "whistle in the dark" - they may hum, sing, and tap their fingers as well.

We sought to test this characterization of avoidance in a pair of recent studies.[12] Specifically, we hypothesized that a chronic response style of avoiding evil would be typified by hypersensitivity to superficial cues suggestive of the "presence" of evil, resulting in intense negative responses that do not involve thinking too deeply about the dreaded object. In the first study we found that among the four responses to evil, avoidance uniquely predicted viewers' guilty verdicts for three teens accused of Satanically-motivated triple homicide in a film documenting the trial. In a follow-up study, avoidance again uniquely predicted seeing a convicted sex offender as evil, as incapable of restitution, and as deserving of annihilation when he was portrayed as enjoying occult (as opposed to "spiritual" or unspecified) reading materials. When the offender was portrayed as enjoying "spiritual" reading (or simply "reading"), avoidance was unrelated to people's reactions. Thus, among people with an avoidant response to evil, traditional symbols of evil - in this case, those associated with the occult - appeared to evoke rigid, punitive responses to the target associated with those symbols.

On the plus side, avoiders seem to take the Christian biblical admonition to "abstain from all appearance of evil"[13] quite literally. More disturbing, however, is the fact that initial reminders of evil may be so aversive to avoiders that they would prefer to make snap judgments in order to forestall more in-depth consideration of the issues at hand. When issues of guilt and punishment are at stake, the consequences of such mental sidestepping could be tragic.

Table 1. How chronic responses to evil may affect the labeling process

	Response to Evil			
	Ignore	Embrace	Attack	Avoid
"Evil" label applied	n/a	slow; n/a	fast	fast
Basis for labelling	n/a	prototype	prototype	symbol(s)
Associated emotion(s)	apathy	empathy?	anger disgust	fear disgust
Behavioural intention	evade respon-sibility	subdue immediate reactions	fight	fight
Additional info sought	no	yes	yes	no
Basis for info seeking	n/a	justify withheld judgement	justify attack	n/a
Elaboration of basis for labelling	low	high	high	low

4. Completing the Circle: How Responses Affect Perceptions

We have thus far discussed what sorts of things people are likely to perceive as or associate with evil, and we have suggested that these perceptions can be understood as resulting from a prototype stored in memory that contains the essential features of evil. We have also presented a model that helps organize people's chronic responses to evil, whatever they perceive it to be. In the final part of this chapter, we offer some speculations with respect to how people's chronic preferences for responding to evil may affect when and why they apply the label "evil." Specifically, we suspect that the tendency to respond to evil in certain ways will affect: 1) how quickly the "evil" label is applied; 2) the basis on which the label is applied; 3) the extent to which people will seek out additional information concerning the situation; and 4) how the act of labelling (or not) may be justified by the labeller (see Table 1 for a summary of our key points).

As we work through each response, it is worth noting that, although we present our speculations as a means of highlighting the distinctive features associated with a person's "predominant response style," we do not assume that a person will only manifest a single response style over time and across situations. That is, although we assume that an individual's style of responding to evil is relatively stable, it is not fixed, nor is it necessarily the embodiment of any one of the four styles that we have presented in "pure" form.

A. Ignoring and Labelling

We have suggested that people whose predominant response is to ignore evil may either be truly lacking a concept of evil or, for various reasons - not the least of which is the desire to evade a sense of responsibility to intervene - may wilfully and disingenuously disavow the concept of evil. Consequently, when faced with a situation in which the "evil" label might be applicable, we would expect ignorers to remain as cognitively disengaged from the situation as possible. We would expect apathy to be the predominant emotional response, and that attention to details of the situation relevant to judgments of harm, intent, or justifiability would be haphazard at best. We would not expect ignorers to consider the concept of evil at all unless coerced to do so, nor would we expect them to seek out additional information concerning the situation to refine their assessment. Indeed, if asked to justify their resistance to apply the "evil" label, we would expect either a minimalist response, akin to a simple denial, or a more elaborate response concerning the irrelevance of the concept of evil that is linked remotely, at best, to the specifics of the situation under consideration.

B. Embracing and Labelling

Earlier we characterized people with a preference for embracing evil as having a healthy respect for what many label as "evil," in part perhaps due to their recognition of their own capacity for destructiveness and consequent internal dialectic. Based on this characterization, although embracers may apply the label "evil" in some situations, we would not expect them to do so swiftly or in a cavalier fashion. Indeed, we might expect embracers to attempt to set aside their immediate emotional reactions in order to assess the specifics of the situation more carefully - specifics that include all three components of the evil prototype. Information and interpretation concerning justifiability may be of particular interest: embracers may attempt, as much as possible, to take the perspective of the perpetrator and to search for mitigating factors inherent in the situation. Such efforts, we suspect, may be motivated by embracers' desire to suspend judgement concerning the "evilness" of the perpetrator. This must not be confused with the apathy and wilful disengagement manifest by ignorers - embracers are not trying to "get off the hook." Quite the contrary: embracers may see themselves as very much "on the hook," such that they cannot label the other as "evil" without also labelling themselves.

C. Attacking and Labelling

Unlike ignorers and embracers, people with a predominant attack response to evil may be swift to apply the "evil" label even based on limited information: two components of the evil prototype - possibly even one - may be sufficient for attackers to label a perpetrator "evil." We would not expect attackers to be particularly attentive to aspects of the perpetrator or situation, such as symbolic evil cues, that are irrelevant to the prototype, however. For example, we found that an attack response was associated with labelling the sex offender as "evil" whether his reading interests were occult (a symbolic cue), spiritual, or unspecified.[14]

We would expect the act of labelling to be accompanied by intense emotional reactions, such as anger or disgust, that are congruent with the desire to eliminate a threatening, offensive perpetrator. Moreover, we would expect attackers to seek out additional information concerning the perpetrator and the situation with an eye toward justifying their own impulse to attack. If asked to explain their rationale for using the "evil" label, we would expect attackers to marshal rather elaborate justifications, reflective of their acute attentiveness to the details that could support their desire to "squash the bug."

D. Avoiding and Labelling

Finally, like attackers, people with a predominant avoid response to evil may be swift to apply the "evil" label based on limited information. Unlike attackers, however, we would not expect avoiders to be particularly attentive to aspects of the perpetrator or situation that are relevant to the prototype. Instead, we expect avoiders to be sensitized to symbolic cues associated with evil when deciding on the applicability of the label. Again, we refer to our study in which we found that the avoid response was predictive of labelling the sex offender as "evil" only when he had occult reading interests.[15] The specificity of this link suggests that avoiders were attending primarily to this symbolic cue, and not to the prototype-relevant information regarding the offender, his crimes, or his victims presented in all three conditions in the study.

As was the case for attackers, we would expect the act of labelling to be accompanied by intense emotional reactions for avoiders, but we would expect fear (and perhaps disgust, but not anger) to predominate. Such reactions are anticipated to be congruent with the desire to run away in true Miss Muffet style. We would not, therefore, expect avoiders to seek out additional information concerning the perpetrator or the situation, and we would expect any subsequently stated rationale for using the "evil" label to have a simplistic, even stilted, quality.

Of course, all responses to evil have the potential to become dysfunctional and counterproductive at their extremes: in the face of horrific injustices, ignorers may turn a blind eye, embracers may become complicit, and attackers may lash out blindly, cheered on by avoiders. If we can understand the emotional reactions and motives behind the differing responses, however, we may perhaps establish a foundation for transforming the more maladaptive or destructive responses to evil as well as the labelling process that allows these responses to thrive.

5. Conclusion

Perhaps the single most important takeaway message of our entire analysis is this: Whatever the precipitating event, *the experience of evil is inescapably psychological*. We have suggested that "evil" is a label that people typically reserve for situations perceived to involve harm that was inflicted intentionally and without adequate justification. As perceptions of harm, intent, and justifiability differ across perceivers, so too do perceptions of evil. Moreover, even if two perceivers were to agree on the applicability of the label "evil" in a given situation, we would not expect that they would necessarily react in the same way, for we have also shown that people's responses to whatever they perceive to be evil - ignore, embrace, attack, avoid - can vary dramatically depending on how personally threatening they regard evil to be, and whether engagement or disengagement is seen as a more fitting response.

"Evil" finds it way into the discourse of philosophers, the exegesis of theologians, the rants of propagandists, the indictments of prosecutors, and the laments of victims. In all cases the same label may have different meanings, and perhaps more importantly, result in different responses. We have not offered a way to unify this diversity - indeed, we do not believe that it is possible - but we have offered a way to understand it. Of course, as with any analysis in its early stages, significant questions remain that have yet to receive even a tentative answer, such as what influences combine to move people toward a predominant style of ignoring, embracing, attacking, or avoiding evil. Nevertheless, we hope that the psychological analysis of evil presented in this chapter helps to shed light on why such an apparently pervasive concept remains the object of some of humanity's most profound disagreements.

Notes

1. Throughout this chapter we will forgo quotation marks when referring to evil as a concept, and include quotation marks when referring to evil as a label.
2. Roy F. Baumeister, *Evil: Inside Human Violence and Cruelty* (New York: W.H. Freeman, 1997).
3. Ibid.
4. Arthur G. Miller, ed., *The Social Psychology of Good and Evil* (New York: Guilford, 2004).
5. Ervin Staub, *The Psychology of Good and Evil: Why Children, Adults, and Groups Help and Harm Others* (New York: Cambridge University Press, 2003).
6. James Waller, *Becoming Evil: How Ordinary People Commit Genocide and Mass Killing* (New York: Oxford University Press, 2002).
7. Baumeister.
8. Nancy Cantor & Walter Mischel, "Prototypes in Person Perception," in *Advances in Experimental Social Psychology, Vol. 12,* ed. Leonard Berkowitz (New York: Academic Press, 1979), 3-52.
9. In this respect, our analysis closely parallels that of Baumeister.
10. For a discussion of uses of the "evil" label in forensic contexts see: Robert I. Simon, "Should Forensic Psychiatrists Testify about Evil?," *Journal of the American Academy of Psychiatry and the Law*, 31 (2003) 413-416; Michael H. Stone, "Sadistic Personality in Murderers," in *Psychopathy: Antisocial, Criminal, and Violent Behavior,* ed. Theodore Millon, Erik Simonsen, Morten Birket-Smith, and Roger D. Davis (New York: Guilford, 1998), 346-355; and Michael Welner, "Response to Simon: Legal Relevance Demands that Evil be Defined and Standardized," *Journal of the American Academy of Psychiatry and the Law*, 31 (2003) 417-421.
11. William James, *The Varieties of Religious Experience: A Study in Human Nature* (New York: MacMillan, 1961).
12. Christopher T. Burris and John K. Rempel, "After the Spider Comes Along: Understanding Responses to Evil." Paper presented at the 7th

Global Conference: Perspectives on Evil and Human Wickedness, Salzburg, Austria, March 13-17, 2006.
13. I Thessalonians 5:22, King James Version
14. Burris and Rempel.
15. Burris and Rempel.

Bibliography

Baumeister, Roy F. *Evil: Inside Human Violence and Cruelty*. New York: W. H. Freeman, 1997.

Burris, Christopher T. and John K. Rempel. "After the Spider Comes Along: Understanding Responses to Evil." Paper presented at the 7th Global Conference: Perspectives on Evil and Human Wickedness, Salzburg, Austria, March 13-17, 2006.

Cantor, Nancy and Walter Mischel. "Prototypes in Person Perception." In *Advances in Experimental Social Psychology, Vol. 12,* edited by Leonard Berkowitz, 3-52. New York: Academic Press, 1979.

James, William. *The Varieties of Religious Experience: A Study in Human Nature*. New York: MacMillan, 1961.

Miller, Arthur G. *The Social Psychology of Good and Evil*. New York: Guilford, 2004.

Simon, Robert I. "Should Forensic Psychiatrists Testify about Evil?" *Journal of the American Academy of Psychiatry and the Law* 31 (2003): 413-416.

Staub, Ervin. *The Psychology of Good and Evil: Why Children, Adults, and Groups Help and Harm Others*. New York: Cambridge University Press, 2003.

Stone, Michael H. "Sadistic Personality in Murderers." In *Psychopathy: Antisocial, Criminal, and Violent Behavior*, edited by Theodore Millon, Erik Simonsen, Morten Birket-Smith, and Roger D. Davis, 346-355. New York: Guilford, 1998.

Waller, James. *Becoming Evil: How Ordinary People Commit Genocide and Mass Killing*. New York: Oxford University Press, 2002.

Welner, Michael. "Response to Simon: Legal Relevance Demands that Evil Be Defined and Standardized." *Journal of the American Academy of Psychiatry and the Law* 31 (2003): 417-421.

How Civilians Became Targets: The Moral Catastrophe of "Collateral Damage"

William Andrew Myers

Abstract: In the history of warfare non-combatants have, from ancient times to the present, been victims of martial violence, sometimes taken as hostages or slaves but more often killed and wounded by accident. Yet in the twentieth century we saw the development of weapons and tactics, especially aerial bombardment that entailed deliberate targeting of non-combatant populations. During the superpower arms race that ensued after the first use of nuclear weapons in wartime, it was part of military doctrine that threatening to destroy the adversary's cities was of the essence of deterrence, and the world settled in for decades of acquiescence in the idea that theoretically, everyone in the world was a potential target. While the arms race has ended, targeting of civilians has not; the more recent perfection of tactics of terrorism has meant that, once again, though on a smaller scale, everyone is a potential target. I make a case for regarding these developments as a moral catastrophe with far-reaching influence on Western culture and self-understanding. More specifically, they constitute an erosion of our most fundamental humanistic value frameworks, revealing a pre-political underlay of nihilism.

Key Words: Non-combatant immunity, World War II, aerial bombardment, Just War Theory, law of war, "collateral damage."

Introduction

Non-combatants have, from ancient times to the present, been victims of warfare, sometimes taken as hostages or slaves or starved to death in sieges, but more often killed and wounded by accident. The twentieth century saw the employment of new weapons and tactics, especially aerial bombardment, that entailed deliberate targeting of non-combatant populations. Along with the concept of total war, these technological developments challenge traditional notions of human life as a value in itself and of warfare as an instrument for human ends. Despite developments in ethical theory and in international law protecting non-combatants and civilians in general from direct assault, military technologies as well as terrorist tactics have rendered these protections moot in many places. The widespread acquiescence of civilian populations to these changes points to an underlying nihilism in society that in turn militates against truly effective measures to curb threats of violence.

1. A Brief History

Prior to the twentieth century, only siege warfare resulted in the deaths of large numbers of civilians. The idea of non-combatant immunity, a slow development of medieval theories of just wars, never strongly applied to sieges. Apart from this exception, warfare that directly targeted civilians was rare and limited by available weaponry and customary practices.[1] Certainly, people who have nothing to do with the conflict of arms have become victims not by accident but by deliberate intent. But on the whole, such events have been exceptional in warfare through most of Western history. Jonathan Glover comments, "At the start of the twentieth century, massacres by soldiers were seen as aberrations." He adds, in light of events at My Lai in Vietnam and more recently in Bosnia, "Perhaps this was too optimistic."[2] Indeed, recent decades have shown us more and more incidents of civilian deaths resulting from military operations, including the deliberate murder of unarmed civilians by soldiers.[3] Nevertheless, the guiding perception of war theorists up to the First World War was that deliberate targeting of civilians was out of bounds.

This all changed with two developments, one conceptual and one technological. The conceptual development was the invention of the concept of "total war," the idea that warfare was not merely combat between opposing military units but entailed the actions, including moral support, of whole societies.

> The concept [of total war] dates to the period after 1919, and is here employed to describe a form of military conflict in which not only armed forces but entire populations are involved.[4]

Van Creveld notes that earlier, especially tribal, societies had, on a small scale, practiced something akin to total war. He cites Rome during the Second Punic War as "engaged on a conflict that was as total as anything witnessed during the twentieth century."[5] But it is only after the Industrial Revolution and the creation of weapons requiring huge support and logistical systems for their deployment that more and more elements of a society at war are engaged in the war effort. The experience of World War I taught military theorists that success in the field depended on total mobilization of the society.

> Since technology had turned war into the question of economic and industrial mobilization, governments set up new departments to coordinate everything from raw materials to wages, and from transport to the number of

> calories to be ingested daily by each citizen. Far from giving rise to unemployment, the war effort resulted in an insatiable demand for labour that could only be met by calling up men, women, and children to serve in fields, factories, and offices. In their most extreme form, these efforts were aimed at turning entire nations into social systems, finely geared and attuned to the creation of the greatest possible military power.[6]

As a consequence, Van Creveld notes, the industrialized form of warfare, employing mechanized vehicles and aircraft, meant that civilian workers were implicated in the war effort as never before.

> War itself extended its tentacles deep into the rear, spreading from the trenches into the fields, the mines, and the factories. Not content with the mobilization of those, it reached further into the design bureaus and, ultimately, into peaceful university laboratories where the most esoteric work was done and the potentially most powerful weapons were developed.[7]

The conceptual framework of total war presents a serious challenge to the application of the ethical tradition of non-combatant immunity, as within this framework it is not merely armed soldiers, sailors in warships, and crews of warplanes who are combatants, but potentially all members of a society engaged in total war.

> If the gearing of entire societies and economies to the war effort constituted the principal characteristic of modern total war, it was aircraft which ended the immunity of those economies and those societies and made it possible to subject them to direct attack. The obliteration of the distinction between front and rear, combatants and non-combatants, followed. The outcome was a crisis in the law of war, and a process of barbarization such as had not been seen in Europe since the second half of the seventeenth century.[8]

Thus the technological development most challenging to the tradition of non-combatant immunity was that of aircraft capable of carrying bombs, and the concomitant development of doctrines of strategic bombing. But the psychological preparation for area bombing as a justifiable means of warfare came during World War I, when British strategists created a naval blockade - a form of siege warfare - that prevented food and other goods reaching Germany. Precise numbers are impossible to establish, but at least 400,000 and perhaps as many as 800,000 civilian deaths can be attributed to the deprivations caused by the blockade, which lasted the duration of the war. "The blockade's importance as a human disaster goes further still. It was a stage in the development of a new psychology of war, a psychology adapted to large-scale killing of civilian populations."[9]

World War II saw the development of technologies of bombing that largely obliterated any useful application of ethical restraints on direct attacks on civilians. The progress of the Allied bombing raids on Germany is a case study in rationalizations, as strategists struggled to justify the manifest imprecision of the raids. In the first phase of the RAF attacks on Germany, civilian targets were banned, but because bombers had to fly at high altitude and at night to avoid German fighters and antiaircraft fire, the crews' ability to find their targets and bomb them accurately was severely compromised. When it became clear early on that civilian areas were being destroyed anyway, RAF Bomber Command faced a "choice between abandoning bombing altogether or intentionally continuing to bomb civilians. What gave way was the ban on civilian targets."[10]

Still, there was considerable resistance, even among the generals responsible for the raids on Germany, to this change in the practice of warfare. Robin Neillands, in his detailed history of the air campaign against Germany, quotes U.S. Army-Air Force General Ira Eaker as objecting to plans for a massive raid on Berlin, "[W]e should never allow the history of this war to convict us of throwing the strategic bomber at the man on the street."[11] This objection, and many others like it from different quarters, was ignored. A quite different line of objection had more success in limiting the scope of air operations. This was the argument that sites of architectural and cultural importance should be spared. Neillands cites

> a note to the Air Minister, Sir Archibald Sinclair, from the chairman of the Society for the Preservation of Historic Buildings, asking for restraint in the bombing of certain historic towns and suggesting that some of them should be bombed only in daylight. This request was taken seriously, and [Air Chief Marshal Sir Arthur] Harris was told not to attack any of these towns without consulting the Air Ministry first and obtaining specific permission. The acceptance of this proposal by the Allied bomber commanders probably

> saved the historic city centres of Rome, Florence, and Paris – occupied cities.[12]

Notwithstanding these arguments, strategic doctrine had shifted profoundly, and the new rationale for what had been happening perforce was that hitting civilian areas could be justified by the idea that damaging civilian morale could count as advancing the aims of the war. The empirical implausibility of this view should have been evident to Allied war planners, had they compared the responses of Londoners during the Blitz to the probable reactions of German citizens to being bombed, but instead, by 1944, deliberate targeting of civilians had become standard doctrine, and the technique of creating firestorms in cities resulted in the destruction of Hamburg and Dresden as well as Tokyo. From these applications of air power it was a quite small conceptual step to the atomic bombings of Hiroshima and Nagasaki. It was against this background that the phrase "collateral damage" was coined to sanitize the inevitable outcome of weapons whose use could not discriminate between combatants and non-combatants.

As the character of warfare has changed, so has its relationship to the societies that engage in it. Van Creveld points out that both world wars of the twentieth century undercut the traditional concept of war as an instrument of national policy. He says,

> Though [World War I] opened with the usual political aims of national aggrandizement, it very soon escaped political control. So far from serving as an instrument of politics, that war and its successor all but swallowed politics, so that what was good for the war was considered good for the nation.[13]

Echoes of this change can be seen in rhetoric that attempts to build civilian support for particular wars, relying as it typically does on an equation between support for the war and patriotism, or negatively, an equation between criticism of the war and treason. In a climate of dichotomy, critique of policy can easily be shouted down, and the momentum of violence can come to advance almost with a life of its own. We might have learned this from World War I, the classic context demonstrating the way war-fighting technologies can easily outstrip the strategic doctrines marshalled supposedly to control them. The resulting casualty rate, for example at the Battle of the Somme with its massive employment of machine guns, shocked and appalled the participant societies, but too late. The trenches were already in place.

As an index of how lethal our species has become, Glover quotes an estimate that "from 1900 until 1986 . . . war killed 86 million people."[14] That figure, stopping at 1986, does not cover the casualties of the Gulf War, the disintegration of the former Yugoslavia, the genocidal massacres in Rwanda, the conflict between Chechnya and Russia, civil wars in the Darfur region and in Sri Lanka, insurgencies in Colombia and other places, and of course, the current Iraq war. Still, despite the fact that the twentieth century was the bloodiest in history, it is also the century in which we see the most concerted attempts to create ethical and legal frameworks to contain the violence.

2. Ethical Frameworks

Against the tide of war-making technologies that seem to have created their own momentum and necessity, ethical and legal traditions have attempted to impose restraints on warfare that express a persistent strain of humanism, in the sense that even in widespread application of our most violent practices, human life remains a value in itself, to be preserved over other values. Here I will only sketch some of the ideas that pertain to non-combatant immunity. The first, Just War Theory, has two main divisions, rules governing when it is just to enter into a war in the first place, the *jus ad bellum*, and rules governing the conduct of warfare once a state is engaged, called the *jus in bello*. The ethical restraints which Just War Theory places on war-making reflect a natural law ethics orientation to the actions of state leaders, in contradistinction to the political "realism" that denies that there is any moral framework applicable to the actions of states toward each other. That is, Just War Theory attempted to put *moral* boundaries around the use of state power.

Jus ad bellum principles fall under three headings: competent authority, just cause, and right intention.[15] Thus a state can justly enter into a war only if the action is initiated by national leaders with the appropriate legal authority; the cause for which the war is begun is sufficiently "serious and weighty" to overcome the "prima facie obligation not to injure and kill others"[16]; and the war is undertaken to re-establish a just order. This last idea rules out wars of conquest or reprisal. As De Lupis points out in her survey of the Law of War, natural law *jus ad bellum* principles have largely been superseded by international law that prohibits aggressive wars, for example the United Nations Charter.[17] Even so, because warfare continues to be an appallingly common state of affairs, rules governing the conduct of war, which in general have had as their primary intent the protection of individual lives, remain relevant.

Thus *Jus in bello* principles of proportionality and discrimination attempt to capture the long standing moral intuition that non-combatants in general, as well as wounded or captured soldiers, should not be subjected to lethal violence. The principle of proportionality requires that military means be proportional to the political and military ends to be achieved.[18] Thus means of warfare aimed at the complete destruction of an adversary's society are forbidden, as this would go beyond what is necessary to re-establish a just social order. "The principle of discrimination prohibits direct intentional attacks on non-combatants and non-military targets."[19] This principle thus rules out the use of weapons whose employment cannot discriminate between military objectives and civilian and other non-combatant assets, i.e., weapons of mass destruction. However, much ingenuity has been applied to the task of validating use of non-discriminatory weapons as theorists (and strategists) bow to the realities of military technologies. William O'Brien, for example, claims that the principle ought not to be regarded as an absolute prohibition of "any use of means that kill non-combatants."[20]

At stake here is a more general moral principle, called the Doctrine of Double Effect. It is always morally impermissible to intend direct harm, and thus "evil may never be done in order to produce a good result."[21] However, it is possible that an action aimed at some good, yet having an unintended (though foreseen) harmful side effect, is permissible, because according to double-effect thinking the harms are not directly intended. If the harms are not actually means to the good end aimed at but unavoidable side effects, the act that brings about those harms may be permissible. Thus use of what have come to be called weapons of mass destruction, which will inevitably kill many civilians, might be morally acceptable so long as the civilian deaths are not directly intended, but are unavoidable consequences of pursuing an acceptable military objective. It is also required that the "collateral damage" be minimized as much as practicable. More limited actions which would violate an absolute principle of discrimination, such as deploying anti-personnel land mines or torpedoing civilian ships at sea thought to be carrying military materiel, might also be justifiable under the Doctrine of Double Effect.

One objection to double-effect thinking hinges on the concept of intention. If I know that my action is highly likely to cause harm (even if only as a side effect) and I intend the action, how can I not be intending the harm? That is, doesn't foreknowledge of an effect of an action automatically entail intention of that effect? On this account, calling the harms side effects (or worse, "collateral damage") does not mitigate the intention, and hence the moral culpability. Applied to contemporary warfare, this objection would undercut the claim that the use of weapons whose use cannot distinguish between combatants and non-combatants is justifiable because the deaths of bystanders are not intended. If those deaths are foreseen, then they are to an extent intended, even though it might plausibly be claimed that if the action could be carried out without the undesirable harms it would be.

Another response to this reading of Just War Theory has been that of pacifists who, O'Brien comments, "rightly argue that war inevitably involves violation of the absolute principle of discrimination. If that principle is unconditionally binding, a just war is difficult if not impossible to envisage."[22] O'Brien rejects this move. Writing during the height of the superpower nuclear arms race, his argument was that the "exigencies of modern war and deterrence" made an absolute principle of discrimination so difficult to reconcile with the realities of military technology and the geopolitical order of, say, the 1980s that it would not provide adequate moral guidance. He opts instead for a view that does not "distinguish an absolute, moral, just-war principle of discrimination from a more flexible and variable international-law principle of discrimination."[23]

But that "more flexible and variable" international law standard should not provide much comfort to leaders using weapons of mass destruction. De Lupis's survey of international law pertaining to warfare, the second major attempt to constrain war-making, shows clearly that a strong principle of discrimination has been incorporated in the Law of War. She summarizes,

> The Law of War has the individual as its exclusive focus and the rationale of all rules can be derived from a common agreement to keep compulsory standards of behaviour. There is no doubt that the use of any indiscriminate weapon is illegal, as no weapon must be used that is not adequately aimed at military targets. There is no doubt that weapons that cause unnecessary suffering are forbidden. There is no doubt that the civilian population and all who are *hors de combat* must at all times be exempt from attack and given necessary medical assistance.[24]

Moreover, the principles developed as part of the Law of War have a different and pragmatically stronger basis than Just War Theory, as a result of their different context of development. For Just War Theory, having developed within Catholic moral theology, can be regarded as (merely) parochial. Adherents of a political realism of the sort associated with Machiavelli or, in our era, Henry Kissinger, the U.S. Secretary of

State during the Vietnam war - or indeed, moral sceptics in general - need feel no compunction about ignoring disputes about the proper application of, say, the Doctrine of Double Effect. The Law of War, on the other hand, is part of international covenants entered into by states and is enforceable by criminal prosecution of state leaders. Structures such as the International Criminal Court constitute practical applications of protections of civilians in wartime, embodying some of the very principles to be found in Just War Theory. In addition, numerous specific weapons, such as poison gas, have been outlawed for use in combat. While the overlap between international law and Just War Theory is far from complete, the development of legal protections for civilians is an important advance in our evolving conceptual frameworks of responses to violence. Non-combatant immunity is much more strongly supported as a binding principle than before World War II.

Nevertheless, some statistics should give us pause, as they indicate that the law has fallen behind both the technologies of warfare and humans' willingness to use them deliberately against civilians. De Lupis says,

> history shows that civilians, despite this protective regime, are increasingly at risk in war. In the First World War some 5 percent of the victims were civilians; in the Second World War this figure had risen to 48, to escalate in the Korean War to 84 and in the Vietnam War to 90 per cent. Not all the increase in this proportion can be explained by difficulties of distinction between combatants and civilians.[25]

Or, put another way, the international legal protections as yet do not provide a sufficient deterrent to war-makers who, for whatever reasons, intend to attack civilian populations.

3. The Catastrophe

During the superpower arms race that ensued after the first use of nuclear weapons in wartime, it was part of military doctrine that threatening to destroy the adversary's cities was of the essence of deterrence, and the world settled in for decades of acquiescence in the idea that theoretically, everyone in the world was a potential target. The term 'omnicide,' coined I believe by John Somerville, was invented to denote a wholly new possibility: that we humans could kill all of ourselves virtually at once. Attempts to supply frameworks limiting the use of violent means such as Just War Theory and international conventions restricting use of specific weapons seem to have been swept aside by the development and deployment of large scale weapons, and by the actions of non-state groups deliberately pursuing policies of indiscriminate murder. In their place we have a *de facto* kind of political realism, crudely pragmatic, in which civilian deaths are regarded either as inevitable side effects of otherwise legitimate means of warfare, "collateral damage," or are treated as themselves means to political ends. Either way, we see the ascendancy of deeply anti-humanistic values.

The paroxysms of shock and rage that followed the events of Sept. 11, 2001, provide further evidence of the disconnect between ongoing reality, the fact that absolutely anybody can be a target, and our determined psychological denial of this fact. What the hijackers did on a small scale was not different in kind from what has been imbedded in military planning for decades: an attack on a city with the intent to kill as many of its inhabitants as possible.

The ethical malaise of general populations with regard to the death of non-combatant immunity may count as another form of what Hannah Arendt called the banality of evil, based as this malaise seems to be, on a kind of thoughtlessness. Her concept of *thinking*, which she described as "the habit of examining and reflecting upon whatever happens to come to pass, regardless of specific content and quite independent of results,"[26] is precisely what is lacking in both the political responses and the ways in which publics have come to think of security. Neither addresses in any useful way the underlying causes of violence against peoples.

In this paper I have treated three large scale interlocking phenomena: the evolution of military technology and the development of the concept of total war; the longstanding ethical framework of Just War Theory; and the development of an international Law of War. It is of course quite difficult to establish empirically the existence and scope of such broad occurrences as ethical malaise. Yet I believe we should regard the almost universal willingness of the peoples of the Earth to regard attacks on non-combatants as inevitable, unavoidable, perhaps even "natural," as a moral catastrophe with far-reaching influence on Western culture and self-understanding. More specifically, it constitutes an erosion of our most fundamental humanistic value frameworks, without which civil society cannot flourish, an erosion that reveals a basic underlay of nihilism in contemporary culture.

Notes

[1] William V. O'Brien, "Just-War Theory," in James P. Sterba, ed., *War and Nuclear Deterrence* (Belmont, Calif.: Wadsworth, 1985), 40.
[2] Jonathan Glover, *Humanity: A Moral History of the Twentieth Century* (New Haven and London: Yale University Press, 2001), 64.
[3] As this is written the press has featured numerous stories on the deaths of twenty-four Iraqis in the town of Haditha in November, 2005, allegedly killed by U.S. soldiers. See *Newsweek* CXLVII/24 (June 12, 2006): 22-31. An event during the Korean War, described in terms strikingly similar to the now infamous My Lai Massacre in Vietnam and the Haditha killings, is analyzed by Marilyn B. Young, "An Incident at No Gun Ri," in Omer Bartov, Atina Grossmann, and Mary Nolan, eds., *Crimes of War; Guilt and Denial in the Twentieth Century* (New York: The New Press, 2002), 242 – 258.
[4] Martin Van Creveld, *Technology and War: From 2000 B.C.to the Present* (New York: Free Press, 1989), 162.
[5] Ibid.
[6] Ibid., 163.
[7] Ibid., 163 – 164.
[8] Ibid., 196.
[9] Glover, 64.
[10] Ibid., 70-71.
[11] Robin Neillands, *The Bomber War; The Allied Air Offensive Against Nazi Germany* (New York: Overlook Press, 2001), 341.
[12] Ibid., 278 – 279.
[13] Van Creveld, 165.
[14] Glover, 47.
[15] James P. Sterba, Introduction to O'Brien, *op. cit.*, 30.
[16] O'Brien, 33.
[17] Ingrid Detter De Lupis, *The Law of War* (Cambridge: Cambridge University Press, 1987), 127.
[18] O'Brien, 37.
[19] Ibid., 39.
[20] Ibid., 41.
[21] Ibid.
[22] Ibid.
[23] Ibid.
[24] Igrid Detter De Lupis, *The Law of War* (Cambridge: Cambridge University Press, 1987), 363.

[25] Ibid., 241.
[26] Hannah Arendt, "Thinking and Moral Considerations: A Lecture, *Social Research* 38/3 (Fall 1971): 417.

Bibliography

Arendt, Hannah. "Thinking and Moral Considerations: A Lecture. *Social Research* 38/3 (Fall 1971): 417 - 446.

Bartov, Omer, Atina Grossmann, and Mary Nolan, eds. *Crimes of War; Guilt and Denial in the Twentieth Century.* New York: The New Press, 2002.

De Lupis, Ingrid Detter. *The Law of War*. Cambridge: Cambridge University Press, 1987.

Glover, Jonathan. *Humanity: A Moral History of the Twentieth Century.* New Haven and London: Yale University Press, 2001.

Neillands, Robin. *The Bomber War; The Allied Air Offensive Against Nazi Germany.* New York: Overlook Press, 2001.

O'Brien, William V. "Just-War Theory." in *War and Nuclear Deterrence*, edited by James P. Sterba, Belmont, Calif.: Wadsworth, 1985.

Van Creveld, Martin. *Technology and War; From 2000 B.C. to the Present.* New York: Free Press, 1989.

Evil and the Loss of Intellect

Wayne Cristaudo

Abstract: Taking my cue from Dante's phrase that hell is populated by "those who have lost the benefit of the intellect," I argue that earthly hells are the result of a certain kind of mindlessness on the part of people entrusted to be the brains of their respective collective. Dante understood that the presence or absence of mind involves more than merely performing cognitive operations. His conception of the intellect is shaped by an ontology in which love is the source of all. Hence where love is absent, or targeting the wrong object, the intellect does not fulfil its real function, and doing evil is bound up with the intellect not being guided by love's light. Concomitantly, those in hell are not there due to an inability to provide "reasons" for their judgments and deeds, rather there is a hiatus between the illusions they have about what they are doing and what they actually do: the damned are unable to see the world they are making until it is too late. Hell becomes inevitable when a group becomes sufficiently steeped in its illusions that it does not see the awaiting terror. Concomitantly, when a group reaches this stage they cannot be touched by true words: the group, then, literally belongs to (the d)evil.

Key Words: Intellect, evil, hell, love, Dante, Baudelaire, Plato, Sade, philosophy, science.

1.

Before evil is a concept it is a reality. The history of the designation of those forces which wreak havoc and unbearable suffering and cruelty is a long one, as is the location of its nature and source. Homer, for example, has Zeus lament the plight of men caught up in the world's war made agony ("there is nothing alive more agonizing than man/ of all that breathe and crawl across the earth"),[1] while elsewhere he insists that while humans blame the gods for their plight, their own recklessness compounds "their pains beyond their proper share."[2] Yet, at other times, as in the death of his beloved Saperdon, Zeus must accept undesired and undesirable fates, which is itself indicative of a limit of faith the Greeks had in how they could deal with evil. Zoroastrians, Manicheans and Christians deviated on precise details about the scope and source of evil, but they were all driven to a considerably common extent by the insight that evil was grounded in a substance, a demonic entity, who was ever in battle against the transcendent/higher good. Monotheisms invariably are pulled into dualisms by the problem of evil, while polytheisms leave evil somewhat dispersed throughout creation. But polytheisms also discern a common species of malevolent forces - demons. What is of significance for the point I wish to commence with is that, in contrast to the widespread moral relativism of our reflexive culture, the accompaniment of our underlying mechanistic metaphysics, which stretches from Descartes to Nietzsche, Foucault and Deleuze, we can, nevertheless, find in all cultures widespread belief in the reality of evil as a force, even if the details of designation may vary.

Nietzsche's division of evil and bad, and master and slave morality was made at the expense of the much more important and more fundamental commonality between Greeks and Christians which is patently manifest in the shared insights about evil detectable in the views that life is tragic and that life is grounded in original sin. Both doctrines alert us to the inevitability of human transgression against the one (for Christianity) or many (for the Greeks) force(s) or powers on which we rely throughout our lives. Likewise, the Platonic and Christian appeals to transcendence and redemption, respectively, commence with the same insight about the reality of evil's inevitability and all-pervasiveness, which, Nietzsche notwithstanding, is also the source of the epic and tragic understanding of life. The difference between Platonists and Christians, on the one hand, and tragedians, on the other, is not in their view of the inescapability of agony and suffering in the world, but in the redemptive/ transcendent *telos* and respective strategies which promise a way out of the very horrors that Homer and the tragedians depict with such power.

I emphasise this point because the overwhelming majority of educated men and women who are employed in sites of social reflexivity in the West believe evil does not exist as such, that it is merely a word. The idea that evil is not real is a cold comfort to those thrown into the chambers of agony for which the species has, with universal consent, reserved the concept of evil.[3] This is not because the word "evil" is invested with any magical powers, but rather because a sign is the means by which we can be orientated to actions and powers which either nourish us or feed a larger destructive field of force. We invariably meet our destruction by participating and living in a linguistic field which disables us in identifying processes at work which actively serve death and cruelty and all its cognates (i.e. the gamut of powers that traditionally were designated as evil). The word evil is simply a means to enable us to identify a plethora of related and connected energies whose coalescence force us into avoidable and terrible sufferings or, to use an archaic word, hell. It is no accident that the terrors of the twentieth century were largely created by cultures which had lost any sense of the notion of the evil of their actions, though not of the actions of others. The great irony was that the philosophies which had prepared our secular culture were largely driven by the faith that once superstitious beliefs in God and the devil had been overcome peace would reign. Marxists saw that a further step would be required, thereby legitimating what was meant to be one last catastrophe, which in fact became the approximately hundred million deaths incurred under Stalinist regimes; while Nietzsche, of course, cared much more about vitalising culture than achieving peace. Few paid any attention to the fact that a great militaristic/nationalist ideology given its then compellingly powerful formulation by Clausewitz, was being brewed, and that it would draw all the world into its Godless and devil-less maw of evil, and all in the name of a belief that the world simply was thus, when it was nothing of the sort.[4]

Of course, one does not need to deny evil's existence for it to occur, simply denying that one's own inflictions of cruelty and carnage are evil by providing moral rationalisations or divine commands suffices.

Present past and future are always separated by veils. That is why faith is not simply a religious category, but, as the late 18th/19th century German philosopher Friedrich Jacobi rightly argued, an ontological category.[5] We cannot know that the good world we think we are building will, in fact, be good. We can have faith that it is, we can hope it is, and we can pray that it is. But faith, hope and prayer (understood as the speech driven by the real end of our devotion) are not luminous in themselves, and only as good as the end that is directing and consuming our energies and talents. Thus it is that people rarely realize when they are building the architecture to "en-hell" themselves and/or their children and grandchildren. Evil loves being in this world: it feeds off our blood, and its preparation requires mass somnambulance. Those who become its under-labourers are absolutely certain that some great reward awaits them. A childlike stupidity engulfs a mass who swarm with activity, convinced that the solution of all the world's problems has been found. Eliminate the Jew, eliminate the bourgeois, eliminate the pagan, eliminate the infidel, eliminate...- it is always the same logic. Invariably, no word spoken will wake them up to the chain of catastrophic consequences their activity is setting in motion. This does not discount the fact that mass evil may occur because a group deliberately undertakes to band together and kill and rape, plunder and maim, etc., but even when these crimes occur on a mass scale, they require some kind of ideological underpinning to galvanize the group, to give their bloody deeds an aura of righteousness. Mass evil requires that the collective, quite literally, loses its mind, i.e., loses its ability to see the world it is making even as it is making it - to see its own present, and no longer just to remain hidden from its future. Its reasons, its evidence, and its vocabulary - every event is semiotically crafted - relate to a phantasm that is as remote from the world that will be as it is from the world that is already there. Concomitantly the group continues to provide rationalisations of its deeds, and there is no way that new information can act as a circuit breaker. The system is hermetically sealed, functioning, as it does, through the circulation of dead information: the group's spirit is as rigid as the minds which form it. The collective then is ready for leaders who will command that it follow through the logic of petrification that it has helped assemble, thus leading them and their victims into the hell they have been making.

In the mid-nineteenth century one figure in particular had a terrifying premonition of where modernity's failure to understand evil was leading. It was a poet, a point which is not without significance, given that modern philosophers from Descartes to Heidegger almost to a man (Kierkegaard and Pascal being notable exceptions) had nothing to say about evil. It was Charles Baudelaire. Baudelaire in many ways is a pivotal thinker of modernity, not least because he realized that the modern process is an alchemical one, and that the great achievement of the modern was the potential to produce flowers out of evil. Some of those flowers - the basic stimulants of sex, narcotics and alcohol - were to be the new forms of the modern's transcendence, rescuing/redeeming him/ her from the peculiarly modern evil/sickness of *ennui*. On the other hand, what he saw with horror was that as modern men and women made their world, they had largely become oblivious to evil's existence.[6] *Flowers of Evil* was his response to the (blindness of) the enlightenment's lack of understanding of evil. His own poems of demonic revolt were to a large extent meant to arrest people against their brainless failure to appreciate evil as an active historic force which has so often been shrouded in life's goods/staples. For Baudelaire this is most notable in religion, which had gained political significance in large part because of its unacknowledged demonic alliances. But even more important for Baudelaire than creating "sympathy for the devil" was his desire to alert people to his presence, a point best summed up in a line from his prose poem "The Generous Gambler": "the greatest ruse of the devil is to convince us he doesn't exist."

In effect this great trick is the counter-pole of the other trick - to get people to think he has poisoned everything - a position powerfully depicted by Dostoevsky in his description of Father Ferapont in *The Brothers Karamazov*. Augustine rightly saw that this view of evil was the central weakness of the Manicheans. For how could destruction not be privative, dependent as it is on an initial act of creation? Evil must have something to negate and defile - whether it be innocence, a reputation, someone's property, someone's life, i.e., some pre-existing good. And to a large extent, secular culture is the response of those who saw too much evil committed in the name of driving out the devil - a point going back to Pierre Bayle's brave claim that atheists were not as inclined as religious adherents to kill each other over doctrines.[7] But Bayle, who was so alert to the deficient understanding of evil in the two greatest philosophies of his time (that of Spinoza and Leibniz), nevertheless missed the more essential point: that evil does not need this or that systemic form to operate, but that it conducts its expansion through the systemic killing of the intellect. It may seem a rather strange claim in our modern/post-modern age, seemingly the most intellectual of all ages, that the spread of evil is bound up with the destruction or loss of intellect, but this is precisely the danger that we moderns face in an age of systems of administration and interaction of such complexity. It is this issue I wish to consider more closely in the remainder of the chapter.

2.

The relationship between evil and lack of intellect goes back at least to Plato's Socrates, who held that "evil is ignorance." He held that if people understood their real good they would not be deceived by the apparent good. Plato's entire moral philosophy is dependent upon this insight. However, it is not a formulation that is without problems, as the philosophy of the Marquis de Sade surely shows. For Sade speaks on behalf of all those who consciously choose evil and not out of ignorance of what will happen to them in their torment, but precisely because they are either already so tormented or so thrilled by torment that doing evil is well and truly done out of intelligence. Along different lines, Shakespeare is the master of showing how a certain modality of the intellect, *viz.*, cunning is one of evil's most important tools. Yet, while Sade may put a spanner in Plato's works, a more nuanced position, and one not derailed by Sade, is articulated in the relationship between intelligence and evil that is put forward by Dante in his *Comedy*.

In keeping with Christian medieval orthodoxy, Dante saw that the pagan concept of the intellect was fundamentally deficient in its failure to appreciate that the virtues of the intellect are incomplete if not conjoined with the forces of faith, hope and love. These forces cannot simply be grasped by the intellect's self-probity. Indeed their potency, for Dante, is only made manifest to the intellect through the contingency of an act (the crucifixion) and group of actors (the earliest and subsequent followers of Christ) whose minds and hearts were dedicated to the creation of the future age of spiritual union.[8] Dante hoped and had faith that that age, also prophesied by his near contemporary, Joachim of Fiore, would soon be realized, once the Holy Roman Empire was no longer plagued by the principle officer of St. Peter forgetting his proper pastoral role and causing havoc in Christendom's complex tapestry of political alliances.

Intellect, in this metaphysical framework, is neither self-generating nor the beginning and end of creation, as Plato and Aristotle would have it, but is itself a force in service to a higher good, a point so fundamental to Jews and then Christians that even such avowed Platonists as Plotinus and Proclus came to systematically embrace it. In this schema, then, it is not the intellect as such - for to repeat, it is not *sui generis*, but as the final and crowning line of *The Divine Comedy* puts it, "love that moves the sun and other stars." Hence, also, it is love that lights the intellect, just as it is the intellect that illumines the lovable. The intellect thus is only really what it is when it is luminous, when it is up-building, and when it works with and for love. Hence, from Dante's position, Sade's "cleverness" is but the perversion of an intellect, a fact that Dante would see in the ruinous worlds of those victims of Sadian appetites. This stands in the closest relationship also to the central deficiency of Sade's conception of love. Sade, like every mechanist, only understands love as appetite. Thus it remains oblivious to the kinds of pleasure that Aristotle made the cornerstone of his love of the contemplative life and the kind of love, *agape*, which is at the heart of charity (*caritas*) and which is invisible to those who only look at love under the rules of *eros*. This too is why even when Freud is at his best, which is when the role of speech is placed in the centre of his theorising (as is emphasised in interpretations of Freud by Lacan, Kristeva and Jonathan Lear) he still frames everything as erotics.

The most fundamental difference between Sade and Dante is that Dante's damned have what they really wanted and they don't like it, while Sade's damnable heroes and heroines love hell, as their appetites are formed by damnable acts and remain directed to damnable deeds. However, Dante is not concerned with the question of whether it is possible to love damnation, only with showing in great detail what consequences flow from what acts, i.e., the worlds that are built respectively by living in either sin or grace. In the case of the former, Dante says that hell is inhabited by "those who have lost the benefit of the intellect."[9] What he means by this is not that they are not capable of performing the functioning operations of the mind - indeed, the transition from a metaphysic such as Dante holds to the mechanistic one of Sade can be briefly summed up, as Ernst Cassirer does, as the transition from substance to function.[10] The substance of the world that is worth living in, for Dante, is a world created by love and intelligence; forces which are complete only with and in each other. Intelligence provides pattern and order and meaning; love provides the *desired* (because it is good and beautiful) pattern, order and meaning.

The functionalist deployment of the intellect is utterly consistent with the metaphysical determinism of mechanistic philosophy and its correlate, a moral but insubstantial free person. Kant's moral philosophy was the perfect way to save freedom for mechanism: it was "a mere idea" having its basis solely in a cognitive operation. And, as is evident in the philosophies of Descartes, Locke, and Spinoza as well as Kant, the metaphysics of mechanism was closely bound up with the invention of a facultative logic in which the mind was but a set of operations. The functionalist understanding of the intellect preserves the very aim it was designed for: the elimination of the idea of nature having ends. But the cost of this view of life in general, and of intelligence, more specifically, was the truncation of the real. We had to take ourselves out of nature, as if nature was completely Other, so that the love and speech of love that generates communities and cultures and, hence individual lives, was reduced, as Pascal saw with such terror, to a deafening silence whose greatest triumph was the creation of anxiety/worriedness, which philosophers by the 20th century (most obviously Heidegger) would come to see as our essence.

Once reality had been thus truncated, the words which were formerly used to describe it now only served to describe a truncated reality which (a) was no longer the reality itself and (b) which most do not realize is truncated. It is this sad state of affairs in which we moderns now find ourselves and which makes us live in a time that is paradoxically more powerful than at any time in history and equally capable of catastrophes even worse than those achieved last century.

3.

In our relationship with love or evil we, as individuals, are not substances (by substance I mean a primary determinative power), which is precisely the opposite of the prevailing modernist superstition which took the ego as the substantive ground of moral right.[11] Another way of saying this is that love and evil are stronger powers than we are, and that in fact we are processes that participate in and are shaped by the substances of love and evil and other forces which sustain or injure us. We are substantive only collectively and in the combination of past (the radiance of still prevailing forces patent in cultures, institutions and even our nature/genes), present (the momentary configuration of past and future) and future (the refraction of real, yet still unrealised events we either hope to realize through our will or which will be released upon us due to an admixture of present and past forces).

The proofs of our accidental nature are (a) the inevitability of our death and (b) the fact that what we become is proactively or reactively shaped by the powers of love and evil in our environments. Concomitantly, another superstition that plagues us is the belief that this or that person is evil, as opposed to the fact that this or that person is in the grip of evil, forms part of an evil field of past, present and future.

The point made here about the individual is also essential to understanding the nature of intelligence. Irrespective of the fact that Hegel's systemic aspirations made him succumb to intellectual overreach, he rightly grasped that intelligence is content-bound, thereby thoroughly undoing the dualisms that had held sway between Descartes and Kant.[12] Content is generated collectively, and so is the corruption of social intelligence. The history of the corruption of Aristotelian thought throughout the Middle Ages is just one prolonged conspicuous proof of how formalism can destroy intelligence. Intelligence is constantly required to do a number of things, which includes processing patterns and being open to contingencies which are thereby integrated into an existing pattern or, to take a point central to Schelling's philosophy of irruptive freedom, generative of a new pattern. When we become conscious of this process it enables us as a species to expand continually (partly by going back to collect past patterns, partly by studying the contemporary patternings, and also being open to the 'new' of the future) the repertoire of patterns at our disposal for grasping our past and present and orientating us into the future.

The philosophical and scientific ideals both require disinterestedness in the face of phenomena. Yet that disinterestedness is itself born by the love that is inherent in philosophy (love of wisdom). There is, as all philosophers know, a major difference between what constitutes wisdom for the philosopher and the scientist. For the scientist has already made a commitment to nature as being the true ground of being, while the philosopher, even when a naturalist, still undertakes meta-level analysis of the "percepts" and categories for its framings. Philosophers, as lovers of wisdom, may play a fundamental role in helping us see evil; scientists as scientists, on the other hand, have no means by which to focus upon evil; although it may help us better deal with specific processes that we designate as evil. That evil has not diminished in the world as science has played an increasing role in it is, in no small measure, due to the limitations of the techniques and purview of (with respect to good and evil, truncated) scientific intelligence. But philosophy is not necessarily a means of salvation. On the contrary, it too can facilitate evil, as is evident by the role of philosophy in the Reign of Terror and in the justifications of twentieth-century mass murderous regimes provided by philosophers as politically diverse as Merleau-Ponty, Sartre, Foucault (his writings on Iran), Heidegger, and Carl Schmitt. In the case of philosophy, such legitimations stem from a dedication to an abstraction of what something can be, but isn't. That is, evil has deployed great intelligence to do its work. Much has been written about intellectuals who have supported evil regimes, but none have bettered expressed the more general point at issue than Albert Camus in *The Rebel*. The key to the book can be summed up in his claim:

> We are living in the era of premeditation and perfect crimes. Our criminals are no longer those helpless children who pleaded love as their excuse. On the contrary, they are adults, and they have a perfect alibi: philosophy, which can be used for anything, even for transforming murderers into judges.[13]

But it has done so by the mutilation of the intellect's quality, which we saw in Dante, as being the service to up-building love and fixating it on a lesser love mingled, most often, with outright hate. I am not making this point to argue that we can learn nothing from philosophers such as Sartre or Heidegger. As Milan Kundera said in "The Deprecated Legacy of Cervantes," if we rejected every idea that came from a 20th century philosopher or writer who made disastrous political choices there would be precious little left.[14] Rather, I wish to emphasize that much 20th century philosophy was politically disastrous because it ignored the task of attunement to evil as such: it ignored the field-like nature of all evil and tended to do its social critique of this or that field by partisanship. This, to repeat, is not to say that life does not force moral choices upon us, but it is to say that even when we side against a more evil regime, that we too are effected by the field of evil in which that regime participates. Nazism and colonialism generated great evils, but that does not mean that the bombing of Dresden was not an evil, that the raping of hundreds of thousands of German women by advancing Russian troops was not evil, that because Saddam Hussein was evil what happened in Abu Ghraib was not, that because the Belgian colonialist army committed evil in the Congo, that the devastating evils that followed their departure were any less evil. Justice and self-defence are two of the more common ways in which (the d)evil is able to achieve its end of "reigning" on earth. Both begin as matters of survival and dire necessity. And it is undeniable that at times the threatening evil is of such a scale that one must fight it or perish. Our resistances to certain evils may well be better than the alternatives, but that only shows us the grimness of a world where evil is a constant presence. Nevertheless, the web of legitimacy that is woven around actions undertaken in reaction to evil (done in the name of justice or in self-defence) repeatedly leads to further acts of evil. Thus it is that justice requires prisons, and prisons are breeding grounds for evil, that defensive wars which turn to total wars are not anomalies but typical of the way in which legitimacy feeds evil. And most of us do not even see that this is what is happening.

The truth of St. Paul's claim that "all have sinned" is that it is a constant reminder of our dark capacities.[15] It is not that "they" are evil and "we" are good, it is that we can all fall under evil's grip at any moment. And because evil has its rewards - its delights and joys - the temptation is constant. Revenge is a joyous act, just as fighting in war can be - "call up the joy of war," says Homer's Achilles in a most revealing line.[16] We can do anything, no matter how terrible, if we believe we can justify it. And our subterranean appetite for blood is constantly seeking a mean for consciousness to give it permission to be satiated. Our hunger for blood, though, is but indicative of our hunger generally. When love fails to nourish, we seek its substitute - and blood is to the generation of flesh as love is to the generation of the spirit.

That is why intelligence as such is never the primary drive of itself - for intelligence is always seeking to satisfy our craving; it is always in service to some higher power, whether benign or malign. Plato thought of it as the good or the appearance of the good; but the dualist traditions of the divine and demonic I think more powerfully express the truth of the ease with which the intellect becomes corrupted, becomes inadequate for helping us flourish in the world that we have made.

Evil inserts itself into every body of believers no matter how pure the doctrine's origin and founders, because there is a willingness by the 'brains-trust' of the collective to accept the inferior or inadequate for the substance it is seeking. That inferior can be the reward of certitude, of status, of belonging. It can be any number of things, but it is always love's surrogate rather than love itself. And the very desire to maintain that surrogate, to serve it, to stabilize it, to keep feasting off it, when it is so empty intensifies the corruption of the collective intelligence.

What better example could there be of this process than the religion which deified Love itself, which grasped the object of desire as a suffering self-sacrificing God? Christianity so thoroughly understood the hunger and the source of its nourishment that it refused to requite evil with evil. Yet that did not prevent it from turning into its opposite and for becoming the spur for inquisition, territorial conquests and witch-burning. When it did so, it did what every deformed loving collective does: it took its mental bearing from the dark chambers of the heart; every capacity of the mind was laid at its disposal. It is irrelevant to (the d)evil's purposes whether logic or rhetoric is the better tool. Evil always uses what it can. We are its stuff. That we momentarily see evil and triumph over it for one minute does not guarantee our response in the following moment. The sense of our own righteousness is a common conceit, and it does nothing but feed evil.

It is, however, not only denial about our own actions that facilitates evil. Denial just as frequently accompanies our failure to discern impending evils which may even threaten our own existence. A voice insists that the evils that are really taking place before one's very eyes are the result of very "complex" causes - hence they are not really evil at all, or that something is just like something else that is not harmful. Corrupted intelligence creates false complexities where there are clear lines of true simplicities, and false simplicities where there are thickets of reasons that require much labour and time to disentangle. Communism, National Socialism and contemporary Islamism have all gained great power through their ability to seduce people into being in denial about their very simple objectives which they all expressed with crystal clarity.

The species has served one phantasm after another in its search for love, and every object of its love has found itself transformed from an up-building to an enslaving power. The transition from life to death is accompanied by a dogmatism of "either you are for or you are against us" thinking. "Either-Or" thinking is always (the d)evil's moment of inevitable triumph, for the triumph is in the antagonism, in the necessity of negation, which does not mean that there are not clusters of forces that are ensconced within traditions which are pernicious and need to be called by their proper names. The idea of calling things by their proper names is one that has tended to vanish in our contemporary relativistic culture. But the basis of that calling is something very simple: it is the calling attention to the cruel and brutal, to what kills and suppresses love. There is a dialogical component that is essential to the intellect's proper function because the addressing of evil is the addressing of another person. That is essential, because evil always spreads through indifference or sheer negation. On the other hand, genuine communion does not mean being silent about the evil the neighbour is generating when he is generating it, nor is it being defensive when the neighbour notes one's own contribution to the world's evil. It is to be in the hard place of the common acceptance of our deficiencies.

The loss of intellect, or more precisely, of that part of the intellect which is most important to its proper and healthy functioning, is a perennial component of evil. But in an age where intelligence is embedded in technologies and large and complex bodies of human associations, the power of such a loss of intelligence is of apocalyptic proportions, as is so evident in the wars of last century and the type and scale of weapons available today.

Evil hides itself until it is ready. Yet it is not a completely invisible power: it is a power that arises among us, and hence it is not part of what we usually designate as nature (hence not part of natural science), any more than the tangible but invisible spirit of any group is. If we observe what we do to each other it is something that we can discern in its development. There are always ways to downplay it, and this problem is compounded by the fact that human choices are so often tragic: we counter one evil by another - e.g., stop criminals by imprisoning them, invaders by war, tyrants by rebellion, etc. And even if we refuse to do this, we can never be sure that our refusal does not contribute to even more evil. The task of the intellect remains, however, to expose its presence, not by simply enabling it to inhabit us in our own fanaticism, to place us one side of an "Or." To perceive life by means of truncating it into contrary segments is one further loss of intellect which prevents us seeing the multiple forms and sites of evil's proliferation. Every organism has its pathologies, every collective its own evils. To become fixated on one type of pathology is invariably a means for assisting another one. Every time evil can have that strata of a society's intelligence focus only on a specific evil, it is victorious and it celebrates the loss of intellect.

While I have emphasised the value of a language which preserves the word of evil, it is true, as I said above, that even the obsession with evil can be evil. But this only shows the extent of the problem, which is both never-ending and always a trial of judgment and intelligence, and, above all, love - the world returning to us the true nature of our loves.

Notes

[1] Homer, *The Iliad*, 17: 515-516, translated by Robert Fagles, (New York: Penguin, 1990).

[2] Homer, *The Odyssey*, 1:39-40, translated by Robert Fagles, (New York: Penguin, 1996). There is no question for Homer that humans are moved by divine powers and "the will of Zeus will always overpower the will of men." *Iliad* 16:805, and see 17: 202. Indeed much, probably most of what humans do is driven by the will of the gods. As Penelope says to Odysseus of Helen: "Some god spurred her to do her shameless work," *Odyssey* 23, 250. Likewise in the opening lines of the *Iliad* Homer asks the question of the conflict between Agamemnon and Achilles "what god drove them to fight with such fury?" *Iliad*, 1: 9. And Agamemnon blames Zeus and Fate and the Fury for his taking Briseis, as he adds "A god impels all things to their fulfilment," *Iliad* 19: 101-4, while Menelaus simply says: "Zeus, Father Zeus, they say you excel all others.../all men and gods, in wisdom clear and calm--/ but all this brutal carnage comes from you." *Iliad* 13: 727-29.

[3] Perhaps the most indicative proof of all is the common strategy of denial after the event by those who do evil that they supply justifications for. Also noteworthy is that thinkers like Nietzsche and Spinoza who deny its very existence react to the concept they are seeking to eliminate by trying to put another in its place.

[4] See John Keegan's powerful, albeit brief, analysis of von Clauzewitz and the tremendous fatality of von Clauzewitz's conviction that "war is the continuation of policy by other means." *A History of Warfare*, (London: Pimlico, 1994), 3-28.

[5] In particular see his writings *David Hume On Faith* and *Concerning the Doctrine of Spinoza* in *The Main Philosophical Writings and the Novel All Will: Friedrich Heinrich Jacobi*, translated .and introduced by George di Giovanni (McGill-Queens Uni Press, Montreal& Kingston, 1994).

[6] When Flaubert had put it to Baudelaire that he had made too much of the spirit of evil, Baudelaire responded: "I have always been obsessed by the impossibility of accounting for some of man's sudden actions or thoughts without the hypothesis of the intervention of an evil force outside him. Here's a scandalous avowal for which the whole nineteenth century won't make me blush." Cited in Jonathan Culler's Introduction to James McGowan's translation of *The Flowers of Evil*, (Oxford: Oxford University Press, 1993).

[7] See the entry 'Clarifications' in Pierre Bayle's *Dictionary*. An English translation can be found in Pierre Bayle, *Historical and Critical Dictionary: Selections*, translated and introduction and notes by Richard Popkin, (Indianapolis: Bobbs-Merrill, 1965).

[8] It is too big a case to make here, but what I am suggesting is that the Christian doctrine of neighborly love (while violated more often than kept), which to be sure partly coincides with Stoic philosophical cosmopolitanism, has been part of the heritage of the modern world, and it is at the basis of all contemporary discourses and practices opposed to discrimination and hostilities to the Other. Amongst others, this position is argued in detail in works by the Christian, Rosenstock-Huessy, the Jew, Franz Rosenzweig (*The Star of Redemption*), and, in several works including *The Fragile Absolute, Or, Why is the Christian Legacy Worth Fighting For?* (Verso, 2001), by the Lacanian Marxist-Leninist, Slavoj Zizek .

[9] Dante, "Inferno," Canto 3, 16-18, *The Divine Comedy*, translated by C.S. Sasson with introduction and notes by David H. Higgins (Oxford: Oxford University Press, 1993).

[10] Ernst Cassirer, *Substance and Function* (1910) later published in English with *Einstein's Theory of Relativity*.

[11] Kant's genius was to provide reasons for this superstition which has outlasted the creaky machinery of Kant's facultative logic.

[12] In fact, modern philosophy reproduced the same patterns of possibility as religions: dualism (Descartes, Locke, Kant), monism (Spinoza), and poly-ism (Leibniz), yet, in this case, dualism started the show and neither Spinoza nor Leibniz escaped it completely, as is evident in the binaries that hold their respective philosophies together, and their common parallelisms.

[13] *The Rebel*, translated by Herbert Read (Harmondsworth: Penguin, 1975 [1951]), 11. What he says here applies to every one of any political persuasion who rationalizes any murder as if it were not a terrible crime. And yet Camus does not give himself the moral luxury and existential cop-out of being an intellectual pacifist.

[14] *The Art of the Novel*, (New York: Grove, 1988 [1986]), 3-20.

[15] Romans, 3: 23.

[16] *Iliad*, 19: 178–9.

Bibliography

Baudelaire. Charles. *The Flowers of Evil*, Introduction by Jonathan Culler and translated by James McGowan. Oxford: OUP, 1993.

Bayle, Pierre. *Historical and Critical Dictionary: Selections*, translated with an introduction and notes by Richard Popkin. Indianapolis: Bobbs-Merrill, 1965.

Camus, Albert. *The Rebel*, trans. Herbert Read. London: Penguin, 1975.

Cassirer, Ernst *Substance and Function and Einstein's Theory of Relativity*. London: Open Court, 1923.

Dante, *The Divine Comedy*, trans., C.S. Sasson with introduction and notes by David H. Higgins. Oxford: Oxford University Press, 1993.

Homer, *The Iliad.* Trans., Robert Fagles. New York: Penguin, 1990.

——— *The Odyssey*. Trans., Robert Fagles. New York: Penguin, 1996.

Jacobi, Friedrich, *The Main Philosophical Writings and the Novel All Will: Friedrich Heinrich Jacobi*, translated and introduced by George di Giovanni (Montreal: McGill-Queens University Press, 1994).

Keegan, John. *A History of Warfare*, London: Pimlico, 1994.

Kundera, Milan. *The Art of the Novel*, (New York: Grove, 1988 [1986]).

Bonds of Authoritarianism and the Embodiment of Political Evil: An Interview with President Echeverría[1]

Alejandro Cervantes-Carson

To the memory of Galo Gómez Ogalde

Abstract: To meet with *the* person whom you had perceived for decades to be the embodiment of political evil can only create a subjective crisis, a crisis of the moral order, and a crisis of ethical standards. The experience of meeting with President Luis Echeverría, in a three-hour long interview, did that to me; all at once, before, during, and after the interview. While the interview was not focused on themes related to the reasons why he was being prosecuted for crimes against humanity in a democratizing Mexico, the spectres of these crimes hung heavily over the entire experience. It was the terrain of the unspoken; it was life and collective memory that were to be silenced. But the symbols were there: they were all there because I read them all to be there. I met his social and political embodiment with my social and political embodiment. In many ways it was not he and I who met, but historical, political, and symbolic forces behind each one of us that were at that meeting. It was a meeting of forces beyond our selves, of signifying circumstances beyond our control, the embodiment of energies (perhaps) that were struggling to define political democracy at that precise historical point in Mexico. This paper is the first exploration into this experience; it constitutes a first instalment of a longer-term research and book project that will try to make sense of these types of encounters.

Key Words: Authoritarianism, Democracy, Tlatelolco, Spectres, Complicities, Political Systems, Subjectivity, Embodiment, Political Sociology, Cultural Sociology.

1. Population Policies as Interview Narrative (or the Unavoidable Spectres of Politics and History)

In August of 2003 I conducted a three-hour long interview with former Mexican President Luis Echeverría. The central purpose of that interview was to explore the paradigmatic changes that so profoundly transformed population policies during his term 1970-1976 in office, and that had a lasting effect over the demographic dynamics of Mexico in the 20th century.

Mexico has been noted and recognized internationally for implementing an incredibly successful family planning program. Since 1973 and for three consecutive decades, governmental programmes had incorporated contraceptives as part of the general package of primary health care services, along with maternal and child care, throughout the country. This well supported and generously funded initiative made these services available to millions of Mexicans living both in urban and rural sites; services that were not even available to women and couples in many so-called developed and industrialized nations at the time. With the financial backing of international foundations and the matching of national funds, the most ambitious governmental programs of the 20th century were launched. The result was a massive and widespread family planning program that created, at once, new rights for citizens and services that were previously unconceivable (ideologically and empirically) to Mexicans.

The dimension of the change can be understood and gauged when compared with the policies of the first three quarters of the 20th century. The Mexican state and its governments firmly believed that the strength of a nation resided in its population. The size of the population was equivalent to the amount of national power: the more populous a nation, the more powerful, so it went. On this conception, Mexico (of course) was not alone, but few countries around the world held so firmly to these ideas. In fact, as early as three years before the policy changes, the distribution and prescription of contraceptives was illegal, and many physicians and nurses found themselves routinely harassed for suggesting or advising on ways to avoid pregnancies. The large exception to this rule is abortion, which continues to be illegal, causing needless deaths and unwarranted pain and grief.

In the last quarter of the 20th century and in a neo-Malthusian international environment, Mexico's policy accomplishments were set up as a standard to follow. Nations like India and China were admonished to understand that effectiveness was not at odds with legal standards based on the respect of human rights. It was the time of the "population bomb" mentality. Ideologies that equated national power with number of citizens were cornered, and suffered dwindling support. The political and ideological environment had changed; population growth was now conceived as the ultimate obstacle for economic development, for the modernization of a society, and for the construction of a modern lifestyle. Population growth rates were established as one of the crucial variables that divided the world into developed and underdeveloped nations, and that categorized countries as first, second or third world. It is not a coincidence, I believe, that the professionals and politicians that authored such indicators and classification criteria came mostly from "developed" nations, and that they found allies in the political elites of the "developing" nations.

Mexico's massive, highly organized, well funded, and effective family planning program caught the attention of world observers, no doubt, but what really created international praise was the effectiveness it had in reducing fertility rates and consequently bringing down population growth. The tipping point, however, was that everything had been set in motion by way of constitutional amendments, and that it had been carried out by an impressively well-oiled and service-oriented governmental machinery. The rights to decide freely about the number of children to have and when to have them were boldly enacted by introducing new articles in the constitution, and hundreds of thousands of physicians and nurses working for the state health-care system were made responsible for the success of the program. The combination of these factors created the rationale behind the award the United Nations gave Mexico in 1986.

It was Echeverría who had launched Mexico onto the scene of international modernization by way of demographic forecasting and policy change. For a developing nation in a neo-Malthusian environment, to reduce your population growth was thought to delimit economic development. "Excessive" births created an inordinate amount of demands and pressure over the national economy and this, in turn, burdened the possibilities of growth. It was Malthus brought from the dead and into the twentieth century; it was Malthus gone astray.

The discourse of development and population growth was only carved out for less developed nations; developed nations did not need to worry about these problems at all. It was the poor nations of the world who needed to control their growth; rich nations with low fertility rates needed, on the contrary, to find ways of enhancing their demographic base and increasing their populations. Within the boundaries of this discourse, it was very clear that population growth was only a problem of poor nations. Malthus was used (perhaps even abused) as a condescending rationale for speaking down to nations that were not able to "feed and sustain" their citizens.

The logic was simplistic at best. If poor countries could not create the necessary wealth for their people (as if distribution of wealth did not matter at all), then they needed to reduce the number of people who were "entered" into the economic and demographic equation of supply and demand. Of course, the most serious problem was that instead of commodities or objects, the discourse actually referred to people as objects. Fewer people meant reducing the demand over national wealth and resources. Not to reduce your population growth was by consequence perceived to be an injudicious decision, in fact, quite irresponsible. How could you not want to free the potential economic development from the burden of population growth? In this way, population control and planning were sold politically to poor nations as routes to achieving an economic development that had remained elusive to them through industrialization, productivity and investment.

That was the discursive equation of the time. Mexico's policy response was praised beyond belief, because it responded impeccably both to all of the "hardcore" requirements of population policy implementation and to the "soft" considerations of human rights.

I had pursued the interview with population policies in mind. And while Mexico's record was clear, my research agenda was fully loaded with political scepticism that had not been well received in many academic forums. After 10 years of research, I had reached an unpopular conclusion:

> While I found no evidence to support the claim that the violations have been massive, there is enough data to argue that they have been, however, systematic. In other words, the data suggest that these violations are not just clusters of mistakes in the provision of services or a series of random events product of individual cases of medical negligence. They suggest patterns of institutional disregard.[2]

Yet I found in the sociology of institutions some of the explanations as to why a liberal legal framework could have generated conditions that were counter to the spirit of the constitutional changes and the design of new rights.

> The establishment of population growth goals and their bureaucratic translation into fertility and contraceptive targets is problematic for reproductive rights in Mexico. Alone, they cannot be blamed for the violation of reproductive rights. However, the implementation of aggressive family planning programs with instrumental objectives, and under the responsibility of medical bureaucracies, has resulted in the formation of a public space more conducive to authoritarian practices that violate rights than to one that respects and fosters the unrestrained exercise of reproductive rights.[3]

My argument was clearly less demographic and more political. And it was unpopular not only for its critique, but also because a political argument made from demographic studies was seen as subjective and scientifically suspect. A positivistic dominant model in demography was not able to deal with the political and subjective dimensions of the production of knowledge in a refined and post-epistemological fashion, within the boundaries and discourse of science. Demography had gotten away with selling itself as a "hard" science, despite being hosted in social science departments throughout the academic world. This scientific credibility came mostly from the techniques used to estimate and construct projections. The hegemony of positivism made the use of mathematical and statistical models a source of scientific legitimacy. Yet as is the case in economics, many times sophisticated statistical models are based on very weak or not very sound empirical assumptions. Being perceived as a "hard" science brought demographers (the world over) credibility, legitimacy, policy leverage and all sorts of scientific privileges, aside from money; that is, huge amounts of funds for research, consulting, and policy design.

On the basis of my research I argued, in essence, that a well conceived population policy in the context of an authoritarian regime had a high risk of being implemented in an authoritarian fashion. And while I had not found a hefty amount of data that could verify a massive violation of individual rights, the evidence was sufficient to sustain my central claims. From a political-sociological perspective the conclusion made perfect sense, yet in demographic environments it was received as ludicrous and even insulting to policy-makers. Nobody can really blame demographers; they have never been known for their political perspicacity and wit. At the end, nevertheless, I believe that they were concentrating more on defending their privileges than debating my results and conclusions. My critiques, along with others coming from sociology, anthropology, and political science were flatly rejected by demographers in Mexico and the U.S., because they undermined their credibility and opened up the terrain for non-positivistic approaches to population studies.[4] Our critiques were perceived as threatening to their privileges and scientific standing.

While the central text of my interview with President Echeverría was population policies, our meeting was inevitably and unavoidably crisscrossed by multiple subtexts that linked our conversations with historical memory and biography, violence and authoritarianism, and of course politics, power, and democratization. These subtexts were all condensed under the metaphor of Tlatelolco: the Mexico City student massacre of October 2, 1968.

Canak and Swanson describe the events and its historical impact in the following way:

> In 1968, a series of large-scale student demonstrations erupted in Mexico City to demand free and mass education. As the protest expanded to include workers, peasants and unions, ideas of democracy and redistribution of wealth were adopted. The student movement was significant for several reasons. First, participation in the demonstrations included approximately 400,000 people ... Second, the student march to Tlatelolco Plaza in Mexico City, October 2, 1968 ended violently with Mexican police and army attacking the [unarmed and peaceful] group: 325 protesters were killed and thousands were injured ... Third, a number of students involved in the 1968 student movement influenced or became leaders of the urban popular movements in the early 1970s.[5]

For many analysts this was a political watershed moment in Mexican contemporary history.[6]

> The student movement of 1968 and the brutal government repression that brought it to an abrupt end deeply disturbed the Mexican people. A political, social, and moral crisis ensued that has not yet been resolved.[7]

Not only was the repressive state reaction excessive and unwarranted, but the systematic cover-up and official denial of the number of dead and injured came to signify the beginning of a political crisis of state legitimacy that did not end until the elections of 2000, when the one-party system was defeated in the presidential elections by the opposition party candidate Vicente Fox. Yet today, and at the end of his six-year term, his unfulfilled promises that he made as a candidate regarding the need to bring justice to this issue continue to stand as a representation of the lack of will on the part of the political elite in Mexico to help heal this historical wound and resolve it in the forum of public acknowledgement and deliberation.

More than three decades later, this metaphor hung as a spectre over our interview. Echeverría was being investigated by a special prosecutor for his alleged involvement in these crimes as Secretary of the Government (Interior Minister) and later as President. My generation had grown up scarred by these events and thinking of him as the embodiment of political evil. In this chapter, I would like to ethnographically reconstruct some of these subtexts, and offer interpretations of their political and moral meaning.

2. Gaze upon the Gaze (or Scrutinizing is a Two-way Street)

"I want to thank you, most sincerely - I said while making a gesture to gauge the hour on my watch - for devoting three hours of your time to us. You have been most kind and generous. Plus, I want to especially thank you for the lavish breakfast you arranged for us. I very much enjoyed it." I was not exaggerating; it had been a five-course breakfast in one of the dinning rooms of his house, not his office, but his private home.

"You are welcome," he said, with a pause that suggested something to follow, "yet I noticed you did not finish your *chilaquiles*!"[8] There was a very subtle smile on his face.

"You are absolutely right," I replied with no hesitation. And then we both engaged a pause that, in my mind, lasted an eternity. It was obvious that I could not but feel obligated to follow that statement with a minor revelation as to why I had not finished that dish. But my thoughts were elsewhere. He had noticed that I had not finished that particular dish, one of five. One detail among many, among thousands that happened during three hours had caught his attention. He had noticed that my plate of *chilaquiles* had enough food on it to warrant a mental note, to warrant the filing of a comment ready to be used in a precise and appropriate moment.

"They were delicious," I offered with honesty. "But you have to understand that I was concerned about the interview. In fact, to be frank, I was a bit nervous about the outcome. It is not that I get to interview a president of Mexico everyday!" His reply was unmistakably ambiguous: he smiled.

I had also noticed the "state" of his plates: he had not left a bit of food on any of them. And I had also made a mental note: at age 81 - I thought - that is one healthy appetite. So, why was I surprised about his observations? Why was I taken slightly aback by his comment? What struck me, I believe, was the minor discovery of the extraordinary behind the obvious.

This was not the first time, in an interview, that my sense of curiosity had been reciprocally shared by an interviewee, but this was beyond that experience. It was not that he was curious to know who I was or my level of sincere engagement with the interview process. What was at stake here was the degree of control over the entire interview process. The gaze upon the observed, it is true, had been turned onto the observer, that is, it had been turned onto me. More importantly though, I believe, this was his way of making two points. First, that I had been constantly under his gaze, systematically scrutinized, and he wanted me to know this. Second, that ultimately he had control over the whole interview process.

Let me be clear though, it is not that there had been any doubt about that: he had controlled the pace, the transitions, the timing, and the dynamics; he also had full control over his team of six advisors that for the first hour tested my knowledge, and my intellectual stamina, until he called them off; plus, it had taken me one full year to negotiate the interview and the conditions under which it would take place. His comment made a claim to a different realm of power: he was conveying and discursively asserting control over the subjective, over the intersubjective bond of interviewer and interviewee. Agreeing to an interview was allowing me to play the role of the interviewer with his express consent and his presidential permission. His comment made evident his gaze, discursively affirmed the control he had over the entire process and reminded me of the permission he had extended for me to play the privileged role of presidential interviewer.

The negotiation of the interview established two things: the theme and the boundaries within which I could inquire. It was out of the question to address anything that was related to the prosecutor's case, which meant nothing that had a connection to the Tlatelolco massacre or to the unrecognized "dirty war" of the 70s. This was never established forcefully. His personal secretary softly sketched the limits and suggested the inappropriateness of crossing them. There were no harsh admonishments, there were no warnings. Using the most skilful of diplomacies, she conveyed them to me, mostly between the lines. Yet I was never constrained about the questions I could ask, as long as I worked within the general issues of population and development policies.

By way of the negotiations I had formally empowered myself for the interview, yet in the same move I had relinquished the power to surprise on thorny issues; in a sense I had relinquished the "real" power of the interviewer. But did I really have an alternative? Was this not the obvious product of negotiating the possibility of having a thematic conversation with a president? Was it not naïve to suppose that a virtual nobody could retain the power of surprise?

Yes, in fact, I was a "nobody" and that was exactly the card that I had played. As a "nobody" I could not be perceived as threatening - that was my thinking. I presented myself as a scholar of population policies, which I was, but I had conveyed that I was only narrowly interested in such a field. In the final stage of the negotiations, I was asked to send along my vita, publications, papers and a rationale for the interview. Never did I suggest that I would use the interview material for other analytical projects. They did not ask and I did not offer. To be completely truthful, though, I never thought I would work a different analytical route with the interview data, I had always thought it would be great material which would be used exclusively for the expansion of my dissertation research. I was a "nobody" and had thought as a "nobody." And a "nobody" can always get away with being naïve, unaware, unsuspecting, and perhaps dull. In many ways it was a reciprocation of their diplomacy. In the negotiation of the interview they had softly set the thematic boundaries and I had softly accepted them. In return, I had made no promises as to how I would use the material and experience. I did not push their boundaries they did not restrict my analytical rights.

"Well, make yourself at home," he said, effectively ending our interview. If you happen to need anything, Juan is here to assist you." He left the room and behind his presence a guard, perhaps a bodyguard, stood in silence and following attentively all our moves, every move we made. Juan became our shadow for the next hour; a shadow that I only noticed when I tried to go to the bathroom and the shadow became a body that blocked my way.

Looking back, years after the interview, the image of a shadow that follows every one of our movements and that protects Echeverría from scrutiny becomes profoundly fitting. The shadow was blocking my way, but it only becomes evident when there is a pressing need. The protection he (and many others in the government) had enjoyed from prosecution (for crimes against humanity) was efficiently possible thanks to the work of shadows or of system-people working in the shadows. For dubious reasons the government had acted with unrestrained and disproportionate force against a student movement that was perceived to be a national threat; a threat to national interests, to the state, to the government, in turn, to the future of the nation.

As part of a campaign to discredit the movement and as a political preface to the massacre of Tlatelolco, the president at the time, Diaz Ordaz, had argued that the movement needed to be stopped because it embodied forces from abroad. This undefined term and reference rang a bell in a xenophobic culture like the one Mexico fostered in the 60s. According to Diaz Ordaz, students were being manipulated by alien forces; they had become puppets of interests contrary to Mexico's. Equating students with aliens meant - in the minds of retrograde Mexico - creating an association with things that were inherently bad and evil. Xenophobic reactions towards foreigners were a cultural currency in a nationalistic environment and closed political culture: what was Mexican was uncritically assumed to be better for Mexicans, for the country. To invoke alien forces was to suggest a veiled and malicious plan of other (wicked) countries to derail the course of Mexico's development and progress. There was nothing worse than what comes from abroad, especially if it comes as rebellion, contestation, and political unrest, especially if it questions "our way of governing", our systems of resolving internal conflicts. Foreign influences were only noticed as malicious forces when they came packaged in political critique.

The interview had ended. The film crew was gathering the video material. I stood in the middle of the room trying to centre myself. What had happened, exactly? Had I just interviewed President Echeverría, the "embodiment of political evil?" Yes, no doubt, my collaborators and friends could confirm that. Yet I still could not believe it. The question was less about the empirical reality of the interview and more about the morality of the experience.

It had taken me a long time to negotiate the interview, but the most difficult part was linked to the moral dimension. Throughout the negotiations I had remained sceptical about the possibility of achieving it, yet every time I considered a successful end to the negotiations I tried to imagine what I would feel and how I would deal with such a complex confrontation. Would I be able to handle the experience of being face to face with him? How would my vantage point, analysis, and critique change about authoritarian politics in Mexico? (That was perhaps the most hurtful question.) This was not a naïve question, I honestly wondered about how this encounter would modify my moral stands and ethical principles. After all I was interviewing the "embodiment of political evil." I was not worried about losing an ethical standpoint, but I frankly did not know how I would be affected by the experience.

As I pursued the negotiations, I felt the moral stakes rising. The closer I got to the possibility of a positive outcome, the more nervous I grew. Yet I was not nervous about the interview itself, but about how I would be affected. The connection between the subjective, the moral, and ethical dimensions concerned me. I literally lost sleep over these issues. There was a point in which the possibility of failing to get the interview actually started to sound appealing. If I were not to get it, at least I would have the perfect justification for not facing up to the moral conflict that was ensuing. It was certainly a very odd period for me.

By all accounts, the experience had been extraordinary, in the strict sense of the word. In an effort to assimilate the encounter, when Echeverría had diplomatically ended the interview, I stood in the middle of that room, there, silently, pensive, and in awe: had I really interviewed the "embodiment of political evil?" I will come back to this question later, hopefully with an answer.

3. Bureaucracy, Rituals, and Politics (or How Identity and Membership are Re-Created in Counter-Intuitive Ways)

One of the campaign promises of Vicente Fox when he was running for president in 2000, was to prosecute those who had been responsible, in previous administrations, for having perpetrated crimes against humanity. When he won the elections, Fox became the first candidate from the opposition to be sworn in as president; the Institutional Revolutionary Party had ruled Mexico for almost 75 years. Of course, he was very interested in appearing as a candidate who promoted justice and opposed authoritarian politics. He was not to be associated with the past. His administration was to be one of the future and of a different Mexico. Campaigns can never be equated with governing, we all know that. Nevertheless, when in office, Fox felt obligated to honour that particular promise; he appointed a prosecutor to look into those issues of Mexico's thorny past. That was the same year that I started my negotiations for the interview.

It was a late Sunday night. As I sat in my dining room, I thought about the number of phone calls invested, the faxes sent, the contacts mobilized, the time that had passed, the number of questions formulated; I was honestly a bit tired: one year, one full year of negotiating!

Yet there I was, dialling the number once again, just to follow the trail, just to be consistent, just to have a story to share with my friends, just to have a narrative to tell in the very likely case of not getting a damn thing! And then the concert of clicks began.

"Hello, hello?" I heard on the other side.

"Hello. This is Dr. Cervantes calling, I was wondering if we could talk about setting a date for the interview." Even when one ignores the threshold of power negotiation, there is a degree of familiarity that develops after repeated phone calls. Many phone calls back I had dropped the introductions and explanations. And in an opaque reciprocation, they had dropped their bureaucratic and seemingly insurmountable distance. One way or the other, in my mind, it was time to define the issue. At that point I felt it was time to push the boundaries of negotiation, time for the uncertainty of the negotiation to be defined or dealt with head-on. I needed a date or else a flat-out rejection. If it is not going to happen, for Nietzsche's sake I needed to know, I needed to be told! I was ready for a definition, for a clear map, for a decisive route.

"Yes of course. Let me try to reach his personal secretary. Can you hold for a second?" Click, click.

In many ways - I thought - one can read bureaucratic procedures as modern rituals and bureaucratic institutions as highly ritualistic modern temples. Mexico has been always full of institutions that ritualized all sorts of procedures. Over the years I had grown increasingly impatient. I had made the remarkably stupid (unconscious) mistake of starting to take bureaucratic delays as personal affronts. I know, believe me I know, but I have to admit that was the case. When one feels it is personal, bureaucracies have effectively won.

However, in my institutional dealings, it was the first time I had gained enough distance to have certain lightness about bureaucracies. Such was the case that I could not but feel surprised. I was no longer tied to an angry or impatient reaction. I was no longer intolerant of bureaucratic intolerance. That felt like a liberation.

Click, click. Click and click. "Dr. Cervantes? How can I help you?"

"Well, I am trying to set a date and time for an interview with President Echeverría." In the lingo of government and politics, once president, always president!

"Yes, yes. Can you hold a second?" Click, click, and click.

At one point in the 70s and 80s, the state was the largest employer of the nation. While on hold, I could imagine hundreds of thousands of people engaging in all kinds of rituals, repeating the same procedures over and over again, delaying and complicating processes, scolding folks for not knowing the precise documents to bring, and treating them like human garbage, scum. But I no longer saw them as mean-spirited or small-minded people out to get the ordinary citizen. Now they appeared, instead, as members of congregations poised to engage in rituals and to follow them from beginning to end. Rituals that they followed and repeated because in addition to everything we know about bureaucracies, there was a social space for identity formation, for membership creation. Yet I think it is important to make the case clearly. These ritualistic followers did not have the religious vein.

These were not fanatics, they were bureaucrats. They did not see themselves as people reproducing rituals of the past. And they were right - I thought - they are our modern (if I may) acolytes.

Click, click. "Dr. Cervantes? Well, I am going to transfer your call to the person that keeps his appointments."

"Great, thank you."

To the extent that their rituals are experienced as jobs, to that extent bureaucrats see themselves as problem-solvers, as satisfying requirements, as developing specific tasks, as following orders. Bureaucrats, efficient or not, are modern subjects. They all participate in complex organizations that rationalize different dimensions of social life, dimensions that are indispensable (should I use quotation marks?) for the functioning of societies. In this sense, it is impossible for bureaucrats to see their activities as rituals. It would make the narrative of the traditional past equivalent to that of the modern present; narratives that are not meant to collapse one into the other. To recognize that their activities could belong to ritualistic procedures would be equivalent to admitting that not all in modernity is rationalization, that many of the things that we modern subjects think of as necessary to facilitate life, to advance ends and shorten means, may exist for different reasons than we imagined.

We conceive of rituals as being at odds with modernity because we are eager (perhaps, even desperately eager) to believe that what we do is better than things in the past, than traditional things. In fact, modern stories, those that we tell ourselves constantly, are predicated on the idea that we have to be better than anything and anybody that came before. All of this is most definitely part of the discursive fantasy of modernity.[9]

"Dr. Cervantes? Sorry for keeping you on hold. We have gotten approval for the interview. All that is left is to arrange an appointment."

"That is no doubt good news," I said. Let's schedule the appointment."

"Oh, no, I still need to transfer you to the person that keeps his appointment book."

"Really? Ok then." Click, click, click; the silence on the other side made me wonder if I was still connected. Yet there I was with the phone in my hand, waiting, hoping to continue being connected.

Modern rituals? Is there such a thing? What are modern rituals? Within a rudimentary binary system of thought that opposes the traditional to the modern, rituals belong to a pre-modern past and bureaucracies are by no means seen as sites of tradition. But they are.

Sure, bureaucracies are not as efficient as they should be, but without them we modern subjects would not know how to survive. True, this was no ordinary bureaucratic procedure I was negotiating. It wasn't a driver's license, a renewal of a passport or a copy of a birth certificate, but actually an interview with a president. Yet the rituals were all there. Each fax and phone call was like a tiny rite of passage, small steps in a one-year journey to the top of the bureaucratic mountain, pieces towards gaining access to the high priest, in fact in a executively centralized political system (like Mexico has been), it was an access to the highest of all priests.

What seems impossible to recognize, in societies that praise themselves of being modern, is how much rituals contribute to our sense of self and belonging. Identity is very strongly made out of our participation in rituals. The public repetition of activities and the sharing of circumstances and organized experiences develop connections and bonds. These bonds, in turn, under certain cultural conditions of recognition, are structural contributors to the formation of identities. However, modern discourses of self-formation hide these connections and bonds. Modern identity claims appeal to ways of identity formation that are slightly different. In a combination of symbolic movements modern identities are thought to be linked to other spheres of activities and made to stand away from rituals.

Click, click. Click, click, and click. "Hello." The voice was unmistakable, it was him; it was Echeverría, himself, on the phone! But how on earth was he on the phone? Nobody had warned me that I would actually be talking to him today. "So, tell me, why would you be interested in interviewing me?" And there he was, putting me through my last rite of passage before the final approval of the interview.

4. Demonizing Subjects and Hiding Complicities (or the Political Games of Blame-Displacement)

The simple yet profoundly thoughtful design of the Truth and Reconciliation process in South Africa has always caught my attention. The idea that entire nations need to live through a collective process of confronting and recognizing the horrors of their social and political past is in and of itself a very powerful idea, that has (in my estimation) ramifications beyond the obvious.[10]

Yet what I find most brilliant has to do with the counterintuitive decision to define the Commission and the process with no prosecutorial and legal consequences. It locates, correctly, I believe, the societal experience of coping with injustices, especially those that are committed in the name of the state, as a collective enterprise, or a national project, in the public realm, the realm of collective consciousness. Lifting the burden of prosecution, trial, and punishment from the Commission created a collective and public space with the mission and capacity to cope with the complexities of the pain and suffering of social and political injustices. Mexico, unfortunately, is still very far from that place and process.

I would never argue or defend the idea that this is enough to heal such deep societal wounds; rather, the claim that I am making is that a process that seeks only legal prosecution misses the central point of collective coping. Collective coping cannot happen or wounds be healed through classic channels of justice procedures. The central reason is because in liberal jurisprudence, justice is defined in individual terms. Justice is reached between individuals by the mediation of courts. But liberal frameworks are ineffectual for reaching justice for groups and collective organizations.

Who we are and what we do socially are inevitably linked to the ways in which we are able to cope with experiences that we feel break our moral and political sense of being or belonging. One can not feel identified with a society that severs our moral sense of being. And this can only be healed by way of a symbolically reciprocal process. That is, a social and public process in which social injustices become acknowledged and part of the landscape of collective consciousness, however complex and imperfect this process might be.

Appointing a special prosecutor to investigate state sponsored human rights violations was the boldest political move that Mexico has witnessed in three decades. But as much as the appointment represents an initiation of a most needed process, it also hides serious flaws. Even beyond campaign promises and insincere discourses, I fear that targeting prosecution will push Mexico to skip over the most important part of the process, that is, a public and collective recognition of the horrors of the past, but most importantly of the intricate network of complicities that allowed the massacre of Tlatelolco to remain in the dark, unaccounted-for, non-recognized.

The massacre was heinous. But the cover-up required a silent and systematic intervention of thousands, perhaps hundreds of thousands of people, both civilians and bureaucrats. There were more than 300 hundred bodies that needed to be disposed of, immediately; there were hundreds of disappearances that became "paranoid stories," and millions of authoritarian actions that were explained-away or tolerated by bystanders. The most important process that Mexico needs to undergo - in my opinion - is the recognition of the intricate and multilayered complicities that society had with the authoritarian regime that ruled the nation for the greater part of the 20th century.

In February of 2006, a report prepared by a team of researchers from the special prosecutor's office was leaked to an academic in the U.S. As a director of the Mexico Project[11] at the National Security Archive, Kate Doyle decided to make the report publicly available by posting it on the Internet. In 800 pages, the report makes the crucial argument that the massacre of Tlatelolco was followed in the 70s and 80s by a 'dirty war' orchestrated by two consecutive administrations: that of Echeverría, from 1970 to 1976, and of Lopez-Portillo, from 1976 to 1982. The dimensions of the atrocities and numbers of victims cannot be compared to those of El Salvador or Guatemala (in Central America) or to those in Argentina and Chile (in South America), but the intention to erase political dissidence was the same. The Tlatelolco massacre was just the beginning of a systematic war against a politically critical and democratically active civil society, and the costs need to be accounted for.

"Nothing more than to think what we are doing", is how Hanna Arendt described her book in the introduction of *The Human Condition.*

As a way of explaining the continuity of her work and the internal substantive connections of her thought before and leading to the report on the "Banality of Evil", Bernard Bergen offers a reformulation of her intellectual intentions: "To think what we are doing by thinking over from the very beginning everything we ever thought we were doing."[12]

I will begin with my part, with my responsibility. I did not expect to find a kind and generous man, but I did, the day of the interview. I was not confronting the embodiment of political evil, yet at the same time, in the same space, but under a different narrative, I was. In this same sense, during the interview I was also an embodiment of the politically critical and democratically active in Mexico, and simultaneously, I was an embodiment of the silent and the complicit.

Notes

[1] I want to start by thanking all my friends and colleagues from the Amelie Restaurant (Barcelona) for carving out a space which ultimately allowed me to write and finish this piece even in the middle of the madness of "Fiestas de Gracia." A million thanks to my old friend and high school buddy Jaime Casillas, without whom the interview would not have happened. He made the initial and crucial contact (through a source who prefers to remain anonymous) and directed the filming of the interview like a master. The basic arguments made of this text and the project in general benefited from the discussions held in my ongoing research seminar ("Spectres of Violence, Authoritarianism, and Biography") held in the spring and fall of 2005 and the spring of 2006. I want to thank all of my students for their enthusiastic collaboration (in alphabetical order: Elizabeth Dowling, María García, Elizabeth Monk, and Emily Schott.) A Faculty Development Grant (from the University of Mary Washington) gave me initial funding for the development of the research project in the summer of 2005.

[2] Cervantes-Carson, Alejandro Cervantes-Carson. *Human Rights, Reproductive Rights, and Population Policies: A Theoretical Intervention, an Analytical Proposal, and an Application to the Case of Mexico*. Ph.D. Dissertation, University of Texas at Austin, 2002, 159.

[3] Ibid.

[4] Aside from my dissertation, examples of two critical articles I wrote that created discomfort in the field and community of professional demographers, especially because they were published in a population studies flagship journal in Mexico appear in the bibliography.

[5] William Canak and Laura Swanson. *Modern Mexico* (New York: McGraw-Hill, 1998), 176.
[6] See Héctor Aguilar-Camin and Lorenzo Meyer. *In the Shadow of the Mexican Revolution: Contemporary Mexican History, 1910-1989.* (Austin: University of Texas Press,1993); Kate Doyle. "Forgetting is not Justice. Mexico Bares Its Secret Past." *World Policy Journal* (summer, 2003): 61-72; Matthew Gutmann. *The Romance of Democracy: Compliant Defiance in Contemporary Mexico.* (San Francisco: University of California Press, 2002); Elena Poniatowska. *Massacre in Mexico.* (Columbia: University of Missouri Press,1992); Paco Ignacio Taibo II. *68.* (New York: Seven Stories Press, 2004).
[7] Paz, Octavio. "Introduction." In *Massacre in Mexico*, edited by Elena Poniatowska, (Columbia: University of Missouri Press, 1992), vii.
[8] There are many regional variations of this dish in Mexico; it basically consists of corn tortillas strips lightly fried and mixed with a cooked hot sauce (chile, tomato or tomatillo, onion, and spices), and meats (chicken, mostly), vegetables or eggs (scrambled or fried) on top.
[9] I find that Zygmunt Bauman makes a very compelling argument along these lines of reasoning. See, *La Cultura como Praxis,*(Barcelona, Spain: Paidós Ibérica, 2002) and also *Identidad,* (Buenos Aires, Argentina: Losada, 2005).
[10] I believe one can cite Julia Kristeva, *Strangers to Ourselves* (New York: Columbia University Press, 1991), as well as Jürgen Habermas, *The Inclusion of the Other: Studies in Political Theory* (Cambridge, Massachusetts: The MIT Press, 1998) to back up this argument. In fact, the argument is also soundly in sync with Bauman (2005), Jeffrey Alexander, *The meanings of social life:* A *cultural sociology* (New York: Oxford Univesity Press, 2003) and Seyla Benhabib, *Situating the self: gender, community, and postmodernism in contemporary ethics* (New York: Routledge, 1992).
[11] George Washington University, Washington D.C.
[12] Bergen, Bernard. *The banality of evil: Hannah Arent and "The Final Solution."* (Lanham, Maryland: Rowman & Littlefield, 1998), xiii.

Bibliography

Aguilar-Camin, Hector, and Lorenzo Meyer. *In the Shadow of the Mexican Revolution: Contemporary Mexican History, 1910-1989.* Austin: University of Texas Press, 1993.

Alexander, Jeffrey. *The meanings of social life:* A *cultural sociology*. New York: Oxford Univesity Press, 2003.

Alvarez, Sonia E., Evelina Dagnino, and Arturo Escobar, eds. *Cultures of politics/politics of cultures: re-visioning Latin American social movements*. Boulder, Colorado: Westview Press, 1998.

Arendt, Hannah. "Communicative power." In *Power*, edited by Steven Lukes, 59-74. Oxford, England: Blackwell, 1986.

Bauman, Zigmunt. *La Cultura como Praxis*. Barcelona, Spain: Paidós Ibérica, 2002.

——— *Identidad.* Buenos Aires, Argentina: Losada, 2005.

Benhabib, Seyla. *Situating the self: gender, community, and postmodernism in contemporary ethics*. New York: Routledge, 1992.

Bergen, Bernard. *The banality of evil: Hannah Arent and "The Final Solution."* Lanham, Maryland: Rowman & Littlefield, 1998.

Camp, Roderic Ai. *Politics in Mexico: The Democratic Transformation*. London, England: Oxford University Press, 4th edition, 2002.

Canak, William, and Laura Swanson. *Modern Mexico*. New York: McGraw-Hill, 1998.

Cervantes-Carson, Alejandro. "Human Rights, Reproductive Rights, and Population Policies: A Theoretical Intervention, an Analytical Proposal, and an Application to the Case of Mexico". Ph.D. Dissertation, University of Texas at Austin, 2002.

——— Política de Población. Nuevas alternativas o viejas premisas para 1989 a 1994?" *Demos, Carta demográfica sobre México*. 3 (1990): 22-23.

———"Planificación Familiar. La preocupación por las metas" *Demos, Carta demográfica sobre México*. 2 (1989): 8-9.

Doyle, Kate. "Forgetting is not Justice. Mexico Bares Its Secret Past." *World Policy Journal* (summer, 2003): 61-72.

Denzin, Norman K. and Yvonna S. Lincoln, eds. *Handbook of Qualitative Research.* Thousand Oaks, California: Sage Publications, second edition, 2000.

Ellis, Carolyn and Arthur P. Bochner. "Autoethnography, Personal Narrative, Reflexivity: Researcher as Subject ." In *Handbook of Qualitative Research,* edited by Norman K. Denzin and Yvonna S. Lincoln, 733-768, Thousand Oaks, California: Sage Publications, second edition, 2000.

Foucault, Michel. "The Art of Telling the Truth." In *Critique and Power. Recasting the Foucault/Habermas Debate*, edited by Michael

Kelly, 139-148. Cambridge, Massachussetts: The MIT Press, 1994

——— "Disciplinary Power and Subjection." In *Power*, edited by Steven Lukes, 229-242. Oxford, England: Blackwell, 1986.

——— *Politics, Philosophy, Culture: Interviews and Other Writings, 1977-1984*. New York: Routledge, 1988.

——— *Power/Knowledge: Selected Interviews and Other Writings, 1972-1977*. New York: Pantheon Books, 1980.

Fraser, Nancy. *Unruly Practices. Power, Discourse and Gender in Contemporary Social Theory*. Minneapolis: University of Minnesota Press, 1989.

Gutmann, Matthew. *The Romance of Democracy: Compliant Defiance in Contemporary Mexico.* San Francisco: University of California Press, 2002.

Habermas, Jürgen. "Hannah Arendt's Communications Concept of Power." In *Power*, edited by Steven Lukes, 59-74. Oxford, England: Blackwell, 1986.

——— *The Inclusion of the Other: Studies in Political Theory.* Cambridge, Massachusetts: The MIT Press, 1998.

Hodder, Ian. 2000 "The interpretation of documents and material culture." In *Handbook of Qualitative Research,* edited by Norman K. Denzin and Yvonna S. Lincoln, 703-716, Thousand Oaks, California: Sage Publications, second edition, 2000.

Kelly, Michael, ed. *Critique and Power. Recasting the Foucault/Habermas Debate*. Cambridge, Massachusetts: The MIT Press, 1994.

Kristeva, Julia. *Strangers to Ourselves*. New York: Columbia University Press, 1991.

McAfee, Noelle. *Habermas, Kristeva, and Citizenship*. Ithaca, New York: Cornell University Press, 2000.

The National Security Archive. *Report Documents 18 Years of "Dirty War" in Mexico,* February 26, 2006, (February 28, 2006). <http://www.gwu.edu/~nsarchiv/NSAEBB/NSAEBB180/index.htm>.

Nicholson, Linda J., and Steve Seidman. "Introduction." In *Social Postmodernism. Beyond Identity Politics*, edited by Linda J. Nicholson, and Steve Seidman, 1-35. Cambridge: Cambridge University Press, 1995.

Paz, Octavio. "Introduction." In *Massacre in Mexico*, edited by Elena Poniatowska, vii-xvii, Columbia: University of Missouri Press, 1992.

Poniatowska, Elena. *Massacre in Mexico*. Columbia: University of Missouri Press, 1992.

Silverman, David. "Analysing talk and text." In *Handbook of Qualitative Research,* edited by Norman K. Denzin and Yvonna S. Lincoln, 821-834, Thousand Oaks, California: Sage Publications, second edition, 2000.

Skidmore, Thomas E., and Peter H. Smith. *Modern Latin America*. Oxford: Oxford University Press, 2001.

Taibo II, Paco Ignacio. *68*. New York: Seven Stories Press, 2004.

Tarrow, Sidney. (1998) *Power in movement: social movements and contentious politics*. Cambridge, England: Cambridge University Press.

Tedlock, Barbara (2000) "Ethnography and ehtnographic representation." In *Handbook of Qualitative Research,* edited by Norman K. Denzin and Yvonna S. Lincoln, 455-486, Thousand Oaks, California: Sage Publications, second edition, 2000.

Wartenberg, Thomas E. "Situated Social Power." In *Rethinking Power*, edited by Thomas E. Wartenberg, 79-101. Albany, New York: State University of New York Press, 1992.

Young, Iris Marion. "Justice and the politics of difference." In *The New Social Theory Reader: Contemporary Debates*, edited by Steven Seidman and Jeffrey C. Alexander, 203-211. London: Routledge, 2001.

Warfare, Pacifism, or Sabotage: Eastern Christian Responses to Political Aggression

Stephen Morris

Abstract: In the history of Byzantine Christianity, three classic responses to aggression developed: fighting back, pacifism, and apparent cooperation in order to subvert. I would like to examine these Eastern Christian responses to the aggression of barbarians onto Roman territory, the aggression of one tenth-century Bohemian prince against his brother, and the aggression of the Soviet state against the Church.

Key Words: Aggression, sabotage, pacifism, Byzantine, subversion, Vaclav, Bohemia, Boleslav

I. Chrysostom's Teaching on the Christian Ruler and Justinian's Realization

"Valour," said Procopius (the sixth century eye-witness and recorder of the emperor Justinian's military exploits), "is unable to dwell with lawlessness but always shuns those who are unholy."[1] Since he is describing Justinian's enemies, it is clear that Justinian is both valorous and holy; bringing law - and therefore, order - to the barbarian world that he is reincorporating into the Byzantine fold. I suggest that Justinian and his Byzantine contemporaries saw these wars as acts of "liberation" bringing freedom to the subjects of tyrants[2] whose rule went hand-in-hand with that of the Antichrist himself. The stage for such a view had been set two centuries earlier by the preaching of John Chrysostom, especially in his homilies on II Thessalonians 2:1-12.

> Let no one deceive you in any way; for that day will not come, unless the rebellion comes first, and the man of lawlessness is revealed, the son of perdition…. And you know what is restraining him now so that he may be revealed in his time. For the mystery of lawlessness is already at work; only he who restrains it will do so until he is out of the way. (II Thess. 2:3, 6-7)

"What restrains?" John asks. Some say the Spirit, he answers, and some say the Roman Empire. John endorses the latter opinion: "I agree with those who say it is the Empire." If the apostle Paul had meant the Spirit, he would have said so plainly, John asserts; he had to speak in code because it was dangerous to say out loud that there would come a time when Rome would not be there to restrain the Antichrist.[3] Even though some of those exercising imperial dominion were wicked (or even *types* of the Antichrist, such as Nero), that does not detract from the central role of the Roman government *per se* (any more than a bad local governor means all "authority" is ill-founded, as John preached in his series on *Romans*). Rome, even pagan Rome that persecutes Christians, staunches the anarchy and chaos that inevitably arise in the absence of a strong civil government; it is in preventing this outbreak of anarchy that Rome restrains the Antichrist who would otherwise seize his opportunity in the confusion following the fall of Rome. Rome is in fact so important in restraining his bid for power that the Antichrist himself will be driven to destroy Rome (the deceiver himself to be later destroyed by Christ at the Second Coming).

Chrysostom considered the Antichrist to be the personification of chaos and destruction. It was the power of Rome (even in her pagan days) that kept complete anarchy and destruction at bay. Rome made the experience of beauty in all its senses possible by making universal peace a reality.[4] Good citizen that he was, Chrysostom thought of himself as a "Roman" living in the "New Rome" of the ongoing "Roman Empire" which continued to restrain the Antichrist. In fact, Chrysostom never lived to see the fall of the Old Rome in the West and therefore would all the more consider himself a citizen of the "One Empire" which had simply moved its political bureaucracy from Italy to the Bosphorus. This trust in the royal figure fending off supernatural evil is a primeval religious idea with deep roots; Chrysostom is here tapping into ideas which had shaped ancient Jewish practice and would continue to be felt for centuries following John's preaching.[5]

When Constantine legalized Christianity in 313 C.E., he was enrolled as a catechumen - a candidate preparing for baptism - and was baptized only on his deathbed. This tradition of imperial deathbed baptisms continued as the violent responsibilities of ruling - such as war and executions - were considered inappropriate and even impossible for baptized Christians to carry out. It was when Theodosius I was gravely ill and baptized at death's door [380 C.E.] but subsequently recovered, that the "birth pangs" of what it meant to be a baptized Christian emperor began. Theodosius I was the first emperor to survive his deathbed baptism and then face the difficulties of being both a baptized Christian and Emperor. The crisis of negotiating both roles - for him personally and for the political make-up of the Empire - is not always sufficiently appreciated, even by Byzantinists. The conflicts of Theodosius with Ambrose of Milan can be seen - at least, in part - as one aspect of this painful process of transition. Furthermore, Theodosius' beginning to dismantle the remnants of classical pagan culture and the legal establishment of Christianity as the official *religio* of the empire (which was finalized under Justinian) can also be seen as the results of Theodosius' wrestling with his conscience in his efforts to determine what was appropriate conduct for an emperor who was actually baptized and not merely a catechumen. Chrysostom's preaching certainly played a role in how the emperor Arcadius (the successor of Theodosius) sorted out what his dual responsibilities were, both as a Christian personally and as political ruler of the Roman world, and how these roles were to be reconciled. Chrysostom's sermon on the occasion of Eudoxia using imperial power to seize a widow's vineyard certainly had ramifications for the imperial couple both as private citizens and political personages. The conflict between personal responsibility as a Christian and political responsibility as imperial ruler continued among the heirs of Byzantine Christianity, the newly converted Rus', as well.[6] It is not inconceivable that Arcadius and subsequent emperors saw their divinely sanctioned function in world politics as complementary to the ministry of Chrysostom himself: the bishop and the emperor were each charged with facilitating and safeguarding the Christian lives of those committed to their charge. It was the two faces of one ministry committed to two different orders in the Church.[7]

Chrysostom's preaching certainly laid the groundwork for the emperors to work out (in their own minds, at least) what it was they were called by God to do in their political and personal lives.[8] John created the climate in which it was possible for later Byzantine political theory to flourish and in which it was possible for Justinian, as both lay member of the Church and as emperor, to proclaim on March 6, 535:

> The greatest gifts that God's heavenly *philanthropia* bestowed upon men are the *sacerdotium* and the *basileia*, of which the former serves divine matters, the latter presides and watches over human affairs, and both proceed from one and the same principle and regulate human life. Hence, nothing should claim the emperor's care so much as the saintliness of the priests, since these constantly pray to God for them [the emperors]. For, if the priesthood is in every way blameless and acceptable to God, and the *basileia* rules justly and properly over the state entrusted to it, good harmony (*symphonia*) will result, which will bestow whatever is beneficial upon the human race.[9]

Two months later, Justinian is even more explicit: "The priesthood and the imperium do not differ so very much, nor are sacred things so very different from those of public and common interest."[10] While not quoting Chrysostom's sermons of more than a century earlier, John's ideas are clearly in the background of Justinian's edicts: the imperial authority is given to the world to act as the primary barrier against chaos, disorder, and ruin. By establishing peace and maintaining order (in Chrysostom's view), the imperial authorities acted out of love and charity for those poor and powerless who would otherwise be destroyed by the greed and might of the powerful. A stable society was more conducive to charity and almsgiving than an insecure society in which each citizen would be too preoccupied with the struggle for his own survival to bother caring for his neighbour. This Roman order itself was the envy of the barbarian kingdoms.[11] While the immediate historical circumstances prompting Justinian's thoughts were very different in their details from the circumstances in which Chrysostom preached, the notion that the *imperium* is given to the world for mankind's protection against disarray and confusion - the powers of the Antichrist - echo in Justinian's assertion that good harmony will result when the emperor and his government rule justly and properly. Justinian's military policy can also be seen as another aspect of the royal function to restrain the Antichrist: by re-establishing Byzantine (i.e. Roman) dominion in the western territories he was not simply extending his own power or the glory of the state but was liberating the western territories from barbarian rule, reintegrating them into the One Empire as opposed to the multitude of smaller kingdoms and warring municipalities. The Roman army in these efforts was itself an image of this idealized Empire: the multitude of nations (represented by the wide variety of the soldiers' ethnic origins)[12] living in harmony and order, under imperial command and sharing the Orthodox faith. Justinian was freeing the barbarians from the confusion and disorder which was inherently a mark of the unholy rule of the Antichrist.[13]

In his *Institutes*, Justinian insists that fighting war and establishing law are the two God-given duties of the imperial office.[14] Even Justinian's choice of generals for these wars can be interpreted as an eschatological act. Of his two principal generals, Belisarius and Narses, one (Narses) was a eunuch[15] - a member of a servant class despised as self-serving, effeminate, and unable/inappropriate to command "real" (lit. "bearded") men in battle.[16] By choosing a member of such a class to lead his army, Justinian was already anticipating the "great reversal" of the End Times, when the last will be made first and the first, last. (Luke 1:52; Matthew 20:16) Justinian's wars to "liberate" the subjects of the sinful, petty tyrants of the Vandals[17] and the Goths[18] were part of the great eschatological battle between darkness and light, good and evil, Christ and Antichrist.

II. Vaclav's *Via Media* as Passion-Bearer

If Justinian fought wars to overcome the political evil of disorder and chaos, Vaclav of Bohemia sought to overcome political evil by non-violence and self-surrender. For the *vita* of Vaclav, we turn to the 1585 version of Matthias Hutsky which he illuminated with reproductions of the scenes of Vaclav's life from the saint's shrine in the cathedral of Prague.[19] This *vita* is based on the 1552 History of the Kings of Bohemia by Jan Dubravius, which "emphasizes historical events, such as were recounted in the earliest Wenceslaus legends" of the tenth and eleventh centuries and "assimilates the influence of European humanism… integrating Czech humanism within the wider European context."[20] The Dubravius' version is clearly attempting both to be faithful to the historical reality of Vaclav and to serve as an instruction manual for contemporary rulers, "a mirror for princes" who could profit from the example of Vaclav.

Vaclav was born in 903 C.E. and raised by his Christian grandmother, Ludmilla. His mother, Drahomira, was a particularly cruel and vengeful pagan queen whose husband Vratislav was easily intimidated by the women in his life: of his two sons, he gave the elder, Vaclav ("who showed greater talent and seemed more promising")[21] to his mother at her behest to be raised as a Christian, while he allowed his wife Drahomira ("who was completely alienated from Christian religion…. [and] showed greater severity and cruelty towards Christians than Jezebel toward prophets")[22] to persecute the Christians. Finally,

> Vratislav died, and having left his sons as heirs, but of immature age, the heathen Drahomira, an extremely cruel woman, usurped the reign in Bohemia and [claiming to rule in the name of Boleslav] immediately revealed her until-then badly disguised hatred of Christians, having decreed that Christians should close their churches and refrain from divine services and long-established ceremonies. Neither the priests…nor the school teachers were to instruct the people. Those who disobeyed were threatened with jail, exile, or death….And if any of the Christians killed one of them [a pagan], perhaps in self-defense, ten paid with their head for one.[23]

Christian judges were replaced by pagans who would support Drahomira's program of oppression. Ludmilla rallied the nobility who opposed Drahomira and together they acclaimed eighteen-year-old Vaclav the prince of Bohemia in 921. He banished his mother to the countryside. He assigned his brother's share of the inheritance to beyond the Elbe, so that the river became the border between the territories on either side.[24]

Vaclav restored Christianity and devoted himself to raising the standards of Bohemian life, especially in the environs of the capital, Prague. He promoted the general level of education, improved agricultural practices to increase productivity, and organized social welfare programs. He was himself involved in tending the sick and needy as well as organizing the redemption of hostages and slaves from the surrounding countryside.

Drahomira and Boleslav were both jealous of Vaclav's popularity and power and angry at having been deposed by the nobles and exiled by Vaclav. They wanted at least that power, if not that popularity as well, for themselves. They continually fuelled whatever flames of discontent there were in Bohemia so as to improve their chances for staging a *coup d'etat.*[25] Although kept at a distance from court by Vaclav, their schemes and spies were everywhere.

Boleslav (either in cooperation with his mother or at her instigation entirely) finally devised a sure-fire scheme to bring about his brother's downfall.

> Invited by his brother Boleslav to celebrate the christening of his baby son, St. Wenceslaus came, having first put in order his affairs at home, confessed to a priest and received the sacrosanct bread to ensure his eternal salvation, because of [a] foreboding of impending doom.
>
> And there at midnight, offering his prayers to God as usual, he [was] killed, struck by the sword of his brother....[26]

According to one version of the story, Vaclav is in fact only wounded in the initial attack and calls on his fleeing assailants to come finish their work, pulling aside his garments to expose his throat or breast to their knives.[27] It was this vindictive anger and hunger for power on the part of Vaclav's mother and brother that brought Vaclav down, in the short term.

Vaclav quickly reasserted himself, however, as pilgrims flocked to his tomb (despite the new ruler Boleslav's anger). Miracles proliferated.[28]

Boleslav the Cruel and Drahomira were subsequently overthrown and killed by the long-suffering populace who invoked Vaclav's intercession and protection, longing for the days of Vaclav's rule.[29] The saintly prince ultimately triumphed over his brother by dying at his brother's hand.

Vaclav accepted Boleslav's invitation to act as godfather, knowing that he was placing himself in a dangerous position. In Boleslav's territory, surrounded by Boleslav's supporters, Vaclav deliberately put himself at risk in the hope of bringing peace to Bohemia. He went, in the words of Isaiah (53:7), "as a lamb that is led to the slaughter" in order to save his people from further strife. If Boleslav was being honest in his pledge to raise his son (Vaclav's nephew) as a Christian, then Vaclav's trust in his brother would pay off with peace in the family now and in the countryside, later. If Boleslav were planning to waylay or assassinate Vaclav (as the prince most likely suspected), then Vaclav's pacifism and non-violent resistance would also bring peace to the land by sparing his people from civil war.

Vaclav was not - strictly speaking - a pacifist at all times or in all circumstances. He led the Bohemians in battle on numerous occasions to defend themselves against attacks from various enemies.[30] Therefore his pacifism in the face of Boleslav's aggression was not part of a general program of non-aggression but a clearly thought-out strategy for dealing with his brother and their mother, Drahomira.

It was this voluntary self-surrender that won Vaclav the title "passion-bearer" in the calendar of eastern Christian saints. He, together with a handful of other political leaders (such as Olaf of Norway [d. 1030], Boris and Gleb of Russia [d. 1015], or John-Vladimir of Serbia [d. 1016]),[31] declined to fight civil wars to defend their prerogatives as rulers - or heirs to the crown - of their various dynasties. They followed the path of innocent suffering for the deliverance of others, that of Christ in His Passion; they considered it was "better for one man to die for the people, and that the whole nation should not perish" (John 11:50) than for hundreds or thousands of innocent men to die fighting a war to keep an earthly king on his temporal throne.

> The East European cult of national rulers had one feature which deserves special mention, partly for its intrinsic interest and partly because it reveals a striking independence of Byzantine hagiographical and political

> models. It found expression in the posthumous veneration of princes who were victims of political murder and whose death was held to be a voluntary sacrifice, made in conscious imitation of Christ's sacrificial death. They were regarded as martyrs, not in the sense that they were killed for the Christian faith, but because, by their act of non-resistance, they chose to die as innocent and voluntary victims in imitation of Him who, by laying down His life for mankind, became the supreme prototype of all martyrs.[32]

The passion-bearers are seen as following not only in the footsteps of Christ but also of David in his one-on-one battle with Goliath. They went toe-to-toe with their adversaries and in some cases triumphed (such as the Byzantine emperor Heraclius against the Persian general Razatis)[33] and in other cases, lost. When they won, their image was assimilated to that of David, shepherd and king, who triumphed against overwhelming odds through his faith in God. When they lost, their image was assimilated to that of Christ, "who reigned victorious from the Tree,"[34] dying that others might live. But there was no way of knowing beforehand if they would survive or be killed: would they follow the path of David or Christ? It was a calculated risk, a political gamble; in either case, an act of faith.

But is such passivity in the face of naked aggression and wickedness ever really acceptable? Is taking the chance of losing a one-on-one battle with evil the action of a responsible leader? It is possible to argue that Vaclav or Boris and Gleb or any of the other royal passion-bearers could do more to save the lives of their people by standing up to and leading an armed force against Boleslav, Drahomira, and the other evil contenders for their thrones.

Here we come up against two very different ideas of what constitute acceptable force in a "means vs. ends" situation: the Western idea of a "just war" versus the Eastern model of "the lesser of two evils still remains evil." The nutshell version of the Western idea begins with Augustine's assertion that

> If the Christian Religion forbade war altogether, those who sought salutary advice in the Gospel would rather have been counseled to cast aside their arms, and to give up soldiering altogether. On the contrary, they were told: 'Do violence to no man… and be content with your pay'

> [Luke 3:14]. If he commanded them to be content with their pay, he did not forbid soldiering.[35]

Its final, classic form can be summarized: an aggressor threatens to murder hundreds of thousands or millions (or more, given modern technology). He can be stopped, but only at the cost of hundreds or thousands (or more) men dying in battle. The cost of war (in human life) is less than the cost of giving the aggressor free rein, and so the war is "justified" to defend those who would otherwise be subject to the wicked aggressor's evil designs. Personally, each soldier in battle is then absolved from his responsibility for - or role in - the killing. He is not guilty of murder, however many of the other side's soldiers he kills.[36]

The Eastern idea differs considerably from this. In the Eastern Christian vision, a war may be an act of self-defense against an unwarranted aggression, but each soldier is still responsible for his battlefield actions. As articulated by Basil the Great and confirmed by the Council of Ancyra, a soldier ought to abstain from Holy Communion for a certain period (from three to ten years, depending on the particular epistle of Basil's cited), "on the ground that they are not clean-handed."[37]

Given this differing vision of responsibility for battlefield deaths, Vaclav's self-surrender to Boleslav's attack fits the Eastern Christian world-view. Bohemia was part of the Central European overlap between Byzantine and Latin missionary expansion and operated "bi-ritually" for another century after Vaclav.[38] Although Vaclav himself practiced Latin Christianity as an adult, all his training in Christian life[39] had been steeped in the principles of Byzantine Christianity.[40] Vaclav, as ruler, was caught between a rock and a hard place (as it were): he would be responsible for any deaths in battle and he would be responsible for the death of anyone at the hands of Boleslav's minions if he did not fight against his brother. In the end, he clearly thought it was worth the risk to walk into Boleslav's trap and trust God to deliver Bohemia in whatever way He saw fit.

III. Vaclav's Response in a Modern Context

Although Vaclav's actions make sense from an Eastern Christian perspective, can modern nation-states operate according to these same principles? It was a question even in the tenth century: "Precisely by placing the terrible question - can a holy man be a fitting duke? - in the mouth of his enemies, the *vita's* author undercuts its validity."[41] The sixteenth century manuscript (based on the tenth century text), which was intended to be a "mirror of princes," clearly endorsed Vaclav's behaviour as a model to be emulated by contemporary rulers. Even if the *vita* intended Vaclav's pacifism to be read as a "parable," not precisely corresponding to what we would call "historical reality," it held up such pacifistic self-surrender as the exemplary behaviour of a political leader. Can a modern leader be called "responsible" if he volunteers to walk into a suspected trap or fight single-handed combat against the enemy of his country and let that single struggle determine the outcome of the war? Can the fate of millions rest on the fighting ability and prowess of a single individual? What if Churchill had volunteered to fight Hitler one-on-one? Could George W. Bush have been asked to walk alone into Saddam Hussein's Baghdad palace? Or into Osama bin-Laden's Afghanistan hideout?

What may be acceptable – and even admirable – for a private individual (remember Terry Waite's decision to travel alone into Beirut, Lebanon in 1987 to deal directly with the Islamic Jihad kidnappers and his subsequent five-year captivity) takes on very different ramifications when practiced by a head of state. Ultimately, this is the same question as that which perplexed Tertullian [42] in second-century North Africa, the emperor Theodosius I in fourth century Byzantium, and others throughout history: "Can a nation-state be ruled by a practicing Christian? Can Caesar be baptized and still remain Caesar?"

Yet a third model for dealing with evil political systems emerges in the mid-twentieth century as bishops of the Russian Orthodox Church reacted to the Soviet regime. "From October 1917, when the Bolsheviks seized power, until around 1988, the year when Russian Christianity celebrated its millennium, the Orthodox Church in the Soviet Union existed in a state of siege."[43] The ancient patriarchate of Moscow, abolished by Peter the Great in 1721, was restored by the 1917 All-Russian Church Sobor [Council] which elected Tikhon Bellavin, the former Archbishop of New York, as patriarch.[44] Shortly after Tikhon's election as patriarch, Lenin and the Provisional Government abolished the private ownership of land (the Church being "thus stripped of its property literally overnight")[45] and then proceeded to publish, in January 1918, "The Law of Separation of Church and State and School and Church." Confiscation and desecration of other church property followed shortly, as did the murder or imprisonment of clergy.[46]

Tikhon denounced this onslaught. He anathematized the Soviet regime and anyone who cooperated with its program of persecution.

> The open and secret enemies of the Truth of Christ have begun to persecute [the Orthodox Church] and are

> striving to destroy [it] ... sowing everywhere... the seeds of malice, hatred, and fratricidal strife.
> ...Bethink yourselves, you senseless ones, and stop your bloody retributions. For that which you are doing is not only a cruel deed; it is in truth a Satanic deed, for which you shall suffer the fire of Gehenna in the future life beyond the grave, and the terrible curse of posterity in the present life on earth.
> By the authority given us by God we forbid you to partake of the sacraments of Christ, and anathematize you....
> We exhort also all of you, the faithful children of the Orthodox Church of Christ, to refrain from communicating with these monsters of the human race in any way whatever....[47]

Tikhon's defiance was endorsed by the Sobor and he remained immensely popular with the general public.[48] He denounced the assassination of the czar ("Whoever does not condemn it will be guilty of his blood")[49] and on the first anniversary of the revolution, Tikhon wrote to Lenin: "he called on them to desist from 'the persecution and destruction of the innocent.'"[50] Even as he condemned the Bolshevik actions, he refused to bless the White army in the Crimea;[51] he also "issued an encyclical ... [in 1919] ordering the clergy to stand aloof from politics of any kind and freeing the faithful from all political obligations on the grounds that the Church and the state had been separated by the Soviet Constitution...."[52] Nevertheless, Tikhon was first subjected to house arrest and then imprisonment and, presumably, torture. In 1923 he issued a declaration from prison in which he "confesses his counter-revolutionary activities," which resulted from his upbringing in a monarchist society and the influence of anti-Soviet persons.[53] He enumerates his anti-soviet activities and

> Recognizing the correctness of the decision of the Court to bring me to trial ... for my anti-Soviet activities, I regret my actions against the State regime and request the Court to do away with my detention, i.e., to release me from arrest.
> I also declare to the Supreme Court that I am no longer an enemy of the Soviet power.[54]

He was released from prison shortly thereafter. "There existed, naturally enough, a great deal of...speculation, whether the text of this declaration had not been dictated to the patriarch by the authorities,"[55] especially as he contradicted certain key points of it in an interview a short time later.[56] Tikhon remained under close watch and died under suspicious circumstances in April, 1925.[57]

The Russian émigré Sergei Bulgakov preached at Tikhon's memorial service in Prague:

> [the Patriarch] in his relations with the State, which under the mask of separation of Church and State was openly hostile to the Church, ... worked for the preservation of the Church's independence. Under the existing conditions, when all possibility of normal interaction between Church and State was excluded – this independence should be realized only by complete aloofness of the Church from the State; in other words, by the Church being non-political and thus indeed separate from the State. Though this state of things was far from being desirable under the conditions, it answered best to the dignity of the Church. The Patriarch preserved the Church from identification with the White movement - inasmuch as that movement was not an expression of the mind of the majority of the people, which had not yet passed out of the disease of Bolshevism. He preserved the Church from any too much connection with any of the political groups, as became apparent after the Karlovitz Synod of the émigré churches. He preserved the Church from being swallowed up by the sinister element of the 'Living Church,' which aimed at making it an obedient tool of the Soviet government.... In open fight with the Church, the 'Living Church' was defeated, and the Patriarch emerged victorious, though a prisoner, but strong in the faith and trust of the people.[58]

Tikhon's initial defiance of the Bolsheviks continued even as he tried to distance the Church from any one particular secular political party, monarchist or Marxist.[59] His post-imprisonment conciliatory attitude is difficult to take seriously, given the circumstances surrounding its promulgation.[60] Tikhon's successor, Sergei followed his lead by insisting (1926) that

> ...while promising complete loyalty obligatory upon all citizens of the [Soviet] Union, we, representatives of the ecclesiastical hierarchy, cannot enter into any special engagement to prove our loyalty.[61]
>
> We cannot accept the duty of watching over the political tendencies of our co-religionists.... Far from promising reconciliation with the irreconcilable and from pretending to adapt our faith to Communism, we will remain from the religious point of view what we are, that is, members of the traditional Church.[62]

It is his declaration of the following year (1927), after imprisonment, which is often seen in the West as "capitulation" to the Soviet authorities.[63] Sergei's declaration asserts that

> We wish to remain Orthodox and at the same time to recognize the Soviet Union as our civil fatherland whose joys and successes are our joys and successes, and whose misfortunes are our misfortunes. Every blow directed against the Union... we acknowledge as a blow directed against us. Remaining Orthodox, we regard it our duty to be citizens of the Union 'not from fear, but from conscience,' as the Apostle has taught us (Romans 13:5).[64]

He goes on to insist that

> ...the clergy abroad [make] a written promise of their complete loyalty to the Soviet government in all their public activities. Those who fail to make such a promise, or observe it, shall be expelled from the ranks of the ... Moscow patriarchate.... Our demand may perhaps cause many to pause and consider whether the time has not come to revise their attitude toward the Soviet regime, so as not to be cut off from their native Church and land.[65]

While the text seems to embrace subservience to the atheistic communist state, it is primarily directed toward Russian émigré clergy whose right-wing, monarchist schism is giving such fuel and ammunition to the Soviet authorities. The authorities use the actions of the émigré schism to justify their continuing harassment of the Church at home and Sergei is asking the clergy abroad to simply stop giving the government material so useful for propaganda.

Periods of "thaw" alternated with periods of renewed intense persecution over the next several decades. One such "thaw" in relations between the Soviet authorities and the Church occurred in 1956, followed by a particularly difficult renewal of persecution in 1959. Khrushchev supported international church contacts abroad as part of his foreign relations program while acting with ruthless abandon against the church at home. A former seminary professor, Ossipov, denounced the Church and religious belief in a series of lectures across the Soviet Union. Metropolitan Nicolai rallied the Holy Synod to excommunicate Ossipov and "all public blasphemers of the Name of God," i.e. all baptized Party members, including Khrushchev himself.[66] Shortly thereafter, Patriarch Alexis of Moscow (Sergei's successor) defended this excommunication in a speech (written by Nicolai, who died in suspicious circumstances not long after) before a large diplomatic gathering at the Kremlin.

Furthermore, Patriarch Alexis offered a surreptitious commentary on Sergei's infamous "Declaration" in a sermon preached in London (September, 1964), which was broadcast by the BBC into Soviet Russia. Sergei insisted on making this broadcast, even knowing that it would create new dangers for him when he returned to Moscow.

> I was very glad, beloved fathers, brothers, and sisters, to pray with you in this glorious temple of God. We express our deepest gratitude to the believers here, the English people, who have extended to us this holy church.
>
> Today we celebrate the Exaltation of the Holy Cross of our Lord. It tells us that the Lord Jesus bestowed on us from the Cross eternal salvation and the possibility to be with Him in His heavenly Kingdom. The Exaltation tells us about this joyous happening even though - through our weaknesses - it is also combined with a sorrowful one. Each one of us carries his own cross: temptations, tribulations, sorrows, illnesses, and all sorts of

> weaknesses. But this is overpowered by the spiritual joy of knowing that Christ Himself is carrying His Cross and helps us carry our own crosses.
> And so, on this day on which the Holy Church celebrates a great feast, we pray with you in the belief that Christ will help us and be with us, both in our joys and in our sorrows.[67]

The patriarch here uses the same phrase as Sergei's 1927 Declaration in order to parse and clarify the meaning of the original statement. Sergei's critics considered the Declaration to be blasphemy and used it to justify their own continuing schism in the Russian diaspora community. Others had seen the Declaration as a way to find salvation through tribulation by its call to "Holy Russia" as opposed to "Soviet Russia." Alexis had been with Sergei when the Declaration was originally issued and, though ambiguity was necessary for survival in 1927, felt that his 1964 interpretation should let no ambiguity remain. He insists that the Cross of Christ is the true source of all joys and sorrows. In addition, by thanking the English Church for the gift of the parish building the London sermon is a rebuke of Khrushchev who had closed more than 10,000 churches in Soviet territory.[68]

The patriarch continues:

> May the peace of God be upon you, all of you, who cherish the historic faith of Holy Russia and the legacy of her great spiritual warriors and who remain faithful….
> The times we live in require us to be deeply understanding. The outer conditions of personal life may not be favourable but heavenly, Christian consolation is available to those who remain faithful witness of Christ's word, both in word and life. The vision of clear duty of Russian Orthodox people remain, wherever we live - whether on her sacred soil or abroad.[69]

Alexis is re-issuing Sergei's call to the diaspora schismatics to refrain from criticizing the Mother Church at home and thereby making her situation even more difficult. But he is also pointing out that the hierarchy has never "sold out" the Church in quite the way it seemed from the outside. He is stressing that Sergei and the other clergy were engaged in a strategic program of resistance which included the apparent cooperation with the political regime to a certain extant while working “from below” to undermine their attacks on the Church. Then Archimandrite (later, Metropolitan) Nikodim had been sure to point out in London (1960) that Alexis had both excommunicated Ossipov, Khrushchev and others as well as publicly defend that action, at great cost to himself and Nicolai.[70]

While some criticize the clergy for not being even more forward in their opposition to the Soviet government, their actions are very similar to those of clergy under another modern, totalitarian regime - that of Nazi Germany. In the case of the Third Reich, most of the German Roman Catholic clergy were no doubt frightened but Spicer points out that one’s definition of “resistance” will affect the answer to the question: “Did the clergy cooperate with the Nazi state or not?”

> There is active resistance and passive resistance, an unambiguous stand and an oblique one, a vigorous opposition and a stoic one - each reflecting the knotty spirit of the resister.[71]

Many clergy, Spicer now demonstrates, quietly participated in the broadly defined *Resistenz* which “indirectly checked the ubiquity of National Socialist control over Germany”[72] whereas fewer participated in *Widerstand* which is considered “the action of those who consciously opposed the Nazi regime on political grounds… [and] who directly challenged the regime for its racist policies against Jews and its anti-Church ideology.”[73] *Resistenz* is, by nature, most often undocumented,[74] while direct confrontation with or support of the Nazi authorities was much clearer, overt, and easier to document - as well as much more rare.[75]

As a case in point, Bishop Konrad von Preysing was one such master of *Resistenz*. He preached repeatedly on the need of each congregant to love his neighbour in need and to offer charity in every “difficult” situation.[76] Just as the Russian bishops, such as Patriarch Alexis, preached against their government’s policies in terms that the government could not criticize, Von Preysing “took a risk making these statements, especially in time of war, [but his] audience could still interpret them however they wished.”[77] One sermon in particular - in which the preacher was able to denounce the political regime but in words which the regime could not disagree with, similar to that of Patriarch Alexis - was preached by Von Preysing in November 1942. He

> announced to his congregation that they also needed to exercise this love of neighbour in a way that reflected

> love for 'the outsider.' To this end, he entreated Christians to 'tolerate and to accept foreign ethnic character.... That is a necessary and daily demand.' ... [Furthermore,] no one should 'be excluded from this love,' including those who 'speak another language or are of foreign blood.... For every person carries the image of God [and therefore] every person has the right to life and love.'[78]

Without pointing out specific groups, the bishop asserted that "members of foreign races" were entitled to freedom, property, and "an indissoluble marriage." No atrocities are allowed against such foreigners and "no people and no groups of people can deprive another people of their right to life."[79] Unable to arrest Von Preysing for the crime of public defense of persecuted Jews because he used such phrases as "every person," the Nazi state allowed Von Preysing to continue his work organizing social relief for all who came to him for assistance. It was his genius in denouncing his enemies to their faces but in words that they could not object to which enabled the bishop to survive. Spicer describes a number of other efforts by several clergy to undermine the population's adherence to National Socialist programs.[80]

Some might contend that any form of engagement with regimes such as the Third Reich or the Soviet Union short of open defiance might be read as "collaboration," but it seems to me that such a reading is overly simplistic and reductive. It does not allow for the complexity of real-world moral positioning. I contend that Tikhon, Sergei, Alexis, and the other clergy of the Russian Church during the Communist period were engaged in such acts of *Resistenz*, using the words and phrases demanded by the authorities in such a way that - simultaneously - the authorities were satisfied and the faithful understood the meaning "between the lines," so that the patriarchs were beating the Communists at their own game. It was this coded language of the official church statements that was lost on the West, until archives were opened and new materials came to light following the collapse of the Communist regime in the late 1980s.

Three paradigms exist for reacting to evil and wicked political conditions: outright aggression, non-violent pacifism, or quiet, underground resistance. Each has good and bad points. The real question is in knowing how and when to apply each appropriately; when is it ethical to fight, when is it ethical to lay down arms in an almost apparent act of suicide, or when is it ethical to seemingly cooperate ("living to fight another day")?

Notes

[1] Procopius, *History of the Wars*, IV.xv.24.
[2] Procopius, *History of the Wars*, III.x.29-31; III.xvi.10-14.
[3] *Homily IV on II Thess.* (*PG* 62, 485-6).
[4] For a further discussion of this point, see my "Clothed in Scarlet, Clothed With the Sun: Thoughts on the Women of Apocalypse 12 and 17" in *Earth's Abominations: Philosophical Studies of Evil* (ed. Daniel Haybron) (Rodopi: Amsterdam. 2002)
[5] Margaret Barker, *The Lost Prophet* (SPCK: London. 1988), 46.
[6] *Vita Porphyrri* (32-54) and Zosimas' *New History* (5.24.1-2); also *The Russian Primary Chronicle* (6502-6504).
[7] While complementary, these two ministries of imperial dignity and priesthood were by no means equal in Chrysostom's thinking: "The office that prevails in the Church… excels the civil office as heaven excels the earth." (*Homily XV on II Corinthians, PG* 61, 507; cited by J. Meyendorff in *Imperial Unity and Christian Divisions*, 36.)
[8] See also my "'Let Us Love One Another:' Liturgy, Morality, and Political Theory in Chrysostom's Sermons on Romans 12-12 and II Thessalonians 2" in *Speculum Sermonis: Interdisciplinary Reflections on the Medieval Sermon* (ed. G. Donavin, C. Nederman, R. Utz) (Brepols: Turnhout, Belgium. 2004)
[9] Translation from J. Meyendorff, *Imperial Unity and Christian Divisions*, 209.
[10] Francis Dvornik, *Early Christian and Byzantine Political Philosophy.* (Dumbarton Oaks: Washington, D.C. 1966)Vol. 2, 816.
[11] Walter Pohl, "Justinian and the Barbarian Kingdoms" in *The Cambridge Companion to the Age of Justinian.* (ed. Michael Maas.) (Cambridge: Cambridge University Press. 2005.), 449.
[12] Walter Pohl, "Justinian and the Barbarian Kingdoms" in *The Cambridge Companion to the Age of Justinian*, 453.
[13] Procopius, *History of the Wars*, IV.xv.23-33; V.vi.9-5.
[14] A.D. Lee, "The Empire at War" in *The Cambridge Companion to the Age of Justinian*, 113.
[15] Leslie Brubaker, "The Age of Justinian: Gender and Society" in *The Cambridge Companion to the Age of Justinian*, 428.
[16] For excellent discussions of the place of eunuchs in late antique and Byzantine societies, see Matthew Kuefler, *The Manly Eunuch: Masculinity, Gender Ambiguity, and Christian Ideology in Late Antiquity* (University of Chicago Press. 2001.) and *Women, Men, and Eunuchs:*

Gender in Byzantium (ed. Liz James) (Routledge: London and New York. 1997.).
[17] Procopius, *History of the Wars*, IV.xv.6-10.
[18] Procopius, *History of the Wars*, III.x.29-31; III.xvi.10-14.
[19] For a full treatment of the history of Hutsky's manuscript and his intentions in producing it, see the essay by Karel Stejskal in *The Life and Martyrdom of Saint Wenceslaus, Prince of Bohemia* (Opus Publishing Limited: London. 1997.) no pagination.
[20] Concluding essay, E. Petru in *The Life and Martyrdom of Saint Wenceslaus, Prince of Bohemia*, no pagination.
[21] *Life and Martyrdom*, no pagination but opposite the reproduction of manuscript page 4.
[22] *Life and Martyrdom,* opposite manuscript page 4.
[23] *Life and Martyrdom*, opposite verso of page 4.
[24] *Life and Martyrdom*, opposite verso of page 4.
[25] Peter Demetz, *Prague in Black and Gold.* (Hill and Wang: New York. 1997) p. 96.
[26] *Life and Martyrdom*, opposite p. 27 (plate XXIII). His preparations before the trip were also appropriate for one about to serve as godfather, as Vaclav was to be for the child.
[27] Demetz, *Prague in Black and Gold*, p. 96.
[28] *Life and Martyrdom*, opposite p. 28 (plate XXIV).
[29] Lisa Wolverton, *Hastening Toward Prague: Power and Society in Medieval Czech Lands*. (University of Pennsylvania Press: Philadelphia. 2001) p. 148.
[30] *Life and Martyrdom*, opposite p. 19 (plates XV and XVI).
[31] Also Stephen Uros III of Serbia [d. 1331].
[32] Dmitri Obolensky, *The Byzantine Commonwealth: Eastern Europe, 500-1453*. (St. Vladimir's Seminary Press: Crestwood, NY. 1971.) p. 401.
[33] See the six silver platter set commemorating this combat of 628-9 (in which Heraclius "advanced to the tray like a second David," in the words of the contemporary Frankish author Fredegar's *Chronicle*) in the Metropolitan Museum of Art in New York City. The platters were executed in 629-30 in Constantinople.
[34] Venantius Honorius Fortunatus, *Vexilla Regis*.
[35] *Ep. Ad Marcel*. Cxxxviii.
[36] See the full discussion of war in Thomas Aquinas' Summa Theologica, II

[37] St. Basil the Great, Canon XIII. *The Rudder of the Orthodox Catholic Church* (Orthodox Christian Educational Society: Chicago. 1957, 1983) ,801.
[38] Obolensky, *Byzantine Commonwealth*, pp. 196-7.
[39] Demetz, *Prague in Black and Gold*, p. 96.
[40] Despite these Byzantine church principles, Byzantine ecclesiastics had deep reservations concerning the sanctity of the Slavic royal passion-bearers. See Obolensky, *Byzantine Commonwealth*, 403.
[41] Wolverton, *Hastening Toward Prague*, 153.
[42] Tertullian, *Apology*, 21. Also, *On Idolatry*, 17-19.
[43] Timothy Ware, *The Orthodox Church*. (Penguin Books: London, 1997), 145.
[44] For a full discussion of the circumstances of the *sobor* and Tikhon's election, see Dimitry Pospielovsky, *The Russian Church Under the Soviet Regime, 1917-1982*. (St. Vladimir's Seminary Press: Crestwood, NY. 1984.) Chapter 1, 25-41.
[45] Matthew Spinka, *The Church in Soviet Russia*. (Oxford: Oxford University Press, 1956), 15.
[46] Spinka, *Church in Soviet Russia*, 21. For a list of bishops imprisoned or exiled to camps and of relics desecrated, see *The Russian Revolution and Religion: A Collection of Documents Concerning the Suppression of Religion by the Communists, 1917-1925*. (ed. and trans. Boleslaw Szczesniak) (University of Notre Dame Press. 1959), 247-250.
[47] Szczesniak, *Russian Revolution and Religion*, 36-7.
[48] Pospielovsky, *Russian Church Under the Soviet Regime*, 38.
[49] Spinka, *Church in Soviet Russia*, 19.
[50] Ware, *The Orthodox Church*, 150.
[51] Ware, *The Orthodox Church*, 150; also Pospielovsky, *Russian Church Under the Soviet Regime*, 39.
[52] Pospielovsky, *Russian Church Under the Soviet Regime*, 39.
[53] Szczesniak, *Russian Revolution and Religion*, 177-8.
[54] Szczesniak, *Russian Revolution and Religion*, 178.
[55] Spinka, *Church in Soviet Russia*, 38.
[56] Spinka, *Church in Soviet Russia*, 38; also Szczesniak, *Russian Revolution and Religion*, 184-5 for the attitude of the U.S. envoy in Riga reporting to the Secretary of State that the text "may have been agreed upon between the prisoner and the legal representative of the Soviet authority."
[57] Ware, *The Orthodox Church*, p. 151; also Spinka, *Church in Soviet Russia*, 41-45.

[58] *Slavonic Review* (London, June 1925), IV, No. 10, 162-3, cited in Spinka, *Church in Soviet Russia*, 47.
[59] See the sermon Tikhon preached upon his release from prison, in Spinka, *Church in Soviet Russia*, 39.
[60] Pospielovsky, *Russian Church Under the Soviet Regime*, 59, 63.
[61] Letter of Metropolitan Sergei (1926), in Spinka, *Church in Soviet Russia*, 157-60.
[62] Ware, *The Orthodox Church*, 152.
[63] See Spinka, *Church in Soviet Russia*, "Chapter II: Patriarch Sergei Capitulates to Save the Church"
[64] Declaration of Metropolitan Sergei (1927) in Spinka, *Church in Soviet Russia*, 163.
[65] Declaration of Metropolitan Sergei (1927) in Spinka, *Church in Soviet Russia*, 164.
[66] Commentary of Bp. Basil Radzianko in the video *Re-Emergence: The Russian Church in the Wake of Its Millennium.* (Holy Archangels Broadcasting Center: Washington, D.C. 1989.) This rare video is extremely difficult to obtain and I would like to thank those who assisted me in identifying and obtaining it: Father George Hasenecz, Hieromonk Joachim Pharr, Matushka Maria Potopova, and esp. Ms. Marilyn Sweezy, who graciously allowed me to borrow her personal copy (one of the few apparently left in circulation).
[67] Sermon of Patriarch Alexis, re-broadcast as part of the video *Re-Emergence: The Russian Church in the Wake of Its Millennium.*
[68] I rely substantially on the video commentary of Bishop Radzianko on the sermon for this information.
[69] Sermon of Patriarch Alexis, re-broadcast as part of the video *Re-Emergence: The Russian Church in the Wake of Its Millennium.*
[70] Again, I rely on the video commentary of Bp. Radzianko, who met with Nikodim on the occasion of the latter's 1960 visit to the West.
[71] Kevin Spicer, *Resisting the Third Reich: The Catholic Clergy in Hitler's Berlin*, by Kevin Spicer (Northern Illinois University Press, 2004),5.
[72] Spicer, *Resisting the Third Reich*, 5.
[73] Spicer, *Resisting the Third Reich*, 5.
[74] Spicer, *Resisting the Third Reich*, 133.
[75] For a more detailed discussion of this, see my review of *Resisting the Third Reich: The Catholic Clergy in Hitler's Berlin*, by Kevin Spicer (Northern Illinois University Press, 2004) in *The European Legacy,* vol. 11, No. 2 (2006). For an analysis of those attempting to create an ecclesiastical body that embraced the ideology of National Socialism, see

---

Doris L. Bergen, *The Twisted Cross: The German Christian Movement in the Third Reich* (University of North Carolina Press: Chapel Hill and London. 1996.).

[76] Kevin P. Spicer, *Resisting the Third Reich: The Catholic Clergy in Hitler's Berlin*. (Dekalb, IL: Northern Illinois University Press, 2004),130.

[77] Spicer, *Resisting the Third Reich,* 131.

[78] Spicer, *Resisting the Third Reich,* 131

[79] Spicer, *Resisting the Third Reich,* 131

[80] Spicer, *Resisting the Third Reich*, 132-138.

The Uncanny and the Feminine Sublime in Japanese Political Fantasy

Charles W. Nuckolls

Abstract: The sensation of the uncanny lies in the fact that something is attention-getting, not because it is unfamiliar or new, but because what used to be familiar has somehow become strange. As Schelling put it: "*unheimlich* is that which ought to have remained hidden, but has nonetheless come to light."[1] It is both frightening and exhilarating because, in psychoanalytic terms, it represents the return of the repressed. Freud defined the uncanny as "something familiar or old-established in the mind that has been estranged by the process of repression."[2] Uncanny events have the power to provoke a sense of dreadful fascination precisely because they are at once strange and familiar. This strangeness is what endows them with a supernatural quality that in Japanese popular culture is sometimes used to relate the construction of a national narrative to the search for authentic origins.[3]

Key Words: uncanny, anime, manga, oni, shojo, feminine sublime

1. Leapfrogging into the Uncanny

Japanese nationalism is a resurgent movement even though "movement" is perhaps too strong a term for the lose set of ideological motifs that inform popular culture. The kind of nationalism I am talking is "banal," that is, so obvious and everyday that it generally goes unnoticed . (Banal nationalism recruits its adherents largely among young urban men and through the medium of *manga* (comic books) and *anime* (animated cartoons). Popular media promise escape from the wearying treadmill of corporate life by offering young Japanese a point of identification in the "mythologization of history" as Kitagawa[4] called it – specifically, the history of Japanese military adventures in the 1930s and 1940s. Media that glorify Japan's imperial history have been increasingly popular since the 1980s.[5]

This is a process I term "generational leapfrogging," whereby the immediately previous generation of parents (those who came of age after the war) are replaced and superceded by the generation of the grandfathers: men who fought in the war on behalf of national ideals which many in Japan believe have been eclipsed in Japan's post-war rush to emulate the capitalist democracies of the West. Generational leapfrogging, however, is not where the story ends but where it begins, since the search for authentic points of idealization it is not limited chronologically. In fact, World War II sometimes turns out to be merely the jumping-off point for a journey in search of the idealized Japan that reaches back hundreds or thousands of years. The purpose of the journey is to find the "real" Japan, the robust nation that existed independently of, or prior to, infiltration by foreign influences. Once found, it is hoped, this entity can form the basis of a new national enterprise as glorious as any in the past.

"Authenticity" in cultural terms is bound up with notions of the good, but in Japan "good" and "evil" do not possess absolute or unchanging qualities. The relationship between the two is better characterized as a process of oscillation. What is evil one moment may become good the next, and the one true danger is to suppress this oscillation for too long a time. Second, and for this reason, anything understood as "evil" or "good" can be seen as uncanny, since beneath the exterior of one exists the only partially concealed possibility that it may turn into the other. Things cannot be completely good or completely bad in a world made up of oscillating images and internally transforming realities. Finally, this oscillation takes place most easily in the realm of supernatural fantasy, and uncanny supernaturalism, I will argue, is a powerful device for the imagination of nationhood.

2. Templates of Uncanny Transformation: The *Oni*

A cultural template for the construction of uncanny "evil" is the *oni,* usually translated as "demon" or "goblin." But "evil" means something very different from any of its assumed Western counterparts. *Onis* are usually represented as red-faced and ugly, and usually come with a horn or two, much like the Christian devil. They have no neck, but a tuft of hair and a big mouth; their fingers are clawed, and their arms somewhat ape-like. Wolfgram describes them thus:

> Throughout Japanese folklore, legend, and religious apocrypha, certain supernatural beings called *oni* exist which incarnate universal forces, sometimes beneficial but most often destructive to the human world. Easily moving between the realms of the living and the dead, these demonic spirits often interact with luckless humans. For Japanese artists, *oni* became a means to depict not only malignant supernatural forces, but one side of the inherent nature of mankind as well. [6]

As Dower notes, however, the *oni* was not a simple creature, but has "a benevolent, tutelary face as well as a demonic one." *Onis* could be subdued and brought over to one's own side. This potentially positive side, he explains, was reflected in certain local festivals, where someone made up to resemble an *oni* marched at the head of the festival procession and drove away evil influences. "In this regard, the *oni* was like the ambiguous stranger of Japanese folk belief in possessing powers that might be used for evil or good." [7]

A good example of the *oni's* inherent ambiguities is the popular children's story, "The Red Oni Who Cried," written by Hamada Hirosuke and published in 1933[8]. The red *oni* wanted to be a friend to people, but humans naturally fear *onis* and rejected him. At the same time his friend, the equally good-natured blue *oni*, offered to sacrifice himself by appearing evil to human beings: a kind of good-cop bad-cop routine, as it were. In this way the red *oni* had a chance to appear good by saving people from the "bad" *oni.* The plan worked, and the blue *oni* disappeared - fearing, it seems, that he might disrupt the red *oni's* friendship with the human beings. The red *oni* is deeply moved by the blue *oni's* self-sacrifice, and cries.

The same uncanny quality, stressing the mutability of good and evil, is also evident in Japan's cartoon depictions of its World War II adversaries. These caricatures appeared on hand-bills and wall posters throughout the war, much like images of Uncle Sam in the United States. Churchill and Roosevelt, for example, were often depicted in popular political cartoons as monstrous *onis* bent on devouring the helpless Asian world. As monstrous as they appeared, however, the *oni*-transformed adversaries still possessed a certain human quality: They are not completely monstrous. This is in keeping with the Japanese belief that even the most terrifying *oni* can be changed into a benign and helpful being. It even suggests an answer to the question posed by Dower in his book *War Without Mercy: Race and Power in the Pacific War:* "After such a merciless war, how can one explain the peaceful nature of the Allied occupation of Japan, and the genuine goodwill that soon developed between the Japanese and the Americans in particular?" [9]

As Dower himself notes, wartime portrayals of an evil enemy on both sides were simply untrue: "The Americans were not demons, as the Japanese discovered when they were not raped, tortured, and murdered as wartime propaganda and rumours had forecast. And the Japanese were more diversified and far more war-weary than their enemies had been led to believe." But there is also another reason. The core metaphor for the Anglo-American enemy in Japanese eyes was the *oni.*

> Acceptance of this new, and lesser "proper place" subservient to the United States was made easier for the

> Japanese because other staples of wartime racist imagery were malleable. Noteworthy here was the positive or beneficent side of the outsider, stranger, or demon [*oni*] that was so deeply embedded in Japanese folk culture. The stranger or outsider always possessed double powers: the capacity to destroy, but also gifts that were entertaining and pleasant, and gifts that could contribute to one's own self-strengthening. The demon - the overwhelmingly dominant persona of the Anglo-American enemy during the war - was also the demon with a human face, the potentially tutelary deity. In occupied Japan, and for many years thereafter, this is the side of the demon that prevailed: large, powerful, human, protective, awkward, vaguely forbidding, generally but not entirely trustworthy. [10]

In other words, the American *onis* changed from being fearsome devils fit only to be exterminated to being tutelary deities from whose largess Japan benefited in the postwar decades. The resurgence of Japanese nationalism over the last twenty years, however, has brought about yet another reconfiguration of the foreigner. The American is once again being cast in the role of the bad *oni.* It is not accidental that the hugely popular (and controversial) manga, *Sensoron,* by Yoshinori Kobayashi[11] features caricatures of Western leaders from Roosevelt to Bush with protrusions that look like hair (but could be horns) on the top of their heads.

The transformative power of the *oni* appears again in the enchanting ogress, “Lum,” featured in the popular magazine series *Urusei Yatsura* (“Those Obnoxious Aliens”) by manga artist Rumiko Takahashi.[12] The 1979-1986 series opens with a fleet of invaders arriving on earth. The leader of the invasion agrees to withdraw if a human can defeat his opponent in a game of tag. The chosen one happens to be Ataru Moroboshi, a sex-obsessed high school student. Ataru refuses to compete until he finds out that his opponent, Lum, is a beautiful girl in a tiger-skin bikini.

Like the mythical *oni,* Lum has two horns located near her temples. She also has fangs and dislikes garlic, a tell-tale *oni* trait. Lum's personality is volatile, and ranges from the cute to the violently angry. She is known for her atrocious cooking, which is extremely spicy (the *oni* are immune to hot spices and use them, leaving a disfiguring effect on humans). Like all *onis*, she is affected by *umeboshi* (pickled plums), which make her drunk.

In their confrontation, Ataru's attempts to grab Lum's horns, but fails miserably until his semi-girlfriend Shinobu promises to marry him if he wins. Thus inspired, Ataru succeeds, but due to a misunderstanding, Lum thought Ataru's marriage proposal was meant for her. She becomes his obsessive wife, and despite his constant flirting with other girls, loves him passionately. Each episode of the comic book series focuses on Ataru's ill-luck, his lechery, or the wide variety of bizarre humans and aliens who interact with Lum and Ataru.

Like the traditional *oni,* Lum represents the uncanny quality of apparently fixed and unchanging values to turn into their opposites. No value is fixed, nor can its embodiment in any form (supernatural or human) be taken as consistent and unchanging. What does not change, however, is that the quality of transformation reveals a grandness of purpose that is cosmic in its proportions. Even Lum reveals this quality, since both her arrival on earth and her activities thereafter implicate all human existence. I find the word "sublime" an appropriate term for the constellation of sentiments this kind of quality is meant to invoke. Beings who embody this quality are fascinating and dangerous, intimate yet wholly other, in the present but simultaneously located in the past and the future.

3. Towards a Concept of the Feminine Sublime

The sublime, said Ruskin, is another word for the effect of greatness upon the feelings: "The sublime is not distinct from what is beautiful, nor from other sources of pleasure in art, but is only a particular mode and manifestation of them"[13] Since well before Ruskin - since Burke, in fact - we have been accustomed to thinking about the sublime in essentially masculine ways. That this is true is most telling in the fact that Burke located the highest expression of the sublime in the Old Testament, where a man, Moses, encounters the divine in the voice in the whirlwind and is shocked to discover both his own mortality and his chosen election to a position of greatness. There is an attitude of masculine empowerment in such images, because the encounter with mortality (whether in the form of God, a waterfall, or the majestic Alps) releases men to a sense of greater vitality, and therefore mastery over themselves.

Kant argues the same point, asserting, in the *Critique of Judgement*, that when the ego comes face-to face with its own possible annhilation, it recuperates itself in the face of this threat. Rational thought is enhanced in this encounter, not destroyed, and becomes the basis for the sublime experience. Drawing on Kant, Battersby remarks:

> The pleasure of the sublime involves fear in the face of the infinite; but it also involves a transcendence of fear. It involves terror and a recognition of that which could overwhelm and destroy the self, but also a simultaneous strengthening of the perceiving "I" by testing its strength against that which could obliterate it.[14]

Nye also finds that in testing "his" resilience in the face of this apparent infinity, the individual "recuperates a sense of superior self-worth because the mind is able to conceive something larger and more powerful than the senses can grasp."[15] The emphasis is on the position of the mindful awareness and rational thought in apprehending the sublime, shifting the attention from "nature" (that which provokes the experience) to the rational "perception of nature" (that which follows the experience as a superior consequent.)

On the other hand, Freeman[16] and others[17] have detected countervailing feminine aspects to the traditional notion of the sublime. Here the idea is that the sublime emerges, not from a confrontation with nature or a strengthening of the powers of the rational self as it contemplates possible annihilation, but rather from nature seen as a friend or sister. As Mellor notes of nineteenth century writers, Mary Shelley and Charlotte Bronte:

> Often their protagonists respond to a mountainous landscape or a radiant sunset with the same loss of ego or consciousness-of-self . . . identified as characteristic of the masculine "negative" sublime . . . [but these women] represent it as a flowing out, an ecstatic experience of co-participation in a nature they explicitly gender as female. For them, this female nature is not an overwhelming power, not even an all-bountiful mother. Instead nature is a *female friend*, a sister, with whom they share their most intimate experiences and with whom they cooperate in the daily business of life, to the mutual advantage of each.[18]

Although Mellor does not describe it thus, her analysis points to the development of eco-feminism in the late 20th century[19] with its characteristic emphasis on an appreciation of the intrinsic value of everything in nature. One could even argue that the so-called feminine sublime of Shelley and Bronte becomes the bio-centric viewpoint of contemporary eco-feminism - but this lies beyond the scope of the present inquiry.

From Charlotte Bronte to Takahashi Rumiko might seem a bit of a jump, but there are reasons for thinking the concepts introduced by Freeman and Mellor can be applied to both. In Jane Eyre and Lum the feminine sublime constitutes an alternative aesthetic pose that challenges culturally dominant models. In Western literature these models are generally masculine, and the aesthetic they construct associates the contemplation of natural forces with the development of the ratiocinative male self. The feminine sublime is the observer, and points to the construction of a self not in opposition to nature but (in some ways) consubstantial with it. Here the sublime possesses inescapable resonances to the maternal. But in the Western sublime there is no sense in which the masculine construction subsumes the feminine, incorporates it, or alternates with it in some grand cycle. To be sure, the two can be combined - this is the basis of the liminal category we call the "grotesque" - but for the most part, Western aesthetics keeps the two distinct and apart.

In Japan the values associated with male and female are configured differently, because the female embodiments of the Japanese sublime do not simply oppose the masculine, but rather represent alternating moments in a cycle of self-conception in which both participate at intervals. The masculine mode, dominant one moment, reveals its opposite the next, and Japanese aesthetics revel in a scary fascination in the fact that the one is partly constituted of the other. This, I suggest, is the very basis of "the sublime" in Japanese manga. And it is also what makes the whole thing uncanny, for the uncanny, in this context, means detecting the alternating opposite of a thing in its most grandiose embodiment. To take one example (to which I will return in a moment): what if the supremely sublime and masculine symbol of Japan, Mt. Fuji, contained within it a feminine component which, sooner or later, must express itself?

4. The Cultural Dialectics of the Japanese Self

One of the liveliest sources of conversation in Tokyo is not the condition of the economy but the condition of the sacred mountain just outside the city. "Is it active?" So often did I hear this and similar questions that I began referring to them collectively as symptoms of a "Mt. Fuji syndrome." Now, it will come as a surprise to no one (least of all the Japanese) to note that Mt. Fuji is a symbol of the Japanese nation. More subtle but just as real is the symbolic identification of Japan's highest mountain with the Japanese self. The speculation one hears in Tokyo is all about the possibility of sudden change, of calamitous eruption that cannot be predicted. Mt. Fuji is a volcano and might erupt, and the same is true, by analogy, of ordinary perceptions of the state, and even of the Japanese themselves as beings with a form of agency both limited and intensified by the demands of living in an (apparently) highly ordered society. What we are talking about is the uncanny sense that everything ordinary and taken-for-granted world might in fact conceal its opposite - and this opposite could emerge volcanically in the flash of a moment.

The concept of agency represented in this analogy - Japanese self and explosive volcanism - is different from personal agency as Americans are inclined to think of it. Agency is not, in the Japanese sense, the expression of individual autonomous needs and wants, centreed in a self that is defined as a unique locus of perception.[20] Of course Americans (especially American men) sometimes describe themselves as possessing "volcanic" temperaments, with a potential for anger that is "seething" or "hot." But the self as the center of volitional action is not located in this set of features, but in opposition to them - hence the importance of expressions like "get yourself under control!" It is the self as seat of voluntary action that directs this action against the passions. Even injunctions to "get in touch with your feelings" reinforce the subjectification of will, and the rational self as synonymous with the will.

In contrast, Japanese culture is sustained by the expectation of an oscillation between bipolar extremes.[21] Both poles demand the sacrifice of individual autonomy, and in this sense they differ radically from American visions that celebrate the exercise of free agency. At one extreme, action complies with structural hierarchy. This is the Japan of the organization, of the nail that is hammered down if it sticks out. It is generally masculine in tone, and finds its characteristic embodiment in the image of the samurai warrior. At the other extreme, action follows from the commands of inner human nature, defined in terms of explosive exuberance and animal passion. In some accounts, but not all, this theory of action is expressly linked to the feminine, and its embodiment is seen as supremely sublime and uncanny. Our inquiry, therefore, focuses on the configuration of the uncanny feminine when it is linked to ideas of nationhood.

5. Yamataika: The Past in the Present

The five volume manga series *Yamataika* by Yukinobu Hoshino first appeared in the late 1980s, at the end (some would say) of Japan's post-war economic boom. It focuses on the story of a young woman who discovers that she is the living embodiment of the ancient shaman-queen Himiko or Pimiko. Little is known of Himiko beyond brief references to her in the Chinese chronicles. There she is described as "occupy[ing] herself with magic and sorcery, bewitching the people".[22] Miwako, her cartoon incarnation, is the daughter of man named "Atarai," who served as a soldier in the Pacific War and was stationed on one of the small islands in the Okinawa chain. This island was the center of an ancient religion whose priestesses worshipped the goddess "Amamiku." There, Atarai met and fell in love with one of the priestesses, a grave transgression of local endogamy and sufficient to get him kicked off the island. The priestess gave birth to a daughter, Miwako, and later to her younger brother, Takahiko, although the two grew up apart - Miwako with her mother and Takahiko with his exiled father.

Miwako is young and nubile, and usually scantily dressed - a bit like the space-alien *oni,* Lum. She is unmarried but usually accompanied by nymph-like attendants always wearing bikinis. She derives her power from her role as a matrilineal descendent of a line of great priestesses. It is the function of this position to call for the performance of the great *yamato matsuri,* or "festival of Yamato," a ritual event that only takes place once every six decades or so. She invokes this power at the beginning of the story, and this is what caused the miraculous events with which it opens: the ghostly battleship Yamato, sunk at the end of World War II, suddenly appears and shells the American bases on Okinawa; a tremendous hurricane develops; and in the sky a great bell, called a *dotaku,* appears.

These events are recognized as portents of transformation by Miwako's father and brother, who rush to the island to see if indeed the great festival is set to begin. What they find when they get there sets the stage for all that follows, including Miwako's discovery that not only is she the incarnation of Himiko, the third century priestess-queen, but also of the great goddess Amaterasu herself whose progeny become the imperial family of Japan.

Yamataika explains that the people of Japan are the "fire people," and that in the past they worshipped volcanoes as divine goddesses and celebrated volcanic eruptions as manifestations of feminine power. The Japanese require these periodic celebrations to revitalize their spirit - *Yamato damashi* - and to release them from the tyranny of convention and hierarchy. If natural eruptions are not available, then, says the manga, artificial ones must be created. As incredible as it may seem, World War II is defined as an eruptive festival occasion - and thus necessary to the expression of the Japanese spirit - and the atomic bombings are its supreme celebratory moment. Now it is time for another great *matsuri,* although the manga does not suggest (as others do) that this can only be accomplished by war.

The manga locates this story in a certain kind of history, according to which the real or original Japanese people are identified with an autochthonous tribe whose only pure remnants are the Ainu, a group now resident in the northern island of Hokkaido and all but wiped out.

The original Japanese were matrilineal and worshipped fire an emanation of the divine. They lived in a domain known as Yamatai, from which the manga, *Yamataika* ("On Yamatai") draws its title. In the sixth century, the story goes, invaders from the Chinese mainland - a patrilineal folk, worshipping male deities and riding horses - invaded Japan and supplanted the indigenous religion. In fact, this is more than just cartoon fantasy; it represents more or less accurately the "horserider" hypothesis introduced by Egami in the 1960s.[23] Their most damaging importation was Buddhism, with its utterly non-Japanese emphasis on withdrawal, contemplation, and distrust of the senses. Over the years there has been a blending, but beneath the exterior pastiche, the vibrant Japanese spirit waits to be released from bondage into ecstasy by a new incarnation of the feminine divine.

The contemporary equivalent of the invading Chinese, according to the manga, is the United States. Like the Chinese, Americans have imposed unnatural structures on Japan, twisting and distorting the Japanese spirit. A certain ambivalence, however, is implicit in the acknowledgment that this imposition was accepted, even welcomed, at the time it first happened. The same is true today. On the one hand, modern life is seen as good to the extent that Japan now possesses and even controls resources the rest of the world considers worthwhile: money, machines, and market share. On the other hand, if that is all there is, Japan no longer deserves to be considered absolutely unique - and this is unacceptable, because if one thing has *not* changed in Japan it is the conviction that Japan itself is like no other country in the world. *Yamataika* is not intended to replace one vision of Japan with another, but to celebrate the uncanniness of Japanese identity by exposing its composite nature and oscillating structure.

The manga sets the priestess, Miwako, on a quest to recover various artifacts of Japan's past, including a great bell (*dotoku*) that symbolizes the ancient power of the Japanese and their female priestesses. It turns out that the bell is to be found within the great Buddha of Todaiji, and Miwako must destroy the statue in order to release the *dotoku*. The Todaiji Buddha - known as "the Buddha that shines throughout the world like a sun" - is significant. It is situated in Nara, the ancient capital in Yamato prefecture, and the place (according to the manga) where the "fire people" of ancient Japan once celebrated their rituals. Todaiji represents the introduction of mainland culture, especially the patriarchal and ranked administrative system of the Chinese. The whole purpose of the manga, in a sense, is to examine the moment of Todaiji's imposition, not to replace it with "fire worship" but to reveal that there is another, even more ancient side to Japanese identity that must be expressed in order to retain its vitality in a world of new threats in which Japan must be both sublimely masculine and feminine.

Once Todaiji is destroyed and reveals the fire-people's *dotoku* at its core, Miwako visits the various sacred volcanoes of Japan, whereupon each one begins to rumble and shake. The people of Japan know, deep down, what is happening, and they begin a pilgrimage to the city of Tokyo at the base of Mt. Fuji. Of course it goes without saying that the greatest volcano in Japan will be the site of the greatest eruption, making Tokyo the only possible location for the ecstatic *matsuri*. Miwako is impeded the whole way by Buddhist priests and the whole institutional structure of modern Japan, including the army and members of parliament. But her progress cannot be stopped, and when she finally arrives in Tokyo, another harbinger of glory appears in the form of the battleship *Yamato*, the same ghost ship that bombarded the American bases in Okinawa at the beginning of volume one.

The battleship *Yamato* - the biggest battleship ever built - is the symbol of the nation, an identity acknowledged and celebrated at the time of its building in 1942. During the war, it was considered too important symbolically to risk in a major naval engagement. It survived until the defeat of Japan was absolutely certain, and in April of 1945 was dispatched on a suicide mission to Okinawa. Since American bombers sank it, the *Yamato* has remained the premier symbol of the imperial state and of Japanese war ambitions, and in terms of its ability to conjure faded glory it ranks in the same league with the *Titanic*.

In the manga, American naval vessels speed to intercept the ghost battleship, but when they open fire, their missiles inexplicably disappear into the sea. Then the *Yamato* itself opens fire with its eighteen inch guns. The American ships are destroyed, and the *Yamato* steams on toward Tokyo Bay, watched via remote video link by thousands of Japanese pedestrians on the giant TV screen outside Shinjuku Station. When the ghost ship arrives, Mt. Fuji explodes in a massive eruption as the sacred *dotoku* floats overhead and rings out the call to *matsuri*. There is rioting and orgy in Tokyo. Young men and women strip off their clothes and dance naked in the streets. Order dissolves in a Dionysian frenzy that lasts days and destroys the city. Significantly, the only men we see at the end, apart from the revellers who join Miwako, are government bureaucrats cowering in their offices as buildings collapse around them.

Finally the American aircraft carrier, Carl Vinson, arrives in Tokyo Bay and confronts the Yamato directly. They steam toward each other and collide, and at that moment a huge nuclear-style explosion takes place. Both ships, apparently, are destroyed, and the bacchanalian frenzy on the streets of Tokyo reaches its culmination. Meanwhile, Miwako and her brother battle a powerful Buddhist monk who tries to prevent the final *matsuri* from taking place. The monk kills Miwako's brother, but not before he drives a stake through the monk's heart. Just before he dies, the monk takes a run at Miwako and impales her on the same stake. They both die, facing each other, a perfect image of the two aspects of Japanese selfhood combined in what could be seen as the implicit message of the manga.

Order is then restored, and life in Japan returns to its modern, patriarchally organized and hierarchical structure. Another sixty years - the traditional period of time between sacred festivals - must elapse before the next orgiastic cataclysm erupts. At that time another priestess-queen must arise - in fact, we are told she already exists as the unborn child of Miwako's father and a side-kick archaeologist friend who plays a minor role in the action.

6. Interpretations

Comic books are a powerful means for the expression of alternative models because, as Kienhorst suggests, the imaginary perspective of speculative fiction lets the familiar - that is, the socially acceptable - become strange.[24] Manga are a speculative arena in which the familiarities of contemporary culture and rendered strange. Gender, of course, figures prominently in such speculation, since it serves as a condensed symbol for a host of cultural values, not all of them consistent with each other. The ordinariness of Japan as a masculine nation premised on values of patriarchal authority is challenged by a manga that sees this Japan as a contingent, almost accidental creation of historical events. It could have turned out differently, the manga implies, and this sets in motion a new challenge - to reconcile the opposed images of the nation in some fashion that preserves their dynamism. The "reconciliation" proposed by *Yamataika* is to redefine the nation as doubled-sided, both masculine and feminine, and to characterize the relationship between them as one of oscillation mediated by explosive ritual.

As Domosh and Seager point out, "representing nations . . . in gendered and sexualized terms most often has enabled the dominant powers to maintain and legitimize their power positions."[25] That is true. But there are always counter-tendencies, and in *Yamataika* the Japanese state is configured as dialectic of forces that oppose but also depend on each other. Emad argues from a similar perspective, to show that Americans imagine nationhood through the comic book icon of Wonder Woman. In different styles at different historical periods, Wonder Woman's body is "both an icon of the traditionally masculine, public realm of nationhood as well as the traditional feminine, private realm of female sexuality. As such, her body serves as a site for oppositional encounters between gender and nation, private and public, bondage and power."[26] The nation is thereby defined as a dialectic of the relationship of these forces which remain in tension and are never resolvable into unity.[27]

Yamataika suggests that the search for an authentic Japan, without the accretions and distortions that result from contact with the outside, culminates in the discovery of a feminine spirit that exists as much in the present as it does in the past. For the last 1500 years or so, this alterative spirit has been hidden or concealed. It emerges only incompletely in moments of uncanny sensation. In *Yamataika,* these moments are chiefly identified with rituals that exist in bits and pieces on the mainland of Japan but perdure nearly intact in peripheral outposts like Okinawa and Hokkaido. The nature of this feminine alternative, however, is not obvious. It is refracted through the several dimensions of the main character's personality.

Miwako is variously depicted as a queen, a priestess, a national emblem, and as a girl, seductive temptress, and childlike innocent. She is also a daughter and a sister, but significantly, never a wife or mother. To some extent this recalls the festishized post-war image of *shojo,* a concept of girlhood epitomized in a genre of manga that bears the same name. The desire that *shojo* represents is for "a state of being unthreatened by the cluster of meanings that burden adulthood, and especially male maturity, almost to the breaking point.[28] *Yamataika* clearly presents a challenging alternative to nation as masculinized ego ideal. But when the manga constructs a feminine alter-ego to this ideal, which feminine - child, girl, vixen, queen - is most important?

The visual presentation of Miwako offers a clue, since, in scene after scene, Miwako appears in close proximity to objects that can only be described as phallic. Sometimes, for example, Miwako appears lying flat on the ground with a stick or pole between her legs. Elsewhere she shows up with a sword in hand projecting up and outward from her hips. One might not wish to make too much of this, but similar imagery appears repeatedly, suggesting a link between the feminine and the phallic.[29] But Miwako represents more than just another phallic female in the mold of Wonder Woman. At the end of *Yamataika*, in fact, Miwako and the hyper-masculine symbol of nationhood, the battleship Yamato, its guns pointing upward and outward, virtually coalesce. The point is that as the masculine and feminine approach each other, each taking on the characteristics of the other, a great energy is released. The instant of their convergence is the sublime moment when the dialectic of masculine and feminine, hierarchical control and ecstatic frenzy, resolve into each other.

Since the relationship between masculine and feminine in the manga's conception of the state is oscillative, the moment of their union is like starting the clock all over again - the cycle begins again, preparing another great matsuri sixty years hence. The manga does not explicitly say so, but the final scenes likely represent a return to "normalcy," with the rebuilding of Japan in its fully patriarchal identity. Is this identity good or evil, or is the question itself irrelevant? By the end of *Yamataika,* the reader understands the author's perspective: Japanese identity is not fixed and there is a feminine obverse to every symbol of nationhood modern Japan takes for granted.

Notes

[1] Sigmund Freud, *The Standard Edition of the Complete Psychological Works of Sigmund Freud*, James Strachey, ed. & trans., vol. XVII (London: Hogarth, 1955) 219.
[2] Ibid., 220.
[3] Kevin Doak, "What is a nation and who belongs? National narratives and the ethnic imaginaton in twentieth-century Japan," *American Historical Review* 102:1997.
[4] J. Kitagawa, "The Japanese 'Kokutai' (National Community) History and Myth," *History of Religions* 13: 1974, 220.
[5] Charles Nuckolls, "The banal nationalism of Japanese cinema," *Journal of Popular Culture* 39: 2006.
[6] Jullian Wolfgram, "*Oni:* The Japanese Demon" in Stephen Addiss ed., *Japanese Ghosts & Demons: Art of the Supernatural.* (New York: George Braziller, Inc., 1985), 91.
[7] John Dower, *War without Mercy.* (New York: Pantheon, 1986), 252.
[8] Hamada Hirosuke, *Mukudari no yume. Naita aka oni / gensaku.* (Tokyo: Kodansha, 1990).
[9] Dower, *op.cit.,* 305.
[10] *Loc.cit.*
[11] Yoshinori Kobyashi, *Sensoron.* (Tokyo: Gentosha, 1998)
[12] Rumiko Takahashi, *The Return of Lum.* Vol. 1. (Tokyo: VizMedia. 1995)

[13] John Ruskin, *Modern Painters*. Vols. 1, 2. (New York: Adamant Media Corporation, 2000), 3.128.
[14] Christine Battersby, *Antimonies: works by Evelyn Williams*. (Warwick: University of Warwick, 1984)
[15] David E. Nye, *American Technological Sublime,* (Cambridge, Mass: MIT Press, 1994), 7.
[16] Barbara Freeman, *The Feminine Sublime: Gender and Excess in Women's Fiction* (Berkeley: University of California Press, 1995).
[17] E.g, Patricia Yaeger, "The 'Language of Blood': Toward A Maternal Sublime," (*Genre* 25: Spring 1992) .
[18] Anne Mellor, *Romanticism and Gender*. (New York: Routledge, 1993), 96.
[19] Greta Gaard and Patrick Murphy, eds. *Ecofeminist Literary Criticism: Theory,Interpretation, Pedagogy*. (Urbana: University of Illinois Press, 1998.
[20] Hazel Markus and Shinobu Kitayama, "Culture and the self: implications for cognition, emotion, and motivation," *Psychological Review* 98:1991.
[21] Nancy Rosenberger, *Japanese Sense of Self*. (Cambridge: Cambridge University Press, 1994)
[22] Walter Edwards, "In Pursuit of Himiko: Postwar Archaeology and the Location of Yamatai." *Monumenta Nipponica* 51:1 (1996), 56.
[23] See Namio Egami, "The formation of the people and the origin of the state in Japan," *Memoirs of the Toyo Bunko* 23: 1964, and Walter Edwards, "Mirrors on ancient Yamato: The Kurozuka Kofun discovery and the question of Yamatai," *Monumenta Nipponica 54: 1999.*
[24] Kienhorst, "Emancipatory projection: an introduction to women's critical utopias," in *Women's Studies* 14: 1987.
[25] Mona Domosh and Joni Seager, *Putting Women in Place: Feminist Geographers Make Sense of the World*. (New York: Guilford, 2001).
[26] Mitra Emad, "Reading Wonder Woman's body: Mythologies of gender and nation," *Popular Culture* 2004:3.
[27] See Charles Nuckolls, *Culture: A Problem that Cannot be Solved* (Madison: University of Wisconsin Press, 1998.
[28] Sherif, Ann. "Japanese without apology: Yoshimoto Banana and healing," In S. Snyder & P. Gabriel eds. *Oe and Beyond* (Honolulu: University of Hawaii Press, 1999), 281.

[29] See Nina Cornyetz, *Dangerous Women, Deadly Words: Phallic Fantasy and Modernity in Three Japanese Writers*. (Stanford: Stanford University Press, 1999)

Bibliography

Battersby, C. *Antimonies: works by Evelyn Williams*. Warwick: University of Warwick, 1984.

Billig, M. *Banal Nationalism*. London: Sage, 1995,

Benedict, R. *The Chysanthemum and the Sword.* New York: Mariner Books, 1989.

Cornyetz, N. *Dangerous Women, Deadly Words: Phallic Fantasy and Modernity in Three Japanese Writers*. Stanford: Stanford University Press, 1999.

Doak, K. "What is a nation and who belongs? National narratives and the ethnic imaginaton in twentieth-century Japan," *American Historical Review* 102 (1997): 283-309.

Domosh, M. and Seager, J. *Putting Women in Place: Feminist Geographers Make Sense of the World.* New York: Guilford, 2001.

Dower, J. *War without Mercy*. New York: Pantheon, 1986.

Edwards, W. "In pursuit of Himiko," *Monumenta Nipponica* 51 (1996): 53-79.

Edwards, W. "Mirrors on ancient Yamato: The Kurozuka Kofun discovery and the question of Yamatai," *Monumenta Nipponica 54 (1999): 75-110.*

Egami, N. "The formation of the people and the origin of the state in Japan," *Memoirs of the Toyo Bunko* 23 (1964): 35-70.

Emad, M. "Reading Wonder Woman's body: Mythologies of gender and nation," *Popular Culture* 2004:3.

Freeman, B.C. (1995) *The Feminine Sublime: Gender and Excess in Women's Fiction*, Berkeley: University of California Press

Freud, S. *The Standard Edition of the Complete Psychological Works of Sigmund Freud*, ed. & trans. James Strachey, vol. XVII (London: Hogarth, 1955), 219-252.

Gaard, G. & P. Murphy eds. *Ecofeminist Literary Criticism: Theory, Interpretation, Pedagogy*. Urbana: University of Illinois Press, 1998.

Hirosuke, H. *Mukudari no yume. Naita aka oni / gensaku.* Tokyo: Kodansha 1990.

Keinhorst, A. "Emancipatory projection: an introduction to women's critical utopias," *Women's Studies* 14 (1987)

Kitagawa, J. "The Japanese 'Kokutai' (National Community) History and Myth," *History of Religions* 13 (1974): 209-226.

Kobayashi, Y. *Sensoron.* Tokyo: Gentosha, 1998.

Mellor, A. *Romanticism and Gender.* New York: Routledge, 1993.

Markus, H. & Kitayama, S. "Culture and the self: implications for cognition, emotion, and motivation," *Psychological Review* 98 (1991): 224-253.

Nuckolls, C. "The banal nationalism of Japanese cinema," *Journal of Popular Culture* 39 (2006): 817-837.

Nye, D.E. (1994) *American Technological Sublime*, Cambridge Mass: MIT Press.

Rosenberger, N. *Japanese Sense of Self.* Cambridge: Cambridge University Press, 1994.

Ruskin, J. *Modern Painters.* Vols. 1, 2. New York: Adamant Media Corporation, 2000.

Sherif, A. "Japanese without apology: Yoshimoto Banana and healing," In S. Snyder & P. Gabriel eds. *Oe and Beyond.* Honolulu: University of Hawaii Press, 1999: 278-301.

Takahashi, R. *The Return of Lum.* Vol. 1. Tokyo: VizMedia. 1995.

Wolfgram, J. "*Oni:* The Japanese Demon" in Stephen Addiss ed., *Japanese Ghosts & Demons: Art of the Supernatural.* New York: George Braziller, Inc., 1985.

Yaeger, P. "The 'Language of Blood': Toward A Maternal Sublime," *Genre* 25 (Spring 1992). 5-24.

Demurring to Doom: The Geopolitics of Prevailing

Lee Quinby

Abstract: This essay focuses on two prevalent and longstanding discourses of evil within U.S. culture, one that emphasizes an apocalyptic sense of doom and divine decree and the other that stresses human agency and social justice. After arguing that apocalyptic literalism is not only reductive but also detrimental, the essay turns to examples of an aesthetic counter tradition in which ambiguity and interdependence are accentuated as foundational to the geopolitics of prevailing.

Key Words: apocalypse, art, doom, evil, Faulkner, geopolitics, literalism, Melville, nationalism

> Evil is unspectacular and always human,
> And shares our bed and eats at our own table,
> And we are introduced to Goodness every day,
> Even in drawing rooms among a crowd of faults;
> W.H. Auden, "Herman Melville"[1]

1. Lot in Life

Can people learn to live non-apocalyptically in a society marred by apocalyptic diatribes against evil enemies and dire warnings of impending doom? Is the apocalyptic use of evil, itself evil? This essay focuses on two contrasting discourses of evil found within American culture, an apocalyptic one in which evil is perceived as a destructive, cosmic force against humanity, and a social justice stance in which evil is the name given to designate harmful human actions. These are hardly exhaustive of the uses of evil in American culture. One need only think of the vast array of horror films that excite our imagination about being eaten alive by the living dead or by the deadly alive Hannibal Lector. Video games and Marvel comics thrive on deadly combat between Forces of Good versus Forces of Evil. Evil doings are also the brunt of much contemporary American humor, from the cartoon boys of "South Park" to the cartoonish cleverness of Jon Stewart's "Daily Show." As I will argue at the close of this essay, there is a benefit to be had from this proliferation of evil discourses. But the two discursive modes of evil I will focus on here have the most entrenched and longest history within American culture and tell us most about prospects for the future, not just for the United States, but indeed, for the world.

I should make clear at the outset that my own stance gravitates toward the second take in which evil is most aptly construed within a human-made framework, a way of describing profound social injustice, betrayal of the public trust, and widespread harm. Nevertheless, I am wary of using even that concept of evil because it so often falls on the well-fertilized and watered soil of an apocalyptic-ready and highly-armed nation. Moreover, it too can take on apocalyptic fervor. Rather than adding fuel to already inflamed forms of moral rectitude, it is possible, and more importantly, desirable, to foster thought that is at home in complexity, change, ambiguity, and artifice. This attitude, or mindset, or standpoint, or pose--as a nexus of ethics, politics, and aesthetics it's something of all of these--is vital for cultivating what I am advocating in Part 3 of this essay as a "geopolitics of prevailing." And that stance, which admittedly requires a significant shift away from apocalyptic categories of belief, encapsulates both a vision and a means more likely to incline U.S. citizens to think of themselves as global citizens, as intimately interconnected with all of humanity and interdependent in the world we live in together. Such a vision offers a vital antidote to apocalyptic fear, its proclivity toward doom, and its appetite for revenge. It entails pursuing an answer to the question that Adam Phillips has posed: "What have we used the conflict between good and evil to stop ourselves thinking?"[2]

In order for such a shift in thought to occur, it is necessary to grasp not only why an apocalyptic view is entrenched within U.S. culture, but also, and more importantly, why the belief itself inevitably misapprehends ways to make the world a more secure place. In fact, accepting that doom is one's lot in life thwarts shared and interdependent global life precisely because an apocalyptic perspective thrives on a stark division of humanity into "with us or against us" categories. This reductive perspective turns socially induced incidents and contingencies of history alike into dualistic forces of total good versus total evil. Foreign policy based on such a premise constitutes what psychiatrist Robert Jay Lifton has called the "superpower syndrome," which he describes as "a medical metaphor meant to suggest aberrant behavior that is not just random but part of a more general psychological and political constellation."[3] The superpower syndrome's way of seeing the world, Lifton argues, stems from the United States' powerful post World War II position as world leader combined with subsequent defeat in Vietnam. The syndrome's doubled sense of excessive entitlement and wounded vulnerability was starkly exacerbated by the attacks of 9/11. Lifton further argues that governmental leaders with apocalyptic dispositions exhibit a simultaneous sense of omnipotence and paranoia that leads to militaristic "solutions" which, in turn, perpetuate cycles of violence.

A similar strong critique has been formulated from an ideological rather than psychological perspective by anthropologist David Harvey. Placing the United States within the context of the growth of world-wide neoliberalism over the second half of the twentieth century, Harvey describes the dangerous complex of a capitalist market economy that favors the wealthy elite and produces devastating global poverty and environmental damage, coupled with a neoconservative insistence on politics motivated by a nationalistic moral purpose. He points out the longstanding "dual character" of U.S. nationalism. This view sees America as a nation divinely mandated toward world power and the envy of all nations. Yet, at the same time, it sees the nation in paranoid fashion as the potential victim of enemies who desire to defeat it.[4] U.S. nationalism is, in other words-or in my words-a coupling of millennialist supremacy and apocalyptic dread.

I single these critiques out here because they provide a valuable fleshing out of my own previous analyses of apocalyptic belief as a dangerous discourse of doom and desire that has become integral to the development and definition of imperial America. By viewing apocalypse as a discourse in the sense of Michel Foucault's concept of a regime of truth that is socially constructed within the particularities of the power/ knowledge format of a given culture, we better understand how it came to permeate U.S nationalism, as Harvey argues, and how it produces a subjectivity characteristic of the superpower syndrome that Lifton diagnoses.[5]As I argued in both *Anti-Apocalypse* and *Millennial Seduction,* apocalypse is most narrowly understood as a discourse of doom, or doomsday narrative, one that foretells the end of the world at the hands of God, as a punishment for sin and corruption of those who have followed forces of evil. In this sense, apocalyptic evil is cast as an ontologized force, a capital E Evil, dualistically opposed to the Good. With this metaphysical dualism of Good versus Evil comes a stance of absolute Truth, moral certainty, and justified violence against the enemy. But as I have also shown, apocalyptic discourse is highly elastic. It stretches from belief in a divine reckoning to technological destruction. It extends from belief in a literal endtime to signaling the end of the world as we have known it. Despite this elasticity, certain recognizable features recur. Paramount among these is the duality of being simultaneously both the chosen and the victimized. As such, the apocalyptic faithful regard themselves as those tapped to be the force of good destined to defeat the force of evil bent on destroying them.

These discursive features of apocalyptic belief are readily and consistently in evidence in the War on Terror declared by the George W. Bush administration following the attacks of 9/11 on the World Trade Center and the Pentagon. President Bush's 2002 State of the Union Address recklessly put forward the theological tenor of the War on Terror in his controversial "axis of evil" declaration targeting Iraq, Iran, and North Korea as ominous enemies of the United States. Despite debate about who actually coined this phrase, speechwriter David Frum or the President, and despite extensive criticism not only about its accuracy but, more importantly about the complications of such an assertion as state policy, pronouncements of the Bush administration sustained this line of dualistic rhetoric over the years following 9/11 and into his second administration.

It was further substantiated, for example, in the online White House Fact Sheet delineating President Bush's "Remarks on the War on Terror" from October 6, 2005. Here the President twice appeals to a concept of evil which is saturated with apocalyptic zeal:

> The evil that came to our shores on September 11th has reappeared on other days and in other places. In cities across the world, we have seen images of destruction and suffering that can seem like random acts of madness but are part of a larger terrorist threat. To combat this evil, we must remember the calling of September 11th - we will confront this mortal danger to all humanity and not tire or rest until the war on terror is won.[6]

President's Bush remarks are typical of apocalyptic fear-mongering that traditionally traffics in the desire for revenge against a declared enemy and a promise for the enemy's defeat. This trajectory from fear to defeat enables the demonization, scapegoating, and stereotyping of the perceived enemy.[7] Also in evidence is the customary calling forth of the force of good that has been divinely appointed. In this case, President Bush's "calling of September 11th" is a calling to arms against the conspiracy of terror. The characterization of so menacing an enemy implies that goodness automatically adheres to the enemy's enemy. According to this logic, America rises to the place of chosen nation, or, as apocalyptic rhetoric would have it, the Elect.

President Bush is hardly alone in marshalling apocalyptic responses in American society. The media often lodges Americans between panic and hope over global viruses, rapidly changing norms around gender and sexuality, arctic meltdowns, and economic decline. Doom-mongering has become a cultural industry. As I mentioned earlier, the entertainment industry knows that fright sells, especially when the demonically evil force can be roundly defeated. The American political Left is no stranger to apocalyptic belief either. Demonization and scapegoating have rendered the Bush administration an easy target of derision over the past several years: Bush, Cheney, Rumsfeld, and Rice cast as hell-spawn gleefully plotting the take-over of the world. From this point of view, the critics of malicious folks are automatically assumed to offer salvation. But such a stance retains the problems of divisiveness and reductive accusation found in that of its "sworn enemy."

The proclivity toward apocalyptic urgency and doom is of long standing in the United States, and it is more pronounced in the U.S. than in other predominantly Christian nations. Polls repeatedly show that the majority of Americans today self-identify as church-going believers in God, Satan, heaven and hell and that at least a third of the population accepts the fundamentalist or literalist view of a coming apocalypse. In part this is due to the results of the post World-War II era, as Lifton and Harvey indicate. But it is also due to the religious legacy of America's colonial period, which has been extended over the past several centuries through the institutionalized presence of conservative Protestantism. Strains of apocalyptic good versus evil resounded mightily as the Puritan colonialists established a theocratic government using the Old Testament as a guide for their laws. Evil for the Puritans was the kind of cosmic force that President Bush now sees as terrorist threat. For the Puritans, their specific enemies included the indigenous population, as well as other colonists like the hedonistic Thomas Morton of Merry Mount notoriety, who rejected their laws and way of life outright. These blatant non-believers in the Puritan way were inevitably seen as pawns of Satan who sought nothing short of world destruction and thereby deserved imprisonment or death. In the centuries that followed, during which a more secular view emerged, the category of evil was maintained but filled with new figures of threat, from the British rulers in the Revolutionary era to the Cold War powers of the twentieth century. Within the logic of apocalyptic belief, and regardless of which group occupies the enemy slot, the sense of urgency and justified defeat of evil remains the same; without the willingness to destroy the enemy, the forces of good will themselves be doomed.

The continuing belief in doomsday in the twenty-first century attests to the pervasiveness of literalism in American society, in which monolithic meaning trumps multiple meanings. As Charles Strozier has demonstrated from a psycho-historical perspective, literalism is a vital feature of American history and shapes the ideology of Christian Fundamentalism. Entrenched within the established Fundamentalist tradition of inerrancy in regard to the *Bible*, deeply rooted in Puritan colonialism, literalism was ultimately accorded the status of dogma in the early twentieth century in the twelve pamphlets titled *The Fundamentals*, which were published between 1910 and 1915. Strozier argues that Fundamentalist Christianity forges circular links between anxiety about death and the impulse toward a literalist reading of the *Bible*. A concentrated focus on doom creates anxiety about personal and collective death that is then held in check by the literalist impulse which provides a sense of "control over sin and badness and ultimately control over death."[8]

In the United States, as Vincent Crapanzano has shown, a tendency toward literalism stretches beyond biblical meaning and extends to the Law in strict construction of the Constitution.[9] In this case too, the erasure of ambiguity seems to be aimed at gaining control, but doing so by refusing to acknowledge myriad meanings carried forth by language, image, and experience. I want to emphasize at this point that literalism is a taught response to texts of all sorts, not just the Bible. So too, a tolerance for ambiguity and the ability to grasp the breadth and complexity of metaphor is not only teachable but culturally transmissible on many different levels.

In light of a cultural habit of literalism, part of the problem we face today in regard to the predominant discourse of evil is the central place that the final book of the New Testament occupies within American society. The "Apocalypse of John," or "Revelation," has for millennia served as the key text of the apocalyptic or doomsday belief system. But is has proven particularly vibrant within the American context. It was vital for the Puritans in their struggle to create a New Jerusalem for the Elect and remains so today for fundamentalist and evangelical Christians who believe it foretells the actual end of the world. But it also occupies a wider arena in American society. Its fantastic imagery is a rich source for superstitions about the number 666, fear of barcodes as the mark of the antichrist, and myriad conspiracy theories.

In its simplest form, "Revelation" is a story of Revenge and Rescue. A man named John has an elaborate vision of world destruction, in which the world deserves to be crushed because Satan's evil has endured in it. In his prophetic vision, tribulations like plagues, boils, rivers of blood, and famine abound. A number of key figures appear, including the whore of Babylon and the antichrist who wears the mark of the beast, the number 666, and who gains control of the earth. He and his forces must be destroyed. The revenge is thus against them. The virginal woman clothed with the sun is rescued and gives birth to the messiah. The final battle of Armageddon is fought and won by the messianic warrior, who rides a white horse. A millennium of harmony follows. Then a resurrection of the dead and the final judgment occur, with the majority of people being sent to eternal agony. The final rescue is for the chosen, more specifically the 144,000 virginal men who, as followers of the lamb, represent the good. They are rewarded by being ushered into the bejeweled New Jerusalem, a heaven on earth, where death and illness are forever banished.

This narrative of overcoming evil and defeating doom while dooming the evil enemy through revenge and rescue took hold as an institutionalized form of religious power but also, as I have indicated, merged with secular forms of government and nationalism. Given this history, in some sense, to be American is to be apocalyptic, that is, to be predisposed toward an adversarial and morally righteous mindset. Because of such deep ideological roots and the literalist impulse, citizens of the Untied States have to struggle consciously to resist tendencies of moral certainty and imperialism. Apocalyptic energy has been consistently renewed at times of crisis, especially around wars, from the Revolutionary break with America's first evil empire, Britain, to the Civil War, in which both sides designated theirs as the divinely ordained one, throughout the Cold War, and right into the current War on Terror and President Bush's condemnation of North Korea, Iran, and Iraq as an "Axis of Evil." It is not surprising, then, that the discursive unity of America and apocalypse has held sway over the centuries, from colony to empire. The most recent bout of apocalyptic fervor and fear began in the years building up to the turn of the millennium and might have diminished shortly after had it not been for the attacks of 9/11. In its use of apocalyptic images to describe both the attack and plans for U.S. retaliation, the Bush administration catapulted an already panic-poised nation onto a war-ready platform.

One might think that the concepts of evil, war, and apocalypse are indispensable comrades in arms, but this is not the case necessarily. In an astute analysis of Bush's characterizations of evil, political theorist Jodi Dean has demonstrated a crucial shift in the use of evil in 20th century presidential speeches. She shows that Presidents Roosevelt and Truman explicitly linked evil with social issues such as "poverty, economic inequality, and the unchecked pursuit of profit."[10] With President Eisenhower, a gradual shift toward religious categories of good versus evil began to emerge and continued to take hold as the Cold War escalated, although Presidents Kennedy and Johnson also maintained notions of poverty and inequality as social evils. Dean points to the most significant shift as occurring within President Reagan's speeches in which she identifies a fusion of the "moral and the ontological".[11] This is not surprising, given Reagan's Christian Fundamentalist acceptance of the Book of Revelation foretelling a final world battle at Armageddon. The current President Bush, she points out, has assumed the mantle of Reagan's fundamentalist Christian approach but adds to it a dimension of his own special role as God's emissary. In his speeches he has portrayed himself as an embodiment of God's will and America as God's chosen nation.

As Dean's treatment of Bush's presidential predecessors indicates, there is more than one way to look at evil. I want to turn now to a second discourse of evil that is also part of an American legacy, one that is inflected in what Dean points to in President Roosevelt's portrayal of poverty and other social ills as human-made and socially alterable evil. It too has a long legacy in the United States. As I have shown in previous work, the writings of Thomas Jefferson, Margaret Fuller, Henry David Thoreau, Maxine Hong Kingston, and June Jordan forge a significant ethical tradition, what I call an "aesthetics of liberty," that portrays evil as a result of social injustice.[12] Their notably non-apocalyptic perspective emphasizes individual and social agency as the necessary antidote to doomsday fatalism and recognizes the place of both contingency and institutional determinism in the making of human history. But the particular example I want to highlight here has special merit because it not only depicts the social view of evil, it also provides a stunning critique of the literalist apocalyptic view of evil as an ontological force. No where in American culture are these two contending portrayals of evil more fully and dramatically developed than in Herman Melville's novel *Moby-Dick*.

Captain Ahab has long been regarded as one of, if not the most, memorable figures of evil in American literature. According to Ahab's view, however, it is the white whale that literally embodies evil; to him Moby-Dick is the actual incorporation of a cosmic force that seeks to destroy him and thus must be destroyed first. Melville's portrait of Ahab is so compelling that it risks readers' mesmerized allegiance to him, as does happen with the ship's crew, including Ishmael, as they vow to follow him to their death if necessary. This is the problem inherent in the kind of literalism that characterizes Fundamentalist belief. I recall as a child being so caught up in Gregory Peck's performance of Ahab in the film version, that for weeks I practiced walking on my own rigged-up whale-bone stump, which I made with belts and a broom stick attached to my bent and bound-up leg. Had I been aboard the *Pequod*, I too would have raised my flask and drunk to Ahab's cause. As the stanza from Auden's poem about

Melville that I have used as an epigraph suggests, evil may be unspectacular but the character Melville created is all about spectacle.

These days, though, I find the novel's most profound insight to be its rejection of evil as a metaphysical, dualistic force precisely of the kind Ahab embraces. This is not the same thing as rejecting the existence of evil, however. Throughout the novel, Melville has his narrator Ishmael point to the injustices and inequalities of the social world with scathing observations about emotionally impaired, self-aggrandizing leaders. Indeed, as Melville shows, one of the most virulent forms of social evil occurs when a leader's personal moral conviction becomes so rigidly absolute that it forecloses on ambiguity and complexity and substitutes for the well-being of those he or she leads. The destructiveness of the monomaniacal Ahab, which brings down his ship and his entire crew except for Ishmael who lives to tell the tale, attests to the dangers of accepting apocalyptic evil as one's enemy-or following a leader who does. Rather than depicting doom as one's lot in life, Ishmael's survival and story reveal that a lot of doom in life stems from human treachery.

2. No! in thunder

As powerful as Melville's account was in his own time, and as relevant as it remains in our time, within the United States today his critique may well remain as isolated as Ishmael afloat in a vast ocean of apocalyptic belief. But is it our lot in life as American citizens to be condemned to a belief system that thrives on doom and fear? One, moreover, that endangers our standing in the world and, indeed, the world itself? To answer that, I borrow the phrase that Melville used to praise Nathaniel Hawthorne as a writer who refused to adhere to the yes-saying status quo: "No! in thunder." As is clear from the brief history of apocalyptic entrenchment I have provided, it is no easy task to dislodge a cultural conviction and habit of life that is so deeply wedged into American identity. And yet, this is surely a time that calls for such change-which is not the same as claiming a calling.

While there is never a "right time" within a non-apocalyptic view, there are ripe times for breaking through the edifice of self-righteous and simplistic explanations endemic to the literalism of apocalyptic belief. I believe this is such a time, not only because the costs and extent of world-wide conflict are so painfully clear, but also because of the saturation effect of apocalyptic belief in contemporary society. There may well be within the United States today, a certain level of apocalyptic fatigue, in particular around political issues, as suggested by declining approval ratings for President Bush and his administration's handling of the war on terror, as well as social resistance to their refusal of rights to same-sex couples and their restrictions on reproductive freedom. The exception to apocalyptic fatigue is to be found within popular culture, where apocalyptic imagery and themes abound in television shows like "Lost," and "Invasion" and films such as "War of the Worlds" and "The Last Stand." Images of the Book of Revelation even adorn Celestial Tea boxes. In these instances, apocalyptic belief fuses with entertainment rather than divine decree. I would also cite the satiric and comedic uses of apocalypse, doom, and evil popularized in segments such as "This Week in God" on "The Daily Show" as part of the weakening effect of apocalyptic drama.

I take these examples of popular culture to suggest that traditional dichotomies of good versus evil have been diminished, which, as should be clear, I applaud. Yet this entertaining and comedic use of evil, while potentially beneficial, is not particularly wise. Nightly spoofs by comedians, helpful though they are to break the hold of moral righteousness, tend to replace it with cynicism. How, then, do we, as individuals and a nation, put deep-set fears aside without succumbing to cynical smugness? How do we place in doubt beliefs that have held sway for centuries, despite ample evidence that their predictions do not occur, without simply replacing apocalypse with belief in nothing? For that kind of vision, literary and visual art has tended to provide greater intellectual sustenance and more robust appreciation for empathy and complexity.

The timbre of these questions and my hope for what I call the "geopolitics of prevailing" take their cue from another American author, William Faulkner, and, more specifically, his Nobel Prize Acceptance speech from December, 1950. Addressing his remarks to aspiring writers, Faulkner states that, "Our tragedy today is a general and universal physical fear so long sustained by now that we can even bear it." This overriding sense of fear, he explains, stems from the nuclear threat deemed paramount in his day. He laments that "There is only the question: When will I be blown up?" and advises young writers to teach themselves that the "basest of all things is to be afraid." For himself he takes a decidedly non-apocalyptic stand. As he puts it, "I decline to accept the end of man," reiterating, "I refuse to accept this." Faulkner concludes his speech on a note of duty and privilege by declaring that the "poet's voice need not merely be the record of man, it can be one of the props, the pillars to help him endure and prevail."[13]

There are several ideas I want to draw on from this speech, which, though explicitly posed to writers, tacitly addresses readers as well. Faulkner's insistence that we must strive to think beyond what he alliteratively terms the "last ding-dong of doom" applies to our own Time of Terror as much as it did to his Cold War Era. His admonition echoes both Adam Phillips's advice that we learn to think "besides" good and evil and Melville's depiction of the narcissistic fear that plunges people into totalistic dramas of destruction. It is no accident that so much of this wisdom comes from literature and art in general, precisely because of what has variously been called literariness or figurativism (as applied to visual arts). In contrast to the impulse of literalism, the pronounced artifice of aesthetic creation invites and enables us to think through ambiguity, to see the intricacies of gray rather than the stark divisions of black versus white. Doing that encourages a shift from the totalizing belief of a single, timeless truth toward the capacity to grasp meaning as context-made and, therefore, re-made and re-makeable. Comprehension of metaphor, in all the arts, not just literature, encourages a swing from certainty about one's lot in life to seeking possibilities for sustaining life, precisely because life is filled with uncertainties. As Faulkner points out, literalism weakens what literature offers us. I would add that it weakens what life offers us. It both stems from and fuels the base kind of fear that, as he says, is nothing short of tragedy.

3. The Art of Security

For me, Faulkner's message and his praise of the "poet's voice" gets to the heart of what I mean by the "geopolitics of prevailing." By this I mean an individual outlook and a national policy that, as Faulkner puts it, "declines to accept the end of man" as its starting premise. When doom is neither cast as the primary threat of an enemy writ large, nor the beginning of a final endtime, when one, in short, demurs to doom, a new space is opened up for human agency. So too, the interconnections between individuals, groups, and nations become more visible, the necessities of cooperation more clear. Faulkner's focus on future writers is worth underscoring even as we look again to past writers who have led the way toward rectifying social injustice. This is evident from the record of the non-apocalyptic writers I mentioned earlier, from Thomas Jefferson to June Jordan. All were influential voices in the leading civil rights advances of their time. They, as well as Faulkner and Melville, provide the pillars we need to help us rethink the geopolitics of our time.

What I am urging, therefore, is a more concerted effort to cultivate an aesthetic way of perceiving and living in the world. As I hope to show in *The Art of Security*, a work in progress that seeks to redefine what it means to be secure, the arts offer us crucial ways of rethinking the geopolitical orientation of the United States. In the close of this essay, I want to give an overview of a geopolitical alternative to the apocalyptic one operative today.

My re-appropriation of the term geopolitics is meant to draw attention to the current policy of the United States, which follows a geopolitical trajectory of empire that uses the discourse of evil and the threat of doom as a means to justify world control. In its most basic sense, geopolitics is a theory seeking to explain world developments in light of geographic space and resources. In historical practice, however, geopolitics was ideologically instrumental in expanding the British empire in the early 20th century and was adapted for similar territorial take-over by the Nazis during the build up of their powers. Geopolitics has, in other words, a totalistic and totalitarian history, one that was founded on assumptions of literalist control over world territory.

The term itself was coined in 1899 by a Swedish geographer, Rudolf Kjellen. But the concept behind it starts 5 years later. That story begins in 1904 with Sir Halford Mackinder, the British geographer who was instrumental in making geography a discipline to be studied in schools. Mackinder's most important contribution is an essay called "The Geographical Pivot of History." In it he suggested that the control of Eastern Europe was vital to control of the world. He formulated his hypothesis with declarative succinctness: "Who rules East Europe commands the Heartland; Who rules the Heartland commands the World-Island; Who rules the World-Island commands the world." Mackinder's Heartland (also known as the Pivot Area) is the core area of Eurasia, and the World-Island is all of Eurasia (both Europe and Asia and some of Africa, thus including the oil rich Middle-East). Essentially oriented toward building and maintaining Empire, this way of thinking about world politics overtly emphasized control and expansion. In Mackinder's case, this was on behalf of the British Empire, but in the early twentieth century in the United States, it specifically guided Theodore Roosevelt's foreign policy in conducting the Spanish American War, taking over Panama, and occupying the Philippines.[14]

As an operative concept and term, geopolitics reemerged in the U.S. during the Cold War, especially through use by Henry Kissinger in the 1960s and 70s, and was further popularized as a foreign policy strategy for the United States during Reagan's administration where the threat of Armageddon was made explicit as a means to curb Soviet power. Within the more recent American context, empire has become less a matter of actually annexing territories and more a matter of extending control over other nations and their resources. Under the first President Bush, through the Clinton administration, and then with the second President Bush, geopolitical control by the United States has been justified in the name of democracy for others but routed through proclamations that Terror is evil incarnate and God is on America's side.

By advocating the geopolitics of prevailing I seek to counter the geopolitics of empire, which thrives on the discourse of doom far more than on the practice of democracy. But we cannot counter the rigidity of apocalyptic belief through mimetic denunciation, which propels the energy of apocalyptic fear, vengeance, and moral certitude. That is the way of Ahab. Worse, it is a way that remains as self-hobbled as I was as a child with my belts and broomstick. Rather, it is worth bearing in mind Faulkner's evocation of immortality understood as the physical act of humankind prevailing. Faulkner was surely correct in appreciating that literary forms of writing more often sanction a world in which ambiguity is a foundational condition, complexity of causes a given, fluidity of perception a virtue, and aesthetic creativity a means by which we may envision many possible futures. These modes of thought and acting comprise a foundation for the geopolitics of prevailing, with its recognition of global interdependency not just as fact of life but also as a social virtue.

As I have wanted to indicate, such a foundation has been laid, with many intellectual resources already available. As my discussion of Melville and Faulkner imply, these resources may be found in works that enable us to resist the dangerous and death-provoking knells of the "last ding-dong of doom." The powerful effects of the aesthetic imagination to combat the limitations and divisiveness of fear may be witnessed in social movements that have envisioned ways for more people to live more justly. Such visions may be summoned in film, literature, and the visual arts, all forms that thrive best when they veer away from the literal and toward the metaphoric as a means to tell truth. To my mind, the greatest insight of the arts is that the literalist concept of evil inevitably falls short of its own goal to eradicate it. The literalist mindset reinforces division, employs surveillance, and strives for control in ways that fuel and perpetuate war and injustice. Learning how to speak, write, and think in the "poet's voice" will not defeat evil for evermore, but it might help us prevail.

Notes

[1] W. H. Auden, "Herman Melville," *The Collected Works of W. H. Auden* (New York: Kingport Press, 1945), 146-7.

[2]Adam Phillips, "Besides Good and Evil," *On Flirtation* (Cambridge,: Harvard University Press, 1994), p. 64.
[3] Robert Jay Lifton, *Superpower Syndrome: America's Apocalyptic Confrontation with the World* (New York: Nation Books, 2003), p. xii.
[4] David Harvey, *A Brief History of Neoliberalism* (New York: Oxford University Press, 2005), pp. 195-6.
[5] Lee Quinby, *Anti-Apocalypse* (Minneapolis: U of Minnesota Press, 1994) and *Millennial Seduction* (Ithaca: Cornell UP, 1999).
[6] Fact Sheet Outline from the Official Web Site of the White House: http://www.whitehouse.gov/news/releases/2005/10/20051006-2.html
[7] Chip Berlet, "Dances with Devils: How Apocalyptic and Millennialist Themes Influence Right Wing Scapegoating and Conspiricism." Available online at: http://www.public eye.org.
[8] Charles Strozier, *Apocalypse: On the Psychology of Fundamentalism in America* (New York: Beacon, 1994), p. 95.
[9] Vincent Crapanzano, *Serving the Word: Literalism in America from the Pulpit to the Bench* (New York: New Press, 2001).
[10] Jodi Dean, "Evil's Political Habitats," *Theory and Event*, 8.2 (2005). Available online at: http://muse.jhu.edu/cgi-bin/access.cgi?uri=/journals/theory_and_event/v008/8.2dean.html.
[11] Dean, online at: http://muse.jhu.edu/cgi-bin/access.cgi?uri=/journals/theory_and_event/v008/8.2dean.html.
[12] Lee Quinby, *Freedom, Foucault, and the Subject of America* (Boston: Northeastern UP, 1991.
[13] William Faulkner, Nobel Prize Acceptance Speech, December 10, 1950. Available online at: http://www.rjgeib.com/thoughts/faulkner/faulkner.html.
[14] See Gearoid O Tuathail (Gerard Toal), *Critical Geopolitics: The Politics of Writing Global Space* (Minneapolis: University of Minnesota Press, 1996).

Bibliography

Auden, W.H. "Herman Melville." In *The Collected Works of W. H. Auden.*146-7. New York: Kingport Press, 1945.

Berlet, Chip. Berlet, "Dances with Devils: How Apocalyptic and Millennialist Themes Influence Right Wing Scapegoating and Conspiricism." Available online at: http://www.public eye.org.

Crapanzano, Vincent. *Serving the Word: Literalism in America from the Pulpit to the Bench.* New York: New Press, 2001.

Dean,Jodi. "Evil's Political Habitats," *Theory and Event*, 8.2 (2005). Available online at: http://muse.jhu.edu/cgi-bin/access.cgi?uri=/journals/theory_and_event/v008/8.2dean.html.

Fact Sheet Outline from the Official Web Site of the White House. Available online at http://www.whitehouse.gov/news/releases/2005/10/20051006-2.html

Faulkner, William. Nobel Prize Acceptance Speech, December 10, 1950. Available online at: http://www.rjgeib.com/thoughts/faulkner/faulkner.html.

Harvey, David. *A Brief History of Neoliberalism.* New York: Oxford University Press, 2005.

Lifton, Robert Jay. *Superpower Syndrome: America's Apocalyptic Confrontation with the World.* New York: Nation Books, 2003).

Phillips, Adam. "Besides Good and Evil." In *On Flirtation,* 59-64. Cambridge: Harvard University Press, 1994.

Quinby, Lee. *Anti-ApocalypseExercises in Geealogical Criticism.* Minneapolis: University of Minnesota Press, 1994.

Quinby, Lee. *Millennial Seduction:A Skeptic Confronts Apocalyptic Culture.* Ithaca: Cornell University Press, 1999.

Quinby, Lee. *Freedom, Foucault, and the Subject of America.* Boston: Northeastern UP, 1991.

Strozier, Charles. *Apocalypse: On the Psychology of Fundamentalism in* America. New York: Beacon, 1994.

Tuathail, Gearoid. (Gerard Toal), *Critical Geopolitics: The Politics of Writing Global Space.* Minneapolis: University of Minnesota Press, 1996.

Post-modern Narratives of Evil and 9-11: The Case of Frédéric Beigbeder

Scott M. Powers

Abstract: In the wake of the Holocaust, theorists including Arendt and Lyotard outlined a post-modern perspective on evil by reconsidering human tragedies as the products of multiple forces and historical conditions that exceed human agency. More recently, post-modern thinkers such as Tzvetan Todorov and Miguel Benasayag, in their analysis of social discourse, have demonstrated how the ways in which we think and speak about evil are themselves implicated in the genesis of events that society considers evil. It remains to be seen how this philosophical perspective on evil translates into fiction. The following paper begins such an inquiry by identifying a post-modern account of evil in Frédéric Beigbeder's best-selling *Windows on the World* (2003), a fictional account of the events of September 11, 2001.

Key Words: Evil, Postmodernism, Fiction, Frédéric Beigbeder, 9-11, French Literature.

1. Evil in Post-Modernity

An investigation into a post-modern perspective on evil risks raising objections to the very possibility of such a perspective. And indeed, it has. When asked to submit an essay on evil and post-modernism, Holocaust scholar Berel Lang responded with an article on why he could not. He argues that

> if post-modernity expected to leave anything behind, [it would be precisely] the nostalgia for the binary or dualistic thinking [that] opposes virtue to vice and then asserts that we can tell [...] the difference between them."[1]

But in fact, Lang claims that despite the advent of the so-called post-modern era, we are not beyond good and evil. Instead of conceiving history in terms of rupture, which the notion *post*-modern implies, Lang contends that our understanding of the world has always reflected a "moral continuum" within history. Accordingly, the wrongfulness of an event, whether we confront it from a pre- or post-modern perspective, appears as evident "as the quality of any human exchange or transaction can be."[2] To illustrate this, Lang highlights the irony of an anecdote in the biography of Nietzsche, the undisputed herald of the post-modern. While strolling through his neighbourhood during the time when he was working on *Beyond Good and Evil*, Nietzsche responded to the cruelty that he witnessed in a cab driver beating his horse by instinctively flinging his arms around the animal's neck in protest. Convinced that contemporary society does not perceive evil in a fundamentally different way than societies of previous time periods, and that post-modernism does not "offer any more compelling [...] explanation of its own," Lang concludes by recognizing the post-modern as simply a *style*.[3]

While Lang's notion that there exists a common denominator across time for events perceived as evil is worth pursuing (and I will briefly do so), this does not rule out the possibility of a new, post-modern perspective on evil. Post-modern thinkers increasingly speak about evil as they begin to sort through the events of 9-11 and respond to the prevailing neo-Manichaeism discourse that ensued in American society. If we can temporarily suspend our objections to a post-modern employment of the term, we may begin to discern what it is about contemporary thought on evil that is new.

2. *Windows on the World*

I would like to initiate such an inquiry through an analysis of *Windows on the World*, a French bestseller and winner of the prestigious *Prix Interallié*. Written in 2003 by Frédéric Beigbeder, one of France's most post-modern writers, this fictional account of September 11 weaves together two alternating narratives. In one, the narrator, who reveals himself as Frédéric Beigbeder himself, spends his mornings breakfasting in the restaurant on the top floor of the Montparnasse Tower, Paris's only skyscraper, as he attempts to imagine what it was like for those who died inside the World Trade Center (WTC). The other narrative, seemingly the product of Beigbeder's imagination, features the narrator Carthew, who, trapped with his two sons inside *Windows on the World*, the restaurant atop the north tower of the WTC, comes to grips with his imminent death.

Beigbeder makes it clear that *Window on the Worlds* is a book about evil. The novel's epigraph - Marilyn Manson's proclamation that the artist's function is "to plunge into the depths of hell" - foregrounds the theme.[4] Just as revealing is Beigbeder's self-identification with Charles Baudelaire, the French writer of evil *par excellence*. In one chapter, after a morning spent reflecting on the events of 9-11 while breakfasting in the Montparnasse Tower's *Ciel de Paris*, Beigbeder visits the poet's tomb in the adjacent Montparnasse Cemetery. There, he takes a photograph of a statue of Baudelaire in the reflective pose of Rodin's *Thinker*. Beigbeder includes the photograph in the chapter, entitles it "Genius of Evil," and accompanies it with a description of the poet's physical appearance, especially his prominent chin. This is an important detail because Beigbeder, in his novels, has often commented on his own protruding chin as his defining facial feature.[5] In fact, critics and fans have come to speak of Beigbeder, synecdochically, by referring to his chin.[6] To be sure, the narrator alludes - through likening his face to Baudelaire's - to a spiritual bond that he enjoys with the deceased poet. Another curious observation that Beigbeder makes is that the statue faces the Montparnasse Tower. The narrator takes a picture of the tower from Baudelaire's "perspective," which he also includes in the chapter. A most likely explanation for this attention to detail is the coincidence that Beigbeder notes between the statue's gaze upon Paris's skyscraper, and the narrator's own interest in towers as an inspiration for his writing. It can be said that in this description of a visit to Baudelaire's tomb, as the narrator looks up to the poet for a snapshot, likewise, Beigbeder looks up to Baudelaire as a veritable "Genius of Evil," and thus as his spiritual father. Indeed, in the tradition of *The Flowers of Evil*, Beigbeder's *Windows on the World* betrays a fascination with evil, and an overarching investigation into the sources of human suffering.

An inquiry into the question of evil inevitably involves two stages: the registering of a case of human suffering, and subsequently, an investigation into the causes. Beigbeder's impetus to write *Windows on the World* was the need he felt to record the human suffering of 9-11. He states that in writing this novel, he has dared to go where even the media dared not go. That is to say, inside the burning towers.[7] The narrative contains numerous scenes that vividly depict the victims' intense emotional distress, the heat, the burnt flesh, the smoke, the vomit, and the bodies sounding like "exploding melons" as they hit the pavement below.[8] Contrary to the media and political discourse, which focus primarily on the symbolism behind the 9-11 attacks, Beigbeder recurrently reminds the reader of the real human suffering that the hijackings caused: "Terrorism does not destroy symbols, it hacks people of flesh and blood to pieces."[9] Verses from a chapter-poem of the novel are a demonstration of the author's insistence on the physical reality of that morning:

> We are metal shrieking
> People hanging out of windows
> People falling from the windows
> An abandoned wheelchair […]
> Blazing fuel in the elevator shafts
> 98 elevators, all out of order

White marble in the open spaces stained with blood [...]

Hands in tatters
skin hanging from arms
like an Issey Miyake dress

Carved-up faces by the coffee machine
A closed space with a fire down below
We roast
We are being roasted like chickens
Smoked like salmon [...]

A rain of bodies over the WTC Plaza.[10]

Far from constituting a callous, insolent recounting of the 9-11 atrocities, such vivid descriptions respond to the moral imperative not to ignore extreme human suffering.[11] Beigbeder states: "In *Windows on the World*, the customers were gassed, burned and reduced to ash. To them, as to so many others, we owe a duty of memory."[12] Halfway through the novel, the narrator takes a trip to New York where he visits Ground Zero and the surrounding memorials to the dead. Beigbeder's initial response is visceral, as he is brought to silence and to tears: "I bring my hand to my mouth. I no longer feel sorry for myself. Here in the midst of this terribly saccharine suffering stood a cynic in tears."[13]

3. Evil and Pain

Both Beigbeder's reaction to the physical pain suffered by the victims of 9-11 and Nietzsche's reaction to a case of animal cruelty would seem to constitute a trans-historical, moral response to what they instinctively recognize as human evil. But perhaps Beigbeder and Nietzsche simply belong to a broader historical era that equates evil with the infliction of bodily pain. As twentieth-century thinkers such as Michel Foucault and Miguel Benasayag have argued, the notion of bodily suffering, and specifically human bodily suffering, has only been perceived as a sure sign of evil since the modern, secular era. In fact, as Foucault shows in *Discipline and Punish*, the public display of tortured bodies in medieval times was often understood as serving a good purpose, as a form of social discipline.[14]

To explain the change in Western civilization's perspective on evil and the body, Benasayag begins by summarizing Freud's definition of a civilization. In *Civilization and Its Discontents*, Freud claims that civilization is made possible when the collective psyche recognizes a common "figure of renouncement."[15] According to Benasayag, this figure represents what society perceives to be the originator of the ontological Law - that which prescribes what is sacred and taboo. By respecting the originator, members of a community renounce their violent impulses. Accordingly, chaos, characterized by one-to-one duels in which the strongest survive, transforms into a civilized state. In any given civilization, evil designates that which violates the common figure of renouncement.[16]

Drawing from historians such as Foucault, Benasayag identifies two distinct types of civilization in history, one religious and the other secular. In pre-modern, religious times, God was understood to be the originator of the Law. Accordingly, evil was perceived as that which desecrated whatever belonged to God, notably divinely appointed kings and the spiritual realm, such as the human soul. Violations included revolution as well as disrespect for the rights of last confession, communion, and proper burial. Any act or declaration that posed a threat to the spiritual order of things was perceived *ipso facto* as evil.[17] Because in pre-modern times evil was equated with acts that violated the spiritual realm, physical suffering alone did not appear as a sign of evil.

During the Enlightenment, a historical shift toward secularisation and thus toward a secular perspective on evil occurred. As described by Benasayag, kingdoms whose authority was perceived as granted by God himself fell to democracies founded on the principles of the "rights of man." Consequently, Man replaced God as the symbol of renouncement for civilized society. As Man was henceforth understood to be the originator of the Law, the figure of Man became equated with the Good. By extension, the human body, as the symbol of Man, became elevated to the position of the sacrosanct, the untouchable. Consequently, tortured bodies not only receded from public view, but also became the very mark of evil.[18]

A well-known illustration of this secular understanding of human suffering is Susan Sontag's description, in *On Photography,* of her initial reaction to the graphic photographs of Holocaust victims as "a negative epiphany," as photographs of evil:

> Nothing I have seen - in photographs or in real life - ever cut me as sharply, deeply, instantaneously. Indeed, it seems plausible to me to divide my life into two parts, before I saw those photographs (I was twelve) and after. [...] When I looked at those photographs, something broke. Some limit had been reached, and not only that of

> horror; I felt irrevocably grieved, wounded, but a part of my feelings started to tighten; something went dead; something is still crying.[19]

In *The Origins of Totalitarianism*, Hannah Arendt similarly responds to the Holocaust atrocities. In light of the Nazis' extreme mistreatment of the human body, from the unbearable conditions inside the freight transports to the endless examples of physical torture inflicted on the Jews upon arrival, Arendt describes the death camps as Hell itself. In fact, as Arendt argues, the infliction of bodily pain constituted a direct attack on the prisoners' humanity. The death camps were a veritable Hell on Earth in the sense that humanity was entirely absent, or rather, eradicated by the daily mistreatment of bodies.[20] Other twentieth-century instances of extreme bodily suffering, especially cases of state-implemented torture, have provoked reactions similar to Sontag's and Arendt's.[21] Elaine Scarry's celebrated work, *The Body in Pain*, epitomizes this modern perspective on evil and bodily suffering by regarding torture as a pure act of destruction. Its sole purpose, she argues, is the destruction of man's perception of the created world and his ability to create. Accordingly, she describes torture as the most immoral of acts, an absolute evil that resists comparison: "[Torture's] immorality is so absolute and the pain it brings about so real that there is a reluctance to place it in conversation by the side of other objects."[22] As a part of this lengthy tradition that equates evil with the infliction of bodily pain, in *Windows on the World* Beigbeder underscores the evil phenomenon of 9-11 through the description of suffering bodies.

Rather than constituting a trans-historical sign of evil, physical suffering seems, rather, to be contingent upon an ideology shared by both the modern and post-modern periods. Despite the many modern ideologies that post-modernity has rejected, the notion of the individual, born with inalienable rights, the cornerstone of democracy, and whose values are symbolized by the untouchable human body itself, remains that which is considered the Good. Benasayag underscores the survival of the individual as mythic figure in the post-modern era:

> The only rock that has survived the historical break occasioned by the demise of the myth of progress, the only credible value of this time of crisis, is the individual [...]. A creation of modernity, the individual is this allegedly autonomous being who occupies the centre of the world. [...] Our era loudly proclaims that

> the entire universe revolves around this central figure:
> the individual.[23]

With respect to what we understand as the outcome of evil, I would agree with Lang that a post-modernist vision does not offer anything new. For contemporary consciousness, as was the case in past centuries, evil's victims are easily identifiable, and recognized by their physical afflictions, their tortured bodies. However, what I believe post-modernism adds to the question of evil is a new perspective on the *origins* of evil, which for the first time, as I hope to show, are not perceived as transparent.

Post-modernism may have been initially used to describe a style of architecture that combines classical structures with modern forms. As a literary hodgepodge of old and new narrative styles, *Windows on the World* can be considered a good example of post-modern fiction. The minute-by-minute diary-like account of one day's events often shifts to other textual forms, including poem reproductions, sometimes of classical verse, sometimes of modern forms. Pop hit lyrics, excerpts from the *Michelin* guide to New York City, questionnaires, and tourist photographs also help shape the narrative. But more than simply an eclectic mixture, the post-modern style in literature has been described by its irony and self-contradictions, the frequent use of parody, its resistance to paraphrase, distillation, and closure, as well as what Brian McHale calls *heterotopia*, or the textual deployment of various contradictory discourses on the perceived reality of the world.[24] These elements of the post-modern style, I would argue, have inevitable implications for post-modernism as a veritable vision of evil. For instance, a text's deployment of multiple, competing discourses reflects, if not occasions, the rejection of those "grand narratives" that attempt to account for all historical events or human behaviour.[25] Indeed, the death of grand narratives such as Marx's economic theories on capital and class struggle and Freud's Oedipal complex constitutes the historical rupture denoted by the "post" in post-modernism. The post-modern cynicism of a single explanation for Being, expressed by a writer's unresolved engagement with competing paradigms, reflects a vision that refuses to identify one overarching source of evil, and a perspective that recognizes the question of evil as multifarious. Below, I will identify the "heterotopic" nature of *Windows on the World*, and how it projects such a vision.

4. The Question of Agency

In considering a post-modern account for evil, a word must also be said about human agency - traditionally one of the most important factors considered by philosophers in the question of evil. To be sure, human agency was already a waning notion during the modern period, in which grand narratives pushed the conscious human will to the wings of history's stage. Today, postmodernists seem to have entirely effaced the notion as they underscore countless biological, linguistic, discursive, social, and economic forces as the veritable actors in historical events. More recently, with the advent of a new information age, philosophers and writers have also looked to various forms of media as powerful manipulators of historical events. The self, no longer predicated on individual agency, constitutes the vehicle, often unknowingly, through which impersonal forces act out. Arendt laid the groundwork for a post-modern vision of evil by portraying the Nazi bureaucrat Adolf Eichmann as an unmotivated evildoer:

> Evil men, we are told, act out of envy; this may be resentment at not having turned out well through no fault of their own (Richard III) or the envy of Cain [...]. Or they may be prompted by weakness (Macbeth) [...]. Or by covetousness[...]. However, what I was confronted with was utterly different and still undeniably factual. I was struck by a manifest shallowness in the doer that made it impossible to trace the incontestable evil of his deeds to any [...] motives.[26]

Arendt's portrayal of Eichmann not as a scheming, demonic executioner with a hatred for Jews, but rather as a simple cog in the wheel of a much larger socio-economic machine, signals a veritable rupture in our understanding of evil by rendering problematic the notion of the "evildoer."[27]

In this post-modern vein, the narrator of *Windows on the World* borrows from the film *Airplane!* the image of a plane with no pilot as a metaphor of present-day society as "an autonomous [system], an organization that ha[s] neither management, nor purpose."[28] Inevitably, the self takes part in a system that exceeds the will, and that is headed toward certain destruction. Carthew, the narrator trapped inside the north tower, expresses feelings of complete impotence as he seeks to comprehend the evil world in which he lives, and the role that he has played in it. At first, Carthew feels unjustly targeted for crimes that he has not committed. After all, he is simply a real estate agent:

> They want us to feel guilty. But guilty for what? I'm not responsible for what my country did when it was

> growing up. Black slavery, the genocide of the Indians, raging liberalism, it wasn't me guys. I came along much later! All I did was be born here, in the Big Guy's house, but I'm not one of them. The only thing I control is my real estate office.[29]

On the one hand, Carthew asserts that he did not willingly cause people harm: "I don't know whether I am the embodiment of Good, but I never wished Evil on anyone."[30] And yet, upon further reflection he begins to recognize that he has participated, despite himself, in a great economic system responsible for poverty and oppression: "Okay, so I'm not so innocent [...]. [But] what could I do if Guatemalan kids were working fifteen hours a day for slave wages to do the job for me?"[31]

Narrator Beigbeder draws similar conclusions about his place in an evil world. While visiting Ground Zero, he reflects on a series of modern-day human catastrophes and admits his complicity in them:

> Nuclear reactor meltdown at Chernobyl nuclear facility, Ukraine, 1986. Wreck of the *Exxon Valdez*, Alaska, 1989. Sarin gas attack, Tokyo subway, Japan, 1995. [...] I stroll among these monstrosities. I would gladly wash my hands of them, I'd like to think that I am not complicit in such horrors. And yet, like every human being, at a microscopic level, I am complicit.[32]

Such observations highlight a common dilemma faced by the post-modern consciousness, that is to say, the feeling of responsibility for something that one did not will.

5. Origin and End

In his attempt to understand 9-11, narrator Beigbeder considers a variety of theories of the causes. For instance, he imagines the motivations of the plane hijackers. He poses the question: "Who are these men capable of such a thing?"[33] In contrast to the Bush administration's portrayal of the hijackers solely as scheming evildoers, Beigbeder considers a variety of interpretations. In fact, he constructs a multiple-choice question that asks who these men are, and then presents the reader with a number of possibilities from which to choose:

> Who are Mohammed Atta, Abdulaziz Alomari, Marwan Alshehhi and their buddies?
>
> Are they (check box as applicable)

Towel-headed fundamentalists? □
Psychotic madmen? □
Neo-fascists? □
Saints in turbans? □
Morons manipulated by a billionaire who is
an ex-CIA agent? □
Heroes of the exploited third world? □
Hardcore post-punks drugged up to the eyeballs? □
Camel-fuckers who need to be napalmed pronto? □
Depressed nihilists? □
Militant anti-globalization activists? □
Kamikazes? (c'mon now, all together!)
Incredible but… TRUE? □

Among this list are the more traditional depictions of the scheming evildoer, including "Towel-headed fundamentalists" and "Psychotic madmen." But Beigbeder also proposes answers such as "Morons manipulated by a billionaire who is an ex-CIA agent" and "Heroes of the exploited third world."[34] Such interpretations suggest that the hijackers, rather than scheming evildoers, were themselves the instruments, if not the victims, of a great economic system that breeds inequality and death.

Elsewhere, Beigbeder targets the role of the entertainment industry and the media in the 9-11 catastrophe. As if an illustration of Guy Debord's notion of the "society of the spectacle" in which reality is increasingly perceived by contemporary society as that which is projected onto the movie screen, the characters trapped inside the World Trade Center restaurant recurrently interpret their life experiences by referring to film scenarios. In an attempt to apprehend the reality of the terrorist attacks, the victims envision themselves playing heroic roles in popular films. Carthew, the narrator trapped in the towering inferno, feels that he should win an Oscar for such a casting: "The tension mounts; we'll have to play a tight game. I deserve an Academy Award! I hold a child's hand in each of mine and play the part of father courage."[35] Meanwhile, Carthew's son imagines him as Clark Kent, preparing for his next heroic exploit: "The tricky thing is there's no phone booth around here. Clark Kent can't turn into Superman with no phone booth to change into his costume. Dad's hardly gonna get his outfit on in front of Lourdes."[36] Narrator Beigbeder is just as guilty as his characters of likening reality to film:

> The "killer cloud," a tornado of rubble, 100-foot steel, girders like train tracks falling from the sky, sheets of glass 100 feet square, sharp as giant razor blades, the killer cloud moved like a tidal wave at 50 miles an hour through the alleys onto Fulton Street, and this, too, is an image lifted from disaster movies: we've seen this same scene in *The Blob*, *Godzilla, Independence Day, Armageddon*, in *Die Hard 2*, and in *Deep Impact*: that morning, reality contented itself with imitating special effects.[37]

Here, Beigbeder compares the events of 9-11 to spectacular films as if the spectacle of Hollywood disaster movies were reality, and 9-11 a mere replica.

The novel illustrates that our dependence on film for the understanding of reality - indeed our confusion of film with real-life events - can have grave consequences. Narrator Beigbeder, aware of the debilitating effects of Hollywood entertainment on the conscious self, speculates that bystanders died in the streets in Lower Manhattan because "they didn't run for cover, so convinced were they that they'd seen it all before."[38] In this spectacle society, the citizen, accustomed to viewing "reality" as it is projected on the screen, indeed becomes a passive spectator in what he perceives to be a simple "show." In a particularly unsettling passage edited from the English translation, Beigbeder states: "Several bystanders died perhaps because they remembered that the last time they saw such a thing, it was while eating popcorn, and one hour later, they had left the theater safe and sound."[39]

Just as disturbing is Beigbeder's portrayal of the role of the media in the perpetration of human catastrophes and warfare. In this information age, entire populations have become the puppets of new forces:

> We live in strange times; war has shifted. The battlefield is the media: in this new war Good and Evil are difficult to tell apart. Difficult to know who the good guys and the bad guys are: they change sides when we change channels. Television makes the world jealous.[40]

Here, Beigbeder suggests that the manner in which "Good" and "Evil" are represented in the media mobilizes nations to wage war against one another. In line with other contemporary post-modern thinkers, such as Tzvetan Todorov and Miguel Benasayag, Beigbeder suggests that society's very representations of good and evil are responsible for events commonly considered evil.[41]

As another explanation of 9-11, Beigbeder also considers the notion of an evil American Empire. Motivated by its dualist perception of the world as a battlefield between an axis of evil and freedom fighters, such an Empire is described by many contemporary theorists as a breeder of terrorism.[42] In a chapter that recounts his trip to New York, Beigbeder visits the United Nations sculpture garden. There, he contemplates a monument entitled "Good Defeats Evil," which depicts Saint George slaying a dragon. Sculpted from the remains of two missiles, one Soviet and one American, the monument celebrates the triumph of good America over the evils of nuclear warfare. Beigbeder takes a picture of the sculpture, which he features in the novel. But rather than ending the chapter with this positive image of American history, Beigbeder juxtaposes this illustration of an America in pursuit of peace with the United States' campaign for war in Iraq. He takes note that during his visit to the sculpture garden, "the members of the Security Council are gathered to vote on a resolution about the war in Iraq."[43] And in a subsequent paragraph omitted from the English translation, Beigbeder argues: "Since 9-11, America is at war against Evil. One may see this as ridiculous, but that's the way it is. The problem is that it's not her job. It's the United Nations'."[44] In an equally disparaging passage, Beigbeder blames American imperialism for giving oppressed groups of people no alternative other than self-sacrificing missions, such as the 9-11 plane hijackings: "America hounds those they oppress into a corner, to the point where, as Brigitte Bardot purred on Serge Gainsbourg's 'Bonne & Clyde': 'The only way out was death.'"[45]

Beigbeder's novel paints a picture of the world subjected to multiple, destructive forces that exceed human agency, including economic systems, the entertainment industry, the media, and society's very discourses of good and evil. This multiplicity, which provides the substance of the narrators' reflections in *Windows on the World,* is characteristically post-modern. But Beigbeder's vision of evil is even more post-modern in its refusal to express with certainty any possible origin of evil. For instance, he does not end his chapter on the multiple-choice question analysed above by providing the correct answer. The reader is left staring at a dozen possible answers with boxes that remain unchecked.

Just as Beigbeder provides no definitive source of evil, he likewise refrains from proposing a definitive remedy for evil. In the chapter on America's usurpation of global political authority also analysed above, Beigbeder proceeds to consider the possibility of a global republic governed by an international parliament, elected through universal suffrage.[46] However, this "solution" is dismissed in a subsequent paragraph, in which Beigbeder relays a conversation that he had with an old friend. In this conversation, his friend describes at length his new obsession with, and political engagement in, the realization of World Democracy. Beigbeder, upon hearing his own thoughts of a global republic spoken from another's mouth, perceives the naïve optimism of such a notion. The narrator ends the chapter by rejecting his theory as simply the best he could come up with, and as a "post-September 11 utopia."[47]

In the chapter that I analysed on the destructive influences of the media, Beigbeder similarly refuses to provide definitive closure. Precisely at the moment in which Beigbeder seems to have deciphered the role of film, television, and journalism in the affairs of the nations, he takes a step back to state:

> OK, I'll stop there, not being competent to analyze everything. If you want to unravel the geopolitical tangle of terrorism, call the offices of Spengler, Huntington, Baudrillard, Adler, Fukuyama, Revel... But I can't guarantee that things will become immediately clearer.[48]

In what could be considered the expression of a meta-post-modern awareness, Beigbeder gives verbal recognition to the tradition of post-modern thinkers that he is following in his account of 9-11. Here, he makes reference to the ambiguous and complex nature of post-modern explanations of the world. Beigbeder admits to the lack of clarity of post-modern accounts. This comes as no surprise, for by definition, post-modern thinkers, including Beigbeder, do not believe the world to be entirely transparent to the conscious self. Instead, he concludes by alluding to the impossible task for a post-modernist to paint a clear picture of the world. Beigbeder ends by leaving his readers with no definitive account of 9-11 or sure voice of authority to refer us to.

The anti-conclusions that leave the chapters of *Windows on the World* open-ended are characteristic of post-modern fiction. However, this "style," far from being evidence, as Berel might suggest, of a post-modernist's inability to provide his own explanation of evil, illustrates rather, a vision that recognizes evil's complexity and affirms the reality of numerous potential sources of evil. In a post-modern vision, the existence of evil is reaffirmed and its victims easily identified. However, post-modernism also constitutes an ongoing, laborious response to an increasingly complex world, aggravated by the advent of the information age. A defining characteristic of post-modern fiction is its attempt to sort through the complex web of extra-human forces. At the same time, post-modern fiction draws attention to its own inconclusiveness. In doing so, I would argue, the post-modern writer forms a position of sincerity that recognizes the limits of human understanding. But even more, post-modern works of fiction constitute a call to vigilance, and propose an ethics that requires us to constantly reassess our ways of thinking and speaking about evil.

Notes

[1] Berel Lang, "Evil Inside and Outside History: The Post-Holocaust versus the Post-modern," in *Evil after Postmodernism: Histories, Narratives, and Ethics,* ed. Jennifer L. Geddes (New York: Routledge, 2001), 11.
[2] Ibid, 13.
[3] Ibid, 21-22.
[4] Beigbeder, Frédéric, *Windows on the World,* trans. Frank Wynne (New York: Miramax Books, 2004), *v*. Unless otherwise noted, all quotes from *Windows on the World* are taken from Wynne's English Translation.
[5] In Frédéric Beigbeder, *Mémoires d'un jeune homme dérangé* (Paris: La Table Ronde, 1990), 17, the author-narrator speaks at length about his "second nose." In Frédéric Beigbeder, *L'égoïste romantique* (Paris: Grasset, 2005), 15, the author-narrator jokingly tells the reader that he must protect his chin from harmful sunrays. There are various other coincidences between the two writers that Beigbeder mentions, such as their Catholic upbringing and that they attended the same high school, Louis-le-Grand.
[6] For instance, in an article aptly entitled "Cyrano de Beigbeider" from the popular French magazine *Le point,* Christophe Ono-dit-Biot refers to Beigbeder as "homme aux deux nez" (the man with two noses). Christophe Ono-dit-Biot, "Cyrano de Beigbeder," *Le point*, 31 March 2005, (8 April 2006).
<http://www.lepoint.fr/litterature/document.html?did=160804>.
[7] Beigbeder, p. 295. Beigbeder states: "Nowadays, books must go where television does not. Show the invisible, speak the unspeakable."
[8] Ibid, 119, 139, 148-49, 167.
[9] Ibid, 167.
[10] Ibid, 145-47.
[11] Unlike the infamous conspiracy theories of 9-11 that French writers have become known for, Beigbeder's account constitutes a sincere attempt

to describe the harsh reality of this day. As an example of a best-selling conspiracy theory on 9-11, see French author Thierry Meyssan's *September 11: The Big Lie.* (Paris: Carnos, 2002).
[12] Beigbeder, 274. The English translation censored parts of this passage. In the original French text, Beigbeder compares 9-11 to Auschwitz, and the restaurant *Windows on the World* to a gas chamber. Frédéric Beigbeder, *Windows on the World* (Paris: Gallimard, 2004), 334.
[13] Beigbeder, 171.
[14] Michel Foucault, *Surveiller et punir: naissance de la prison* (Paris: Gallimard, 1975), 61, 121, 125.
[15] Miguel Benasayag, *Utopie et liberté* (Paris: Editions La Découverte, 1986), 43.
[16] Ibid.
[17] Ibid, 43-70.
[18] In *Utopie et liberté*, Benasayag observes that contemporary states go to extreme measures to hide their practice of physical torture. Moreover, they categorically deny such practice when accused, for fear of losing their legitimacy as the arbiters of civilized society.
[19] Susan Sontag, *On Photography* (New York: Farrar, Straus, and Giroux, 1977) 19-20.
[20] Hannah Arendt, *The Origins of Totalitarianism* (New York, New York: Harcourt Brace & Company, 1979), 438, 445-47, 453, 459). Arendt specifies that what she means by "humanity" is "spontaneity," which she considers the essence of the human condition.
[21] See, for instance Miguel Benasayag, *Utopie et liberté* (*op. cit.*), which presents state-implemented torture as contemporary society's "absolute evil." See also Laura Tanner, *Intimate Violence* (Indianapolis: Indiana University Press, 1994).
[22] Elaine Scary, *The Body in Pain: The Making and Unmaking of the World*, (New York: Oxford University Press, 1985), 145, 60.
[23] Miguel Benasayag, *Le mythe de l'individu* (Paris: Editions La Découverte, 1998), 9-10 (Translation is mine). As the tone of this passage suggests, Benasayag not only highlights the supremacy of the notion of the individual in the postmodern era, but also seeks in his book to reveal it as a dangerous ideology that needs to be abandoned.
[24] Brian McHale, *Post-modernist Fiction* (New York: Methuen, 1987), 163. For a description of post-modern narrative structure, see also Steven Connor, "Postmodernism and literature," in *The Cambridge Companion to Postmodernism*, ed. Steven Connor (Cambridge, Cambridge University Press, 2004), 62-81.

[25] François Lyotard defines post-modernism as "incredulity regarding metanarratives, that is to say, "grand stories about the world and the place of inquiry in it." François Lyotard, *The Post-modern Condition: A Report on Knowledge*, trans. Geoff Bennington and Brian Massumi (Minneapolis: University of Minnesota Press, 1984), xxiii-xxv.
[26] Hannah Arendt, *The Life of the Mind: Volume One* (New York: Harcourt Brace Johanovich, 1981), 3-4.
[27] Hannah Arendt, *Eichmann in Jerusalem: A Report on the Banality of Evil* (New York: Penguin Classics, 1965). Arendt's analysis of Eichmann in fact implies that the Nazis themselves were the victims of socio-economic forces, in particular the disintegration of class society and the concomitant emergence of a European mass society.
[28] Beigbeder, 203.
[29] Ibid, 286.
[30] Ibid, 287.
[31] Ibid, 286-87.
[32] Ibid, 125.
[33] Ibid, 264.
[34] *Loc.cit.*
[35] Beigbeder, 75.
[36] Ibid, 207.
[37] Ibid, 266.
[38] Ibid, 266.
[39] Beigbeder (original French version), 324. English translation mine. A handful of passages such as this one were omitted from the English translation, purportedly to respect the sensibilities of American readers. In the "Author's Note" of the English translation, Beigbeder states: "Merging fiction with truth - and with tragedy - risks hurting those who have already suffered, something of which I was intensely aware when rereading the novel in English - the language in which the tragedy *happened.* There were, I felt, moments when it was starker and perhaps more likely to wound than I intended. Consequently some scenes have been revised for this edition." Ibid, 307.
[40] Ibid, 111.
[41] Several contemporary post-modern thinkers have made this point. See for instance, Tzvetan Todorov, *Mémoire du Mal, tentation du Bien* (Paris: Robert Laffont, 2000), and Miguel Benasayag and Edith Charlton's *Cette douce certitude du pire* (Paris: Editions La Découverte, 1986). See also David Schalkwyk, "Truth, Reconciliation, and Evil in South Africa," in

Truth, Reconciliation, and Evil, ed. Margaret Sönser Breen. (Amsterdam: Rodopi, 2004), 3, 13.
[42] Consider, for instance, Noam Chomsky's *9-11* (New York: Seven Stories Press, 2001).
[43] Beigbeder, 245.
[44] Beigbeder (original French version), 301. My translation.
[45] Beigbeder, 110.
[46] Beigbeder (original French version), 301. My translation.
[47] Beigbeder, 247.
[48] Ibid, 111.

Bibliography

Arendt, Hannah. *Eichmann in Jerusalem: A Report on the Banality of Evil.* New York: Penguin Classics, 1965.

——— *The Life of the Mind: Volume One.* New York: Harcourt Brace Johanovich, 1981.

——— *The Origins of Totalitarianism.* New York: Harcourt Brace & Company, 1979.

Beigbeder, Frédéric. *L'égoïste romantique.* Paris: Grasset, 2005.

——— *Mémoires d'un jeune homme dérangé.* Paris: La Table Ronde, 1990.

——— *Windows on the World*, translated by Frank Wynne. New York: Miramax Books, 2004.

——— *Windows on the World.* Paris: Gallimard, 2004.

Benasayag, Miguel. *Le mythe de l'individu.* Paris: Editions La Découverte, 1998.

——— *Utopie et liberté.* Paris: Editions La Découverte, 1986.

Benasayag, Miguel et Edith Charlton. *Cette douce certitude du pire.* Paris: Editions La Découverte, 1986.

Chomsky, Noam. *9-11.* New York: Seven Stories Press, 2001.

Connor, Steven. "Postmodernism and Literature." In *The Cambridge Companion to Postmodernism*, edited by Steven Connor, 62-81. Cambridge: Cambridge University Press, 2004.

Debord, Guy. *The Society of the Spectacle.* Translated by Donald Nicholson-Smith. Cambridge: MIT Press, 1995.

Foucault, Michel. *Surveiller et punir: naissance de la prison.* Paris: Gallimard, 1975.

Freud, Sigmund. *Civilization and Its Discontents*, translated by James Strachey. New York: W. W. Norton & Company, Inc., 1989.

Lang, Berel. "Evil Inside and Outside History: The Post-Holocaust versus the Post-modern." In *Evil after Postmodernism: Histories, Narratives, and Ethics*, edited by Jennifer L. Geddes, 11-23. New York: Routledge, 2001.

Lyotard, Jean-François. *The Post-modern Condition: A Report on Knowledge*. Translated by Geoff Bennington and Brian Massumi. Minneapolis: University of Minnesota Press, 1984.

McHale, Brian. *Post-modernist Fiction*. New York: Methuen, 1987.

Meyssan, Thierry. *September 11: The Big Lie*. Paris: Carnos, 2002.

Ono-dit-Biot, Christophe. "Cyrano de Beigbeder." *Le point*. 31 March 2005. <http://www.lepoint.fr/litterature/document.html?did=160804>. (8 April 2006).

Scarry, Elaine. *The Body in Pain: The Making and Unmaking of the World*. New York: Oxford University Press, 1985.

Schalkwyk, David. "Truth, Reconciliation, and Evil in South Africa." In *Truth, Reconciliation, and Evil*, edited by Margaret Sönser Breen, 3-41. Amsterdam: Rodopi, 2004.

Sontag, Susan. *On Photography*. New York: Farrar, Straus, and Giroux, 1977.

Tanner, Laura. *Intimate Violence*. Indianapolis: Indiana University Press, 1994.

Todorov, Tzvetan. *Mémoire du Mal, tentation du Bien: enquête sur le siècle*. Paris: Robert Laffont, 2000.

You Are What You Eat: Cannibalism, Autophagy and the Case of Armin Meiwes

Roger Davis

Abstract: This paper addresses the German cannibalism case of Armin Meiwes. After a brief summary of events, the essay examines the figure of the cannibal as outside institutionalized discourses and considers the self-cannibalism, or autophagy, of the cannibal's victim, Bernd Brandes. Drawing upon psychoanalytic perversion and the configuration of the perverse couple, the essay argues that the self-destructive autophage could be a response to the appetites of the modern industrial world. The autophage reveals the cannibal to be a projection of Western appetite and correctly re-situates the appetite in the image of the Western subject consuming itself.

Key Words: cannibalism, autophagy, psychoanalysis, perversion, psychosis, identity, appetite

1. A Matter of Emphasis: Cannibalism and Autophagy

The title of this paper will shift the emphasis in the cliché phrase "You *are* what you eat" to "*You* are what you eat," so the subject literally consumes itself in an act of self-cannibalism or autophagy. My topic is the cannibalism case of Armin Meiwes, and I am attending to two issues: after giving a brief account of events, I will address the eccentric position of the cannibal in the modern industrial world and examine the so-called victim of this crime, Bernd Brandes, who volunteered to be eaten, consumed his own flesh and then agreed to be killed. Situating these events in terms of psychoanalytic perversion, I will suggest that autophagy may be read as a perverse attempt to reveal the falsities behind the West's understanding of its own identity and appetites.

The facts of the case are quite straightforward. In 2001, over the Internet, Meiwes solicited a willing victim to be cannibalized: one of his emails read "I search for a boy, if i can real kill him and butchering him. I am a cannibal, a real cannibal."[1] He had several replies, and a few would-be participants individually visited Meiwes' house at different times. However, when faced with the actual killing, each man backed out. Meiwes even rejected one man "for being too fat."[2] Meiwes allowed the men to leave, even socializing with some after they backed out, which demonstrates that this is not a predatory killing. When Brandes arrived, Meiwes had his willing participant. According to reports, Meiwes and Brandes engaged in sexual relations, and, shortly thereafter, Meiwes cut off Brandes' penis at the latter's request. They fried it up and apparently ate it. After Brandes took a bath, Meiwes suggested that he finish the act, and Brandes consented. Meiwes cut Brandes' throat, thereby killing him, and proceeded to dismember his body and pack it for freezing and later consumption. Meiwes videotaped the night's events. When police finally arrested Meiwes, he had consumed approximately 20 kilograms of Brandes' body. The prosecution of Meiwes proved difficult, as cannibalism is not illegal in Germany. The court sentenced Meiwes to 8 ½ years in jail for two different crimes: killing upon request, which carried a five-year sentence, and disturbing the peace of the dead, which carried 3 ½ years. The prosecution appealed the ruling, and, during the appeal, in March 2006, German courts banned the release of the film *Rohtenburg* which is arguably based on Meiwes' acts. In May 2006, at the conclusion of the retrial, the court convicted Meiwes of manslaughter and sentenced him to 15 years in prison, arguing that the killing was not made upon request but motivated by sexual impulses.[3]

The various media reports, responses, critiques and condemnations of Meiwes' acts have invoked numerous discourses: legal, psychiatric, anthropological, psychoanalytic. Each discourse attempts to contain Meiwes' actions in some kind of rational framework in order to regulate, to control or to explain the inherent violence and horror of the deed. However, the cannibal figure remains largely outside of institutionalized discourse, and, if addressed, it is often othered or abject. First, legal discourse proves ill-equipped to deal with the nature of Meiwes' crime, as the law has not classified or even recognized cannibalism as a crime. Perhaps the wickedness is self-evident. Moreover, it would appear obvious that cannibalism would require murder, and the law could prosecute accordingly. Yet, as we see here, the cannibal could eat just a part of the victim and leave him alive (in this case, temporarily), or the victim could consent to his own death. The non-aggressive nature of Meiwes' act forces the law to address cannibalism not as murder but as mercy killing or killing for sexual gratification. The act of consuming another person is not at issue; the death is at issue. Neither the criminal nor the ethical questions of cannibalism are ever addressed. As Meiwes himself stated after hearing his initial sentence: "I'm relieved. At least I'm not being branded a murderer."[4] Apparently, it is preferable to be a cannibal than a murderer.

Second, psychiatric, medical and psychoanalytic discourses have attempted to explain the reasons behind Meiwes' acts through variations on Freudian approaches. On the simplest reading, Meiwes and cannibals in general must be insane. However, professionals deemed Meiwes to be of sound mind: "a court-appointed psychiatrist testified that he was not suffering from 'diminished responsibility' at the time of the killing."[5] Insanity is the reason for neither the crime nor the defense. Therefore, psychoanalytic discourse searches for the unconscious or repressed reasons for the act. Roger Boyes, a reporter of the trial, explains Meiwes' relationship with his mother who died in 1999: "He never left home[.] He was completely dependent on his mother - in an unhealthy way."[6] He adds, "He is reminiscent of a Norman Bates character, from the Hitchcock film *Psycho*....[His mother's] dressing gown is laid out on the bed and a mannequin's head lies on the pillow."[7] Also, Luke Harding reports that Meiwes "felt lonely and neglected as a child after his father walked out on the family. He had fantasised about having a blond 'younger brother', who he could keep forever by 'consuming him.'"[8] The problem, therefore, is his dependence on his mother coupled with the fact that he had no strong male role model. While these characteristics are quite typical of popular understandings of the dynamics of psychoanalysis, they are in danger of rationalizing or harm-reducing Meiwes' acts rather than developing the complexities of this case. To aid this development, I turn to a third possible reading of cannibalism: anthropology.

While I cannot rehearse the voluminous body of literature on anthropological study of cannibalism, one common ritualistic motive for cannibalism is to retain the qualities of the other in the self.[9] It occurs in war as exocannibalism - to acquire the strengths of your foe - and it occurs within a community as endocannibalism - to retain the memory of a family member or loved one. We see endocannibalism in Meiwes' case; he desired a friendship, and he sought it through cannibalism. Meiwes states, "With every bite, my memory of him grew stronger."[10] And, we see exocannibalism, too; Harding reports that "Brandes spoke good English...and since eating him [Meiwes'] English has improved."[11] In reporting such statements, the media tend to trivialize the nature of these acts as bizarre ritual rather than horror. Typical to much discourse about cannibalism, ritual forms of cannibalism often arise in discussion of the other, as occurring in lands far away geographically or far removed historically. The difference in Meiwes' case is that this potentially ritualistic cannibalism occurs in industrialized Europe, not some fictional or remote village halfway around the world. The cannibal is no longer the other but the self. Because this ritualistic reading is so seldom applied to so-called civilized culture in public space, the West has difficulty accepting the self as cannibal and trivializes or sensationalizes the matter. Of course, this is a common observation about myths of cannibalism; that is, the accusation of cannibalism in a different culture is a means to dehumanize the other, often to justify militaristic or colonialist projects against them. To turn this against the self is to recognize our own barbarity. In a sense, to acknowledge ritualistic cannibalism in Germany is to admit that the West is, to some extent, the cannibal.[12]

Indeed, we see the response to this discomfort in some of the attempts to humanize the cannibal when he appears in industrial culture. During the trial, Meiwes' lawyer Harald Ermel defended his client's humanity: "My client is not a monster" and "My client has dignity. My client has a personality."[13] Meiwes' new girlfriend gave similar testimony: "He's not a monster, he's a good man."[14] While from obviously biased sources, these comments deal in rather blunt binaries of the human and the monstrous and attempt to reconstitute the boundary between the two, which Meiwes' acts had dissolved. Simultaneous with these assertions of humanity is an infantilization: his girlfriend says, "He is very childish....He is a child himself."[15] Roger Boyes (who reports on the case) echoes this claim: "He was caught in different roles including that of a child" and "He's like a naughty schoolboy making faces."[16] One investigative reporter who surveyed online cannibal chatrooms notes that he discovered "how much [cannibals] craved respectability" and how "cannibals are ordinary people."[17] He even suggests that cannibals do not want "mere tolerance...but applause."[18] Of course, not all reports on the crime are sympathetic in nature. Another reporter calls Meiwes' videotape a shameless act where "terrible crimes are recorded as if they were home movies or family portraits. It is as if human nature had changed."[19]

However, it is not that human nature has changed; rather, we are largely unable to categorize or accept this kind of cannibalism under our existing knowledge of human nature. In all three discursive sketches, the institutionalized discourse cannot adequately address cannibalism. Either it finds nothing wrong, or it labels cannibalism a juvenile, pre-modern or prehistoric aberration. When the charge of cannibalism is directed back against the West, the response is to try to normalize, rationalize or reduce the nature of the crime. It is self-defense. And, we see this quasi-exoneration in Meiwes' own apologies for his actions: "I had my big kick and I don't need to do it again....I regret it all very much, but I can't undo it."[20] Apparently, he, like a child, did something wrong and has learned his lesson. Similarly, in Western culture, we acknowledge our primitive, possibly cannibalistic past but recognize, surely, that we are beyond it. Yet, conventional moral instincts are uncomfortable with such excuses when faced with this incident.

While the media focus on Meiwes' cannibalism, they largely ignore Brandes' autophagy. One type of cannibalism is news; the other, curiously, is not. In terms of acceptance and denial, Meiwes accepts his identity as cannibal but denies it as murderer, and the West accepts its primitive past but denies its continued presence. Similarly, the media sensationalize cannibalism, but they ignore autophagy. The second topic of this paper addresses the possible logic(s) behind autophagy, which is ultimately the destruction of the self, not the other, through cannibalism. I do this through psychoanalysis' concept of perversion for two main reasons. First, Meiwes' and Brandes' acts would fit popular definitions of perverse acts, yet, as I will demonstrate, perversion is more complicated and relevant than simple abnormality. Second, much like cannibalism's eccentric position in common discourse, perversion is similarly eccentric in psychoanalytic theory: "perversion, even in the Lacanian era, has always remained an outsider."[21] The external or abject positions of perversion and autophagy create a potentially fruitful link between the two concepts. One difficulty for such an analysis, however, is that very little is reported about Brandes and autophagy; therefore, it is hard to examine the events, let alone begin to understand his motives or desires, if any. Before discussing autophagy, it is necessary to outline some features of perversion and the perverse couple.

2. The Nature of Perversion

My task here is not to differentiate between the numerous interpretations and complexities of perversion. Rather, I use perversion as a framework to situate these events in contemporary theoretical discourse and to consider their effects on our conceptualization of the Western subject. In very general terms, psychoanalysis has three major structural categories: psychosis, perversion and neurosis. Moreover, for the purposes of this discussion of perversion, it is necessary to distinguish between a perverse act and the perverse structure. A perverse act does not necessarily correspond to the logic of the perverse structure. In other words, a perverse act could be performed by a psychotic, perverse, neurotic or normal individual. If we momentarily consider cannibalism to be a perverse act, then we can think about it in relation to these different structures. For example, it is perhaps easy for someone to imagine a psychotic performing a cannibalistic act, where he unpredictably or malevolently eats a part of another person. Clinical literature includes many such examples. However, reports of cannibalism occur in survivalist stories where people in emergency situations will resort to cannibalism to avoid starvation. A famous example is the 1972 plane crash in the Andes mountains of Uruguayan rugby players who ate crash victims to stay alive. Of course, we would not consider these people perverse, let alone psychotic. Therefore, the mere occurrence of an act does not necessarily indicate the existence of a structure, whether psychotic, perverse or neurotic.[22]

The structure of perversion exists between psychosis and neurosis, and these structures are differentiated from each other by psychoanalytic concepts of alienation and separation. In Bruce Fink's formulation, "although the pervert has undergone alienation, he has not undergone separation. The psychotic has undergone neither, while the neurotic has undergone both."[23] In other words, the Name-of-the-Father is only partially complete in perversion. The pervert recognizes he is not the object of his mother's desire (recognizes that she has a lack), yet he does not fully surrender to the Name-of-the-Father that redirects his desire towards something other than his mother. In rejecting the paternal law, the pervert is unable to enter the symbolic realm of language, thereby failing to name desire and become a neurotic or normally functioning subject. Rather, the pervert attempts to restore or to retain his position as the object of the mother's desire, and he will do almost anything to fulfil his function. Jacques Lacan's short phrase defines the pervert as a subject who "makes himself the instrument of the Other's *jouissance*."[24] Or, as Fink phrases it, "the pervert, as subject, plays the role of object: the object that fills the void in the mOther."[25] Therefore, the pervert sacrifices himself in order to satisfy the desire of the Other.

One outcome of the partial failing of the paternal law is that the pervert understands that the law exists, yet he does not understand his relationship to the law. Unlike the psychotic who acts independently of and indiscriminately towards the law, the pervert is anxious about the law, and his actions often try to invoke the law as a means to orientate himself in the world. Yet because he fails to understand the symbolic realm, the only law for the pervert is the desire of the other. The pervert's actions often force the other to pronounce a law, sometimes "exposing the fantasy of the other and the various social lies that such fantasy necessarily enforces."[26] The fantasy comprises the symbolic properties of normal desire to which the pervert has no access. Consequently, normal desires and satisfactions are illusory to the pervert. The pervert endlessly seeks a law beyond these fabricated desires, and the only avenue he understands is to be the phallus for the mother. In this way, "the pervert calls upon or appeals to the father, hoping to make the father fulfil the paternal function."[27] The pervert wishes the law would manifest itself so he could achieve separation, yet it always fails and is illusory.

To use Meiwes as an example, he solicits willing victims. He assumes the role of cannibal to satisfy the other's desire, yet in pressing the issue, he forces his victims to admit they are only fantasizing. He is not predatory; rather, he creates anxiety in the other to the point where the other abandons his fantasy, invokes the law, ends the encounter and redirects his desire. Similarly, Meiwes fulfils his perverse function by acknowledging his crime, satisfying the status quo's desire to see a guilty conscience or rehabilitation. All the while, with his smug satiety in accepting the cannibal label as morally preferable to murderer, he reveals the superficiality of such simplistic public moralizing, and the public is, again, disgusted with him. Read in this way, Meiwes would fall under the perverse category of sadism.

Now, it is possible that Brandes is also perverse. Clearly, he will sacrifice himself to satisfy Meiwes' desire in a very direct manner. At this point, one major issue arises: a configuration of a perverse couple. Jean Clavreul's writing on the perverse couple defines at least three configurations. First, the simple case of a pervert and normal person. Second, the relationship between a psychoanalyst and a perverse analysand. Third, he gestures towards a couple comprised of two perverts, and it is this third configuration which is relevant here.[28] Clavreul isolates the perverse structure from the perverse act, and he theorizes the couple in terms of love. He argues that love as a discourse allows us to examine the authenticity of the couple's bond; more specifically, he questions whether or not a pervert can love - the highest accomplishment in a couple, according to Clavreul - or whether the pervert is merely fulfilling his perverse function in the relationship by only satisfying the desire of the other. He does not directly answer these questions; rather, he leaves the complexity of the problem in terms of a "complementarity"[29] between the pervert and his partner. Clavreul carefully points out that an appeal to *love* as a general term opens up the possibility for the pervert to undermine the popular understanding of love, which would be a fulfilment of the pervert's function to point out the lies of the law of the status quo.

A couple comprised of two perverts presents some challenges. First, a primary goal for the pervert is to satisfy the desire of the other, yet, if both parties are attempting to achieve this, then a circularity results: the first pervert would attempt to satisfy the desire of the second pervert who desires to satisfy the first pervert. Second, another primary feature of perversion - that the other invoke the law - will potentially never be satisfied, as each member of the couple will continue self-sacrifice to the other and never invoke the law. Each would potentially sacrifice *ad infinitum*. In not fully recognizing the paternal law, neither pervert has the ability to invoke it. One possible conclusion of such a configuration is manifest in the destruction of one half of the couple: Brandes ultimately sacrifices his entire being to Meiwes.

3. *Folie-à-deux*

The perverse couple raises another possibility within psychoanalysis: *folie-à-deux*. First outlined in medical discourse in 1877,[30] *folie-à-deux* is a psychotic condition where a dominant psychotic individual communicates, projects or shares his psychosis with a more submissive partner who may or may not be psychotic. C. Lasègue and J. Falret outline the basic conditions for *folie-à-deux*: it contains an active and passive member; the couple has lived "a very close-knit existence in the same environment for a long period of time"; and, the delusions are of a relatively probable, believable, almost rational character.[31] Moreover, the couple usually lives in isolation from others, and each person's particular desires support or confirm one another. At first glance, the case of Meiwes and Brandes fits this characterisation of *folie-à-deux*. Meiwes appears to be the active member, and their desires definitely complement each other.

However, several characteristics create problems for this model. First and most obviously, Meiwes was deemed non-psychotic and fit to stand trial. One cannot share a non-existent psychosis. Second, Brandes was living with a male lover just prior to his decision to visit Meiwes. Brandes is not socially isolated in any direct sense.[32] Nor do Meiwes and Brandes live together in isolation from others; they had never met, except over the Internet. Third, it is open to question how close a bond the two men could have formed over the Internet. The Internet offers the potential for alienation or community, depending on its function. Popular culture is filled with Internet love affairs, marriages and friendships as much as it is filled with Internet predatory abductions and sexual assaults. This case can represent the psychotic or perverted predator luring in willing victims, or, as the extensive forums on cannibalism evidence, it can represent an online community exploring common ideas, fantasies or experiences of cannibalism, if legal and ethical questions are momentarily suspended.

As a brief aside, *folie-à-deux* has been linked to suicide pacts where two or more individuals agree to commit suicide under certain conditions, usually at the same time.[33] Like *folie-à-deux*, suicide pacts usually occur between individuals who live or interact closely. However, like the problems with *folie-à-deux*, the suicide pact model fails in this case, since Meiwes does not desire to die. Brandes apparently is suicidal, although the suicidal impulses seem secondary to his function as cannibal victim, self-mutilator and autophage. Rather, his desire to be killed - which would fulfil his perverse function of satisfying the desire of the other, the cannibal - is more prominent than his desire to die. In other words, Brandes desires to die not in and of itself but in a particular manner.

Folie-à-deux is a rare occurrence, and while this case shares many similarities, significant differences call into question the applicability of the theory. As current clinical literature points out, *folie-à-*

deux "occurs to fulfil needs of both the source and recipient of the psychosis, though the exact nature of these needs remains the subject of debate."[34] Its inclusion here demonstrates the ambiguities that exist between *folie-à-deux* and the perverse couple. Both structures satisfy the desires of each member, yet one follows a psychotic structure and the other a perverse structure. This is not surprising, given that perversion lies between psychosis and neurosis; indeed, as Clavreul indicates, "The danger that the pervert is always bordering on - I must repeat it here - is psychosis."[35] The difference for Clavreul between psychosis and perversion is the presence of the fetish: for the purpose of this present study, the fetish is cannibalism, autophagy, or consumption more generally.

Clavreul outlines a further ambiguity within perversion: it simultaneously disgusts and fascinates the viewer.[36] Specifically, by positioning perversion in relation to conventional love, Clavreul argues that an appeal to conventional love relegates a normal person to a rather mundane sexual and emotional existence. He suggests that the discourse of perversion - whether enacted literally or only in fantasy through literature, for example - allows a more creative or adventurous subjective experience. Therein lies the ambiguity: the perverse act compels and intrigues the witness, but the witness would be uncomfortable performing the perverse act. For this reason, Clavreul highlights the necessity of a third party in the perverse couple.[37] The third party can be someone as simple as a witness to a perverse act, but the more important implication is the third party as law, social convention or the Other. The law must witness and judge the perverse couple, yet the judgment lacks conviction. Clavreul states that the third party is "present but only insofar as [it] is blind or an accomplice or impotent."[38] In terms of the present study, the third party is mostly blind to the existence of cannibalism in the industrial world. It is an accomplice in several respects: in largely ignoring or othering cannibalism, it may conversely allow or enable its practice; technology, particularly the Internet, facilitates solicitations for perverse practices, as evidenced by Meiwes; the media sensationalizes the case, creating an appetite for such stories, etc. The third party is impotent because it does not or cannot do anything about cannibalism; most obviously, the fact that it is not illegal and cannot be tried. Relevant to Meiwes' calm defense of his actions and the media responses to the acts, Clavreul notes that the "transfixed observer will never fail to be astonished in remarking how perverts reconcile their extreme delicateness with the total disrespect for the other that their practice implies."[39] This is the challenge of the pervert and the perverse couple to the status quo: we are implicated in the situation, partly because of our reliance on received notions of love and morality more generally. Meiwes mutilated, killed, butchered and consumed Brandes, but he performed these acts with care and compassion. He did it out of love, but a perverse love.

Perverse love, then, functions to satisfy the other by attempting to remain the phallus for the mother. The pervert facilitates the jouissance of the other, yet he also attains some level of satisfaction for himself in the process. However, another feature of perversion is that the pervert is only ever temporarily satisfied. If we recall the night's events, Brandes desires to be eaten; that is, he will satisfy Meiwes' appetite. Recall also that Meiwes desired a male victim. Yet, we see that Brandes begins to undermine the cannibal's desire. As Meiwes tells the court, "It was important to [Brandes] that his member be cut off and that he witness it."[40] At the instant that Meiwes begins his cannibal act, Brandes is emasculated, possibly feminized, and he partially disrupts Meiwes' desire to eat a man, as he renders the rest of his body de-sexed or, at least, sexually mutilated. After satisfying Meiwes' literal appetite, the pervert Brandes now must satisfy other appetites. As Judith Feher-Gurewich explains, "For the pervert, there is no comfort in the success of his operation. The fun is in the process, not in the result."[41] In other words, Brandes must continue to feed the desires of the other. Meiwes further describes the event: "[Brandes] screamed terribly and jumped around the table but after a while he said he was surprised it didn't hurt and was very pleased that the wound bled so strongly."[42] With this menstrual imagery, Brandes surmounts the pain in order to continue the perverse interactions, and he allows Meiwes apparently to assert his identity as cannibal by continuing with the killing.

4. Auto-cannibalism

Part of Brandes' desire is for self-mutilation: literal castration. Like cannibalism, self-mutilation can serve different ends, ritual or otherwise. Armando R. Favazza's study of self-mutilation surveys a wide spectrum of clinical and cultural examples.[43] Cannibalism and autocannibalism (Favazza's term) enter into his study. Interestingly, Favazza contextualizes his references to cannibalism in terms of literature, myth or uncertainty: his examples include Ovid's *Metamorphoses* and unverified reports of cannibalistic customs, including the Caribs of the Caribbean whose name is the etymological root of the current word *cannibal*. His references to autocannibalism arise in terms of psychosis or mental illness, and he cites several clinical cases. In a literature survey documenting mutilation of the self, Favazza clearly establishes self-cannibalism in the West, yet the study curiously and perhaps unconsciously reinscribes cannibalism as largely fictional in the other.

This furthers the claim that cannibalism frequently indicates more about the self than the other, and it is important to highlight the fact that the cannibalism present in Western culture is autophagy, not consumption of the other.

Moreover, autocannibalism or autophagy need not be associated strictly with psychosis as in Favazza's work. Mark Benecke reports on a non-psychotic autophagic woman who ate portions of her own skin which she removed.[44] Reading autophagy as non-psychotic, he contextualizes self-mutilation and self-consumption as types of body modification. Benecke's report characterizes autophagy as one practice among others, including tattoos, piercings, scarring, etc. The difference he elides between these other practices and autophagy is that tattooing and such do not involve consumption. Mutilating the body and eating the mutilated body are quite different acts. In analyzing the woman's case, Benecke states that the subject has no history of domestic, familial or sexual abuse or other common social problems which might lead to such behaviours. Overall, Benecke concludes that "it may be difficult to decide whether body modification can be understood as self-therapy or as an 'unwanted behaviour.'"[45]

Given the severity of Brandes' self-mutilation, "self-therapy" and "unwanted behaviour" seem inadequate descriptors for his act. Similarly, a desire for castration is hardly a simple form of body modification. Favazza discusses male genital self-mutilation in cases which are non-psychotic, yet all the cited cases are instances of a desire to be female: transsexualism.[46] None of the instances involves autophagy. In terms of Favazza's and Benecke's examples, Brandes represents a unique act of non-psychotic genital self-mutilation and autophagy without an explicit desire to be female. Of the autophagic woman and people involved in body modification more generally, Benecke suggests that "the underlying psychodynamics of their behaviour may include feelings of disconnection from their body or certain emotions."[47] These "feelings of disconnection" are important to perversion because the pervert experiences alienation yet fails to achieve separation, and the act of self-mutilation allows the pervert to alienate himself from his body and quite literally achieve separation from himself, although not from the Other. And, autophagy paradoxically re-incorporates the severed body part back into itself.

As a way to possibly understand this paradox, it is worth examining Ofra Eshel's clinical analysis of perversion as a version of biological autotomy which she defines as "the capacity of some living creatures to waive the wholeness of their body as a means of survival."[48] For Eshel, this analogy represents the pervert's self-sacrifice to the Other. One part "is left behind to be devoured by their predator, and another that thus succeeds in escaping and surviving, and later regenerates," with survival understood as the psychic survival of the pervert (and perverts need separation from the Other).[49] However, the difference in autophagy is that the sacrificed part is consumed by the subject. And, in this case, the killing is not predatory, yet the big Other may be construed as a predator if there is no separation. Autophagy, then, helps to signal a shift in Brandes' perversion as a doubled self-sacrifice both to the Other and to the self: he is both cannibal and cannibalized. Brandes' perverse autotomy satisfies Meiwes, yet his perverse autophagy satisfies himself: both are attempts at psychic survival.

Moreover, Eshel situates perversion in the realm of Pentheus, not Oedipus.[50] The Penthean model has the subject "torn to pieces and devoured alive by his mother," which can result in perverse acts such as "sado-masochistic violence and cannibalistic murder."[51] In autotomy, the other cannibalistically murders one side of the split self; in autophagy, the one side of the split self murders the other side of the split self, cannibalistically and suicidally. The autophagic act conflates the self and the Other. It facilitates the jouissance of the other (which is perverse), yet it destroys the barrier between self and other (which is more in line with psychosis and *folie-à-deux*). On the one hand, Brandes sacrifices himself to Meiwes in a perverse scenario. On the other hand, his autophagy enacts the desire of the other, thereby eliminating the alienation which separates psychosis from perversion.[52] The separation in autotomy for survival is offset against the separation in autophagy for self-destruction. This perhaps makes sense in a perverse couple, as neither pervert will invoke the law, and self-sacrifice will continue unabated. Therefore, given the lack of information about Brandes, it is unclear if his acts better fit perversion or psychosis, as elements of both are apparent.

In moving from perversion and self-mutilation through autotomy and into autophagy, we see the paradoxical nature of autophagy: it is self-destructive, yet the re-incorporation of the body provides sustenance to the body, whether gastronomically, psychically or metaphorically. Given the dearth of information about Brandes, a sustained analysis of this event will necessarily draw upon other disciplines to construct interpretations of these acts, and, up to this point, I have mostly drawn upon discourses of cannibalism and psychoanalysis. Now, I wish to examine the metaphorical implications of the paradoxical nature of autophagy and situate it in the larger context of contemporary Western culture. While I do not wish to obscure the real death of Brandes, I will examine the implications of the figure of the autophage for identity construction in the contemporary world. Earlier, I argued that conventional discourses attempt to contain or to rationalize horrific deeds, and I am aware of the contradiction in attempting an analysis of Brandes' acts; that is, attempting any analysis - psychoanalytic or metaphoric - is to structure the arguably unstructurable. However, considering the lack of reporting on Brandes, a failure to analyze and interpret his actions would only further obfuscate or ignore the situation of the autophage.

One of the most engaging cultural analyses of autophagy occurs in Maud Ellmann's *The Hunger Artists*.[53] Ellmann configures autophagy not as the literal dismemberment and subsequent consumption of the body but as the self-destruction of the body through hunger. In experiencing the lack of food, the body begins to consume its own materials. Ellmann incorporates numerous examples of hunger including famine, hunger strikes, eating disorders such as anorexia, religious fasts and the American obsession with dieting. She draws an analogy between Michel Foucault's analysis of sexuality and her analysis of hunger. Where Foucault argued that sexuality was "subjected to intense scrutiny"[54] in the nineteenth century, Ellmann asserts that the contemporary world is obsessed with food, starvation and the body. Regarding sexuality, she writes, "ironically, the doctors, educators, and psychiatrists who probed and codified its shameful secrets actually invented new perversions in the very effort to exclude them from the norm."[55] She uses similar reasoning to claim that hunger in its various forms can often result less from a scarcity of food than from the management, presentation and representation of food; that is, hunger is a result of social and cultural forces, not strictly natural disaster or lack of production. In this way, she proposes "not to find the cause of self-starvation but to follow the adventures of its metaphors."[56] Often, the metaphors represent resistance which is in direct response to the "intense scrutiny" or control of dominant political, spiritual, legal, economic or other forces.

Ellmann is particularly useful in this context because by linking Foucault's reasoning about sexuality and her writing about hunger she states that "now the kitchen rather than the bedroom has become the theater of temptation and the scene of sin."[57] In a rather grotesque move that is perhaps tangential to Ellmann's intentions, we can apply both the sexual and gastronomical elements to the perverse sexualized cannibalism between Meiwes and Brandes: the kitchen and the bedroom converge. Moreover, connections between sex and food - both very base and material needs - are ubiquitous in literature and everyday speech. And, as Maggie Kilgour has argued, "Like eating, intercourse makes two bodies one, though in a union that is fortunately less absolute and permanent."[58] Kilgour's focus on incorporation highlights the corporeal dimension of cannibalism, and it is worth reiterating Meiwes' endocannibalistic desire to incorporate the other into the self. In comparing Ellmann's focus on self-consumption through hunger and Kilgour's consumption of the other into the self, we see that the autophage assumes the appetite of the cannibal yet devours the body of the self. Beyond the mere sexual desire which Meiwes and Brandes satisfied, each man desired a more permanent form of incorporation. For Meiwes, the fetish is cannibalism; for Brandes, the fetish is autophagy.

Ellmann's emphasis on regulation is relevant to my earlier discussion of how differing discourses attempt to regulate or explain these cannibalistic acts. To a large extent, whatever establishes the terms of regulation also establishes the terms of perversion. Similarly, Kilgour's argument tentatively attempts to avoid conventional binary thinking by positing the prominence of the relation that "plays an important role in the conceptualization of all antitheses, that of inside and outside."[59] Kilgour argues that the relative position of the subject in terms of inside and outside offers a useful model because any subject must establish limits in order to regulate the border between inside and outside. For Kilgour, obviously, cannibalism is the movement from taking the other as outside and making it inside. Considered in this manner, Ellmann sees autophagy as eating oneself from inside, often in response to something outside. This distinction is important to the structure of perversion because the pervert is outside the symbolic realm of language; therefore, he performs acts which are outside of the law.

5. Autophagy and Discourse

For Ellmann, a necessary feature of autophagy is discourse; in other words, for the autophagic act to have any human meaning, it must be narrated. She argues that a silent death is suicide, and only language can give the act meaning.[60] Therefore, for the media largely to ignore Brandes' autophagy denies the act meaning. One can only imagine the actual pain and suffering of Brandes' castration and subsequent death, yet the media focus on Meiwes as German cannibal. Discursively, the cannibal moves from the outside to the inside, and the autophage remains outside. One effect of situating the cannibal inside the West is that the public understands the cannibal to have an appetite for the other, and this generates a fear of being eaten. Despite reports that establish Meiwes as a quiet neighbour aside from his cannibalistic urges, the media rely on the demonized figure of the cannibal to generate fear or disgust coupled with perverse fascination. In part, this acknowledges the presence of a disturbed appetite in the West and serves as a warning to control our appetites, to ensure that we consume properly within well-regulated limits. To ignore Brandes is to ignore an examination of our own appetites beyond the obviously destructive and undesirable forms represented by cannibalism or other abnormalities.

Therefore, the media representations regulate the figure of the cannibal within contemporary culture. Media permit the cannibal to exist but only in very well-defined terms, as an aberration against which we can define the self, which serves to reinforce dominant modes of consumption. To focus on Brandes would be to force us to try to work out our incomprehension of autophagy: to focus not on the consumption of the other but on the consumption of the self. Rather than invoking the terrible image of the cannibal which is so coded in historical ideas of the barbaric other, we would be imagining ways in which we are destroying ourselves, how our own appetites are destroying us. The autophage does not project the destructive appetite on to the other; rather, he relocates appetite in its original position, the self. In doing so, the autophage potentially raises the question of the responsibility for the effects of our appetite, and the dominant media fail to acknowledge, let alone pose, the question. If anything, the autophage is suppressed.

The media's sensational treatment of this case affirms the public's role as witness to the perversity of the act. Perverse acts are increasingly becoming the subject of media images and reports. Researchers argue that the media play a "role of management in contemporary culture....[The] logic of excess dominates. An excess of offers and products mobilizes anyone and everyone with a promise of enjoyment that never ends. As we can see, post-modern logic lies very close to perverse logic."[61] Viewers become implicated with perverse acts, fascinated with and disgusted by the events. In this way, we feed off the other cannibalistically, and even unconsciously enjoying the images of their suffering or excess. The autophage represents the conscious turn towards consuming ourselves; specifically, he forces us to realize the exploitative nature of our enjoyment and internalizes it within the self, not the other. This is the perversity of the autophage: the conscious, willing self-sacrifice to the other, whether the media, the cannibal or something else, to offer himself up to the enjoyment of the other. The pervert knows the appetite of the other and acts accordingly. And, the autophage knowingly participates in the perverse structure of the act of consumption, demonstrating his understanding of the desire of the Other.

In his discussion of technology, media and the film *The Matrix*, Slavoj Zizek articulates the pervert's worldview: "What the pervert enacts is a universe in which, as in cartoons, a human being can survive any catastrophe; in which adult sexuality is reduced to a childish game; in which one is not forced to die or to choose one of the two sexes."[62] In the case of Brandes, his response to literal castration only reinforces his disavowal of castration. In having his penis severed, he denies his sexuality and subordinates the practical consequences of the action to the enjoyment of the other. Perversely, he simultaneously literalizes the force of paternal law, forcing it to assert itself in his castration. He embraces his suffering and seeks further suffering. The momentary satisfaction he experiences necessitates a further excessive act, ultimately resulting in his self-destruction. In his endless pursuit to satisfy the Other, the pervert potentially exhausts all avenues of satisfaction, leaving only himself to be offered up for consumption.

Referring to Max Horkheimer and Theodor Adorno's work, Zizek re-states their assessment of Pierre Flourens' analysis of medical anesthesia: "while we are butchered alive on the operating table, we fully feel the terrible pain, but later, after awakening, we do not remember it."[63] In overcoming the pain of his submission to the Other, the pervert makes explicit the fact that "unknowingly we are our own greatest victims, butchering ourselves alive."[64] The conscious knowledge of this destruction differentiates the pervert from the unknowing neurotic. The autophage extends the conscious realization of this fact by actively participating in the very process of destruction. To ignore the autophage is to repress the knowledge that the history of cannibalism, the history of colonialism and the history of the West are, to a large extent, about appetite and consumption. After exhausting all other resources, whether through persecution, exploitation or some other mechanism, what is left but to turn on ourselves? Zizek's example of *The Matrix* is fitting here, as one of the food sources for the human batteries in the film is the liquefied remains of exhausted, dead humans: all humans have become cannibals.

Whether or not he is conscious of the Swiftian irony, Meiwes is reported to hold "deluded ambitions for a world in which eating people could solve problems of famine and overpopulation."[65] Where Swift employs cannibalism to critique the British and the Anglo-Irish for forcing the Irish into poverty through political and economic practices, Meiwes fails to recognize what Ellmann articulates: the problem of famine and overpopulation is a misreading of our appetites when faced with a supposed scarcity of resources. The solution for famine and overpopulation is not to feed our appetites more fully through cannibalism but to check the appetite itself. Conceptualized as a transformation of the cannibal, the autophage reveals the self-destructive nature of the West's appetites and our inability to regulate them.

If it is true that the cannibal figure represents the appetites of the West as projected on to the other, then the autophage is perhaps an appropriate figure to supplant the myth of the cannibal in response to recent reconfigurations and re-readings of past cannibal narratives and experiences. If one of the true horrors of the cannibal is the disproportion of the West's appetite, then the marginalization of the autophage is an unsurprising manifestation of the West's anxiety about coming to terms with the realization of overconsumption. While we may react with horror to cannibalism or a willing victim, Brandes' perverse autophagy is perhaps the ultimate horror which reveals the falsity of the law we invoke to judge these acts. Specifically, by turning the cannibalistic appetite against itself, we are horrified not simply by this specific instance of autophagy but by the realization that the very nature and voracity of our own appetites, if left unchecked, make us all autophagic.

Notes

[1] Franky, "search for a real boy from Europe," *Google Groups*, 18 April 2002, <http://groups.google.com/group/alt.sex.snuff.cannibalism> (30 September 2005).

[2] Roger Boyes, "Cannibal Put Off by Man's Obesity: 'My Mother…insisted on lean meat," *Calgary Herald*, 23 December 2003, sec. A, 16.

[3] For a journalistic, true-crime narrativisation of this case, see Lois Jones, *Cannibal: The True Story Behind the Maneater of Rotenburg* (New York: Berkley Books, 2005).

[4] Roger Boyes, "Cannibal: Roger Boyes in Kassel Reflects on an Extraordinary Trial," *Times Online*, 30 January 2004, <http://www.4law.co.il/cann31104.htm> (23 September 2005).

[5] Mark Landler, "Cannibal Advertises for Victim, Devours Man who Volunteered," *Times-Colonist*, 31 January 2004, sec. A, 5.

[6] Boyes, "Cannibal Put Off."

[7] Ibid.

[8] Luke Harding, "Victim of Cannibal Agreed to be Eaten," *Guardian Unlimited*, 4 December 2003, <http://www.guardian.co.uk/germany/article/0,2763,1099477,00.html> (23 September 2005).

[9] For an overview of anthropological approaches to cannibalism, see Shirley Lindenbaum, "Thinking About Cannibalism," *Annual Review of Anthropology* 33 (2004): 475-498.

[10] Harding.

[11] Ibid.

[12] Maggie Kilgour, "The Function of Cannibalism at the Present Time," in *Cannibalism and the Colonial World*, eds. Francis Barker et al. (New York: Cambridge University Press, 1998), 238-259.

[13] Harald Ermel, "Anderson Cooper 360 Degrees," *CNN.com*, 22 December 2003, <http://transcripts.cnn.com/TRANSCRIPTS/0312/22/acd.00.html> (30 November 2005).
[14] Roger Boyes, "Girlfriend Defends Cannibal in Court," *Calgary Herald*, 10 January 2004, sec. A, 14.
[15] Ibid.
[16] Boyes, "Cannibal: Roger Boyes."
[17] George Jonas, "Craving Respectability - and Human Flesh," *National Post*, 29 March 2004, sec. A, 14.
[18] Ibid.
[19] Gerald Owen, "Crimes and the Camera," *National Post*, 22 May 2004, sec. RB, p. 2.
[20] "Jailed Cannibal Regrets Killing," *Leader Post*, 31 January 2004, sec. D, 12.
[21] Judith Feher-Gurewich, "A Lacanian Approach to the Logic of Perversion," *The Cambridge Companion to Lacan*, ed. Jean-Michel Rabaté (New York: Cambridge University Press, 2003), 191.
[22] For a more thorough discussion of the distinction between perverse acts and perverse structure, see Paul Verhaeghe, "Perversion I: Perverse Traits," *The Letter* 22 (2001): 59-74, and "Perversion II: The Perverse Structure," *The Letter* 23 (2001): 77-95.
[23] Bruce Fink, *A Clinical Introduction to Lacanian Psychoanalysis: Theory and Technique* (Cambridge: Harvard University Press, 1997), 179.
[24] Jacques Lacan, *Ecrits: A Selection*, trans. Alan Sheridan (New York: W. W. Norton & Co., 1977), 320.
[25] Fink, 175.
[26] Feher-Gurewich, 192.
[27] Fink, 181.
[28] Jean Clavreul, "The Perverse Couple," *Returning to Freud: Clinical Psychoanalysis in the School of Lacan*, ed. Stuart Schniederman (New Haven: Yale University Press, 1980), 215-233.
[29] Ibid, 232.
[30] C. Laségue and J. Falret, "La Folie A Deux ou Folie Communiquée," trans. Richard Michaud, *American Journal of Psychiatry* 121.4 (1964): 1-23.
[31] Ibid, 18.
[32] Deutsche Welle, "German Cannibal Victim's Will Found," *Current Affairs*, 14 December 2002, <http://www.dw-world.de/dw/article/0,,714339,00.html> (February 2, 2006).

[33] Sundararajan Rajagopal, "Suicide Pacts and the Internet: Complete Strangers May Make Cyberspace Pacts," *British Medical Journal* 329 (2004): 1298-1299.
[34] Carl L. Tishler and Janet Meltzer, "Folie à Deux in Children: An Emergency Room Presentation," *Clinical Case Studies* 3.1 (2004): 49-56.
[35] Clavreul, 225.
[36] Ibid, 216.
[37] Ibid, 218.
[38] Ibid, 219.
[39] Ibid, 221.
[40] "Cannibal's Confession Shocks Court," *Toronto Star*, 4 December 2003, sec. A, 29.
[41] Feher-Gurewich, 204.
[42] "Cannibal's Confession."
[43] Armando R. Favazza, *Bodies Under Siege: Self-mutilation in Culture and Psychiatry* (Baltimore: Johns Hopkins University Press, 1987).
[44] Mark Benecke, "First Report of Nonpsychotic Self-Cannibalism (Autophagy), Tongue Splitting, and Scar Patterns (Scarification) as an Extreme Form of Cultural Body Modification in Western Civilization," *The American Journal of Forensic Medicine and Pathology* 200 (1999): 281-285.
[45] Ibid, 285.
[46] Favazza, 183-186.
[47] Benecke, 285.
[48] Ofra Eshel, "Pentheus Rather Than Oedipus: On Perversion, Survival and Analytic 'Presencing,'" *International Journal of Psychoanalysis* 86 (2005): 1071-1097.
[49] Ibid, 1077.
[50] Ibid, 1080.
[51] Ibid, 1080.
[52] Fink.
[53] Maud Ellmann, *The Hunger Artists: Starving, Writing, and Imprisonment* (Cambridge: Harvard University Press, 1993).
[54] Ibid, 4.
[55] Ibid, 4.
[56] Ibid, 15.
[57] Ibid, 22.
[58] Maggie Kilgour, *From Communion to Cannibalism: An Anatomy of Metaphors of Incorporation* (Princeton: Princeton University Press, 1990), 7.
[59] Ibid, 4.

[60] Ellmann, 18-19.
[61] Ana Boczar, et al, "Discontent in the Era of Consumption: 'I Enjoy, Therefore I Exist," *International Forum of Psychoanalysis* 14 (2005): 206-209.
[62] Slavoj Zizek, "The Matrix, or, the Two Sides of Perversion," *Lacan Dot Com*, <http://www.lacan.com/zizek-matrix.htm> (11 July 2005).
[63] Ibid.
[64] Ibid.
[65] Roger Boyes, "Accused Cannibal Spills Details of Global Man-Eating Network," *Calgary Herald*, 6 Jan 2004, sec. A, p. 8.

Adorno and the Guilt of Thinking

Anders Johansson

Abstract: There has been an increasing scholarly interest in the problem of evil during the last decades. The essay discerns two opposed approaches to evil in this trend, each of them with its fallacy: evil is either treated as a practical issue, and thus trivialized, or as an ontological issue, and thus mystified. This dilemma is one explanation for the widespread notion that literature is better suited than philosophy for understanding and relating experiences of evil. A problem with this supposedly post-metaphysical approach is that it implies a metaphysical conception of an inherent goodness in literature. To find a more critical approach, the paper turns to Theodor W. Adorno, and his comments on poetry after Auschwitz. From his perspective evil is just as present in the interior of every artwork as in society in general - literature is no less evil than anything else. Due to its material character, however, every artwork does harbor a possibility of understanding and reconciliation that philosophical thinking lacks. Finally, two examples are used to illustrate Adorno's points: Michael Haneke's film *Funny Games*, and the Swedish novel *Äldreomsorgen i övre Kågedalen* by Nikanor Teratologen. Both could be seen as two extremely cruel narrations of evil, totally lacking all reconciliation. However, a reconciliation can be found in the interior of the works. In that way, the two works demonstrate a sensibility of the immanent violence of their own form.

Key Words: aesthetics, aporia, Auschwitz, Michael Haneke, non-identity, post-metaphysical, reconciliation, Nikanor Teratologen

1. The Return to the Problem of Evil

Evil is hip. Or, to put it in more austere academic terms: the concept of evil has gone through a renaissance in the humanities and social sciences during the last decade. There are several ways to understand and explain this turn. Michael Ignatieff serves us one option:

> Why can't we just call acts by their proper names and conduct ourselves accordingly? The name for this is evil. Many people bridle at this word and think it inhibits understanding the deeper grievances that fuel resentment and violence. [...] But it is worth holding the line that separates understanding from justification, the line that divides understanding from explanation. That is

> the work that the word 'evil' does. It holds the line. In any event, full understanding is God's work alone.[1]

From this angle, the resurgence of the concept of evil appears as a sound dissociation from the threat of relativism, a return to the ancient truths of religion. Evil is simply evil; let's not complicate things.

The Peruvian sociologist Gonzalo Portocarrero approaches the issue from another angle:

> From my own experience, I believe the generation I belong to neither could, nor wanted to see evil. This blindness was a result of the bedazzlement produced by the modern project and its relative, socialism. In fact, the idea was that the problems originated from the social structures and its manifestations, like the ignorance of the people.[2]

Seen from this angle, the concept of evil is connected with a post-theoretical humbleness, and a newborn interest in the ethical freedom and responsibility of the subject. "Evil" is first and foremost an expression for the blind spots of enlightenment.

No matter which side we concur with, one conclusion is already clear: it would be a mistake to give "the evil turn" *one* single explanation or interpretation. The point is rather that in a secularized world, the originally theological problem of evil subsists, transformed into a question about the pretensions and limitations of reason. From one side evil is a reality, an ontological category; from the other side "evil" is a word we put on certain unwelcome things, a social construction. From one angle, evil is a request that human reason should hold itself back for religious or ethical reasons, and humbly be aware of its limitations; from another angle, "evil" implies, on the contrary, an ethical cry for more thinking, more theorizing, more reason. In short: evil is what *can't be* explained; evil is what *must be* explained.

The American philosopher Susan Neiman has traced the origin of these two attitudes to the early Enlightenment, and the dispute between Voltaire and Rousseau: "The one [tradition], from Rousseau to Arendt, insists that morality demands that we make evil intelligible. The other, from Voltaire to Jean Améry, insists that morality demands that we don't."[3] Her comment is remarkably pregnant: it catches both the difficulty in relating rationally to evil, and the simultaneous necessity of doing exactly this. What's at stake here are the ethical implications of thinking or theorizing: are there cases when theorizing as such is irresponsible, disrespectful or outright harmful? Or may it, on the contrary, be irresponsible to abstain from thinking, explaining and theorizing?

In this general form these questions may appear strange; they become more meaningful if we use an example. Let's say there was an academic conference on evil in Rwanda in 1994. Inside the university a group of international and Rwandan scholars were discussing the concept of evil, the Holocaust, murder, rape, serial killers, evil in fiction, etc. Meanwhile, outside the university, thousands and thousands of people were systematically being slaughtered. Through the windows we could see and hear the killings, while we continued our discussions.

It goes without saying that this would be a totally perverse situation. Nonetheless, it differs from reality only with regard to the distance between the academic discussions and the reality of the evil deeds. It's not that we don't *know* about the killings going on today in, say, the Sudan, Nigeria, Congo, Iraq, Sri Lanka, Palestine, etc.; we are informed but we realize that we, as scholars, can't do much about it. So we continue our discussions, arguing that that may be the most responsible thing to do. After all, as Neiman points out, if we give up the attempts to explain evil theoretically, we also give up the possibility to confront and defeat it in practice.[4] The theoretical and the practical sides cannot be separated. In the end it is hard to deny that the task of philosophy is to reduce the evilness around us, as the Norwegian philosopher Lars Fr. H. Svendsen states. From his angle evil isn't primarily a philosophical, theological or metaphysical problem, but rather a concrete and practical issue.

Hence, it is logical that his book - *Ondskapens filosofi* (*The Philosophy of Evil*) - ends in a discussion on UN charters, the notion of "the just war", the NATO bombings of Serbia in 1999, and so on. In that way he avoids the danger that he may be caught in "abstractions and lose the concrete evilness, which was the outset for the reflection, out of sight".[5] On the other hand, the problem with this sobriety and pragmatism is that it borders on triviality. In turning to practical issues, the possibilities to investigate *in advance*, with the help of thinking, what the judicial system administrates *afterwards* gets lost. The productive distance to evil disappears.

In that perspective there is a point in maintaining the philosophical distance, even though one agrees that evil primarily is a practical problem. A good example of this attitude is the German philosopher Rüdiger Safranski's *Das Böse oder Das Drama der Freiheit* (*Evil or The Drama of Freedom*). Unlike Svendsen, Safranski doesn't look for solutions, but rather for an understanding of the history and genealogy of the problem of evil. What is paradoxical about the history - from Hesiod to Nooteboom - he sketches, however, is that it *conceals* rather than reveals the very historicity of evil. One symptom of that tendency is the presence of recurring formulations such as "For Einstein the 'wholeness' is a unity of...", "For Schelling God is...", "The radical rationalism [...] was convinced that...".[6] Slavoj Zizek once pinpointed the inadequacy of this kind of construction: they reduce the history of ideas to a series of contingent opinions. What gets lost here is the historic logic, the sensation of how one idea surges from the inconsistencies of another idea.[7]

This is exactly what happens in Safranski's book: evil becomes an ahistorical mystery beyond both the history of ideas and the mundane reality we all know. Accordingly the book ends with a coda that primarily underlines the unchangeable character of existence ("Human freedom remains enigmatic." "It was certainly always like that..."[8]) and the futility in every attempt to bring about a change ("Human thought has never liberated itself from that." "today [...] one is just as wise as before, when one said: man thinks, God rules"[9]). Time passes, but evilness endures. The drama of freedom that Safranski set out to draft eventually escapes him.

There are, of course, other views and positions than those Svendsen and Safranski represent. Still I believe their respective fallacies are paradigmatic: either one comes too close, or one ends up too remote; evil is either trivialized or mystified. Is there perhaps even a causal connection between those opposing views, between the difficulty and necessity of coming to terms with evil, and does this aporia in fact contain an answer to why the concept of evil has returned? Is the problem of evil crucial to the human and social sciences just *because* it is evasive? Is evil the infected wound that gives rise to the theoretical thinking of the humanities? Or, seen from another angle: shouldn't the fact that evilness doesn't disappear - in spite of all enlightenment, technical progress, civilization - but on the contrary only seems to increase in strength and dimensions, shouldn't that fact be an acute problem to virtually all thinking, including philosophy, art, literature etc.?

2. Philosophy and the Goodness of Literature

It would obviously be naïve to look for a solution to or way out of this dilemma. Nonetheless every scholar who approaches the problem of evil is forced to try. To enter the discourse and either turn only to the facts (too close), or just present a general theory (too remote) is simply inadequate. It's easily and often done, for sure, but is there really a need for a philosophy presenting us with the reality of evil? Are we not familiar with it already? And, on the other hand, don't all of the moral theories that are still being presented tell us more about the morality of the philosopher than about evil?

This difficulty is probably one reason why philosophers turn to art in general, and literature in particular, when they discuss evil, a trend that has become more evident after the so-called fall of the Grand Narratives. The standard explanation is that literature - or rather *storytelling* - contains a form of knowledge that philosophical thinking cannot reach. Unlike philosophy, moral philosophy or theology, whose theories and dogmas are aiming at the general, so the argument goes, literature contains a possibility to do justice to the particular experience. As Peter Levine explains,

> Literature is better [than philosophy] at depicting recalcitrant details, ambiguous situations, and tragic dilemmas. If we face problems that actually lack clear solutions, then stories can offer us rough but decent answers.[10]

In the same spirit Colin McGinn states that

> fictional works [...] combine the particular and the general in ways we find natural and intelligible. The general is woven into the particular which gives the particular significance and the general substance.[11]

Martha Nussbaum, arguably the most influential advocate for this attitude, argues in the same way: through its complex and allusive form, literature stands closer to life than conventional philosophy. Nussbaum talks about "the ability of narrative to evoke emotional activity in the reader", or how novels, through their own indeterminacy, "characterize life more richly and truly – indeed more precisely – than an example lacking those features ever could".[12] This sensibility to the particular experience is what another commentator, María Pía Lara, following Walter Benjamin, calls "the power of storytelling".[13]

One objection is close at hand: are not all of these praises of literature's power to do justice to the particular, its closeness to life, its power, etc. dubiously general as such? Significantly enough, it isn't *Moby Dick*, *The Trial* or *Don Quixote* that draw attention, but Literature, the Novel or Storytelling *in general*. Certainly, the general ideas are demonstrated by particular examples, but the impression remains: the way of thinking seems to contradict exactly what should be proved.

There are, however, more important objections to be made. What tends to be disregarded among the scholars mentioned is that every narrative also contains generalizing traits: all narrating forces the singular narrated fate into a language, a literary tradition and a genre, all consisting of very tangible limitations and demands. The singular is thus necessarily subordinated to the general, even in the most innocent or original of literary narratives.

A yet more important objection is that the scholars mentioned are united in an - implicit or explicit - claim to have left the grand narratives, philosophical systems and metaphysical truths behind. Nonetheless their arguments imply a highly metaphysical (I insist on this word due to the post-metaphysical pretensions) notion of the inherent goodness of literature. One turns to literature because it can help us get around in the world, not leading us astray; what is aesthetically praiseworthy is presupposed to be ethically praiseworthy as well; literature is presupposed to be connected with "the good life", not with the bad, unworthy, futile or empty life; literature is a means against evil, not in favor of evil. In short, literature is presupposed to be on the good side of an implicit division between good and evil. There is nothing wrong with that stand or valuation as such; in fact, it is a notion which is extremely hard to leave behind.[14] The problem is the fact that it is silently taken for granted. In that way the attempts to treat evil in a "post-metaphysical" manner imply another, more persistent metaphysics.[15]

This doesn't mean that these philosophical attempts to use literature in order to understand evil are totally misleading. From the perspective of traditional academic literary criticism they may, on the contrary, appear very fruitful in the way they confront literature with the 'big questions', instead of technicalities interesting only to the extreme specialist. In that sense they give literature an importance that is all too often lost in traditional literary discourse.

3. Adorno and the Aporias of Art

If evil is hip, so, at least to some extent, is the German philosopher Theodor W. Adorno. This is a strange situation, given that Adorno's ideas always have tended to be out of touch with their time. Obviously during the rise of Nazism in Germany in the early thirties, but also during the exile in the capitalist liberalism of the UK and USA during the second world war, as well as during the student revolutions of the sixties, and - posthumously - during the academic Marxism of the seventies, the textualism of the eighties, and the post-colonialism of the nineties. Still, something in his thought has obviously maintained its attraction all through these intellectual climate changes. One possible explanation for this vigor is the tension between immediacy and theory, materiality and spirit, reification and truth, reality and possibility that his writings stress and develop through their characteristic dialectic. In any case, this is the reason why I believe his position is very productive in the case of evil in general, and the dilemma described earlier in particular: how to do justice ethically to concrete suffering, and at the same time maintain a productive distance to the issue. In fact, Adorno's entire work - above all his writings on art and aesthetics - could be seen as a search for an answer to this problem.

To try to summarize Adorno's philososphy, or even his aesthetic theory, would be a mistake since in every single paragraph it fights the simplification of summaries. Let's instead focus on one famous - or rather infamous - feature of his work: his remarks on the barbarity of writing poetry after Auschwitz. The statement is first made in the end of the essay "Cultural Critique and Society", written in 1955.[16] Adorno's point is that society has grown so totally reified that it has become virtually impossible for "the mind" (*Geist*) - including both poetry and, significantly, Adorno's own critique - to emancipate itself from reification. There is no position outside of reification - no safety zone, no innocence, immunity or radicalism. Evilness thus also encompasses the philosophical and literary efforts, which all too often take their distance from evil for granted.

Seven years later, in the essay "Commitment", Adorno defends his - by now heavily criticized - statement, and goes on to raise the question whether, given the recent regression of society, art may exist at all anymore. But he also adds that the paradoxical task of contemporary art is to refuse to give in to this situation. For although art has lost its right to exist, there still is a great *need* for art. On the one hand the excessive factual suffering around us (condensed in the name "Auschwitz") makes all art appear either cynical or naïve; on the other hand the same suffering "demands the continued existence of the very art it forbids; hardly anywhere else does suffering still find its own voice, a consolation that does not immediately betray it".[17]

Another four years later, towards the end of *Negative Dialectics* (1966), he underlines this aspect and admits, incidentally, that his earlier statements on poetry after Auschwitz might have been false, since "Perennial suffering has as much right to expression as a tortured [person] has to scream".[18] He immediately adds, however, that one rightly might ask whether it is at all possible to *live* after Auschwitz. The earlier exaggeration is withdrawn - only to be replaced with a new, yet stronger hyperbole. What looked like an aesthetic problem is made into an existential one.

At least one overarching tendency in these three remarks is clear: every time Adorno returns to the issue it becomes more complex, more paradoxical, or rather aporetic, *and* more important. It seems as if he is forced to come up with a stronger exaggeration every time, in order to avoid his own thought becoming reified, becoming merely another public opinion. In fact, this reflects to some extent the point that was visible already on the first occasion: the need for poetry, literature, art, philosophy or any attempt of the human mind to break free from reified circumstances, to rise above the evilness it confronts, becomes harder and harder, but thus also more and more crucial.

In that sense Adorno's remarks on poetry after Auschwitz - which actually could be seen as a *mise en abyme* for his entire aesthetic theory - is an answer to the dilemma discussed earlier: the necessity and impossibility to approach evil rationally. Once again: you *can't* write poetry after Auschwitz, it would be a perversity, if we really keep in mind what happened; you *must* write poetry after Auschwitz, the unfathomable suffering demands it. In other words all spiritual activity - philosophy, literature, theology - in the modern age is enclosed in an ethical aporia. Every single thought, every poem written down encapsulates a guilt. The more vehemently it denies this, the bigger the guilt.

So how does Adorno cope with this aporia? In a way he follows the two streams Neiman discerns, the one from Rousseau *and* the one from Voltaire; he tries to do what Svendsen does and what Safranski does *at the same time*: keep the distance *and* stay as close to the problem as possible. Or, as Adorno himself puts it in the very last aphorism of *Minima Moralia*: "The more passionately thought denies its conditionality for the sake of the unconditional, the more unconsciously, and so calamitously, it is delivered up to the world." It is, however, only from this very aporia that we can gain some hope, Adorno immediately argues: "Even its own impossibility it must at last comprehend for the sake of the possible."[19]

In other words, Adorno acknowledges the double ethical demands on thinking that Neiman outlines, but he understands these demands in the opposite way. If Svendsen shuns abstractness and metaphysics exactly in order to contribute to the making of a better world, Adorno turns to metaphysics in order to maintain hope for a better world - to maintain a possibility, as the last quote says. And while Safranski humbly takes a step back from concrete suffering, arguing that evil is beyond our understanding, Adorno remains in the concrete suffering for the very same humble reasons. Paradoxically, one could almost say that Adorno maintains the metaphysical perspective for practical reasons, and sticks to materiality for ethical reasons. We're stuck in the empirical circumstances that produced Auschwitz, and we're forced to wring some hope out of this hopelessness. This is where art - above all music and literature - enters the picture.

There are indeed important similarities between Adorno's position and the recent philosophical interest - in Lara, Levine, McGinn and Nussbaum for example - in literature. (One could mention the idea of a truth content of the artwork, the resistance to relativism as well as positivism, the idea of a relatedness between philosophy and literature, etc.) The differences may be harder to distinguish, but they are certainly important. While Nussbaum approaches literature with the question "How should one live?",[20] Adorno's question would rather be "Is there still life?" And while Lara treats literature as a general, historically indifferent solution (the form - storytelling - is silently presupposed to exist as an ever present possibility before and independently of the formed - the experience of evil),[21] the outset for Adorno is a fundamental doubt about the very possibility of art.

This doubt is connected to what Adorno calls the "double character of art": if the artwork is *autonomous* in relation to the capitalist logic of modern society, it is exactly this autonomy which gives it a social function and a value - that is: makes it *heteronomous*.[22] If this dialectic is a dilemma, it is also from this dialectic that art draws its strength, according to Adorno, its ability to offer a consolation that isn't a betrayal. In order not to lose this ability, the artwork is forced continuously to turn against itself, its own form and even the very concept of art. Consequently there is nothing certain, stable or self-evident about art anymore, "not its inner life, not its relation to the world, not even its right to exist", as is stated in the very first sentence of *Aesthetic Theory*.[23]

But this uncertainty, which results in a constant obligation to produce its own conditions, also implies a certain amount of violence. There is something instrumentally violent already in the conception of a modern work of art, from Adorno's point of view. Already through its forming of a material, every work of art takes part in the purposive violence which characterizes modernity, a violence which the artwork, as an autonomous formation, at the same time distances itself from. However innocent its purposes, every work of art reproduces the evil it is supposed to mediate.[24] Accordingly the difficulty in narrating evil, from Adorno's point of view, doesn't reside in the moral content of the experience recounted, but in the very *singularity* of the experience. The crucial question is how to avoid the particularity of the singular experience being subordinated to a general form, how to create a form that is tolerant towards its amorphous counterpart. Or, with Adorno's Hegelian terminology, how to create an identity between *identity and non-identity*. As this is a difficult but crucial point, it needs further explication.

In the Preface to his *Logic*, Hegel stipulates "the identity between identity and non-identity" as the basis for all thought.[25] This is a passage Adorno returns to over and over again. In a way, he agrees with Hegel: what actually happens in thinking is that an identity is established between the identical and the non-identical, that is, between thought and the subject of thought. In other words, all thinking presupposes a certain kind of reconciliation. The problem is, however, that this identity or reconciliation implies that everything alien to thought or the concept - "the other", the non-identical - is forced into the identity of conceptual thinking, where it disappears, so to speak. No matter if the world is reasonable or not - that is what we *make it*, in our very act of thinking. Adorno's critical conclusion is that conceptual thinking consequently cannot do justice to reality in its irrationality, multiplicity, singularity, materiality - in its non-identity. We are stuck in our own identity, which will always be a *false* one, since it contains no sensibility of non-identity. This is, in principle, Adorno's objection to Hegel.[26]

In broad terms, this is the problem that Lara, Levine, McGinn and Nussbaum pointed out, the reason why they turned to literature (cf. above), and it is also the fundamental reason for Adorno's interest in art. For the rationality of the artwork constitutes, contains a possibility to establish an identity that *can* harbor the non-identical in its non-identity. In other words, Adorno would agree with McGinn, for example, that the artwork can do justice to the singular experience (of evil, for example) in a way that conceptual thinking cannot. The reason for this, however, is not that artworks are less rational or general than philosophy, or that they are less evil, guilty or reified than anything else in this world, but that the material and mimetic qualities of the artwork make it more adaptable, more vulnerable, and thus in a way less violent than the rationality of conceptual thinking, whose identity is always established by force.[27]

But although art can thus be seen as a more tolerant discourse than philosophy, the efforts of the work of art cannot really succeed. Every artwork stretches against a *true identity*, a reconciliation which isn't a deceit, but due to the inevitable heteronomy of the work of art, this identity is never really reached. In this failure to reconcile the identical with the non-identical, we can, however, experience the *possibility* of a true reconciliation, a consolation that isn't a betrayal, a utopian possibility which reality under the present conditions denies.[28]

So far, it might look as though Adorno, in a traditionally idealist manner, sees an opportunity in the artwork to rise *above* evil, to present a possible reconciliation *beyond* the limitations and discriminations of modern society. There is, however, another possibility of interpreting his idea of an aesthetic reconciliation. As indicated above, that possibility is connected to the materiality of the artwork. The artwork, in contrast to conceptual thinking, *needs* the material, the approximate, particular, amorphous which at the same time nonetheless is an obstacle to its necessary unity.[29] Accordingly, the unity of the artwork is nothing but the immanent tension between identity and non-identity. But what is more important is that this unavoidable tension or dialectic also has to be understood as a moment of a micro-logical reconciliation, an unrestrained unity between form and "otherness", an image of a truth free from violence.[30] Rather than a transcendent truth, we thus face an immanent reconciliation, a utopia within the already known.

4. First Example: Michael Haneke

The Austrian director Michael Haneke's film *Funny Games* is an extremely cold narration about sadistic violence, a naked study in extreme evil, reminiscent of Stanley Kubrick's *A Clockwork Orange*.[31] It tells the frightening story of how two young intruders, seemingly just for the fun of it, terrorize and finally kill a family, locked up in their stylish weekend cottage. In its total lack of all compassion and reconciliation it is quite a scary movie. Personally, I can't remember ever seeing a film where a happy ending was so distant. Without doubt one could read the film metaphorically (for example, the helpful/cruel attitude of the intruders - all dressed in white - opens the door for a postcolonial interpretation in which the murderers represent western imperialists). In any case, *Funny Games* seems to illustrate Lara's points about "the power of storytelling" and the experience of evil: it certainly tells us more about evil than most philosophy books do. The problem is that there still is something routinely comforting (Adorno would call it a *false* reconciliation) in the storytelling itself: whatever the intention, the evilness is already made well-known, ready-to-hand and almost enjoyable, by being forced into the regular film format. Haven't we, after all, seen it all before? And isn't that recognition a condition for our appreciation of every story?

But the film expresses a consciousness about this. At one point in the film, one of the murderers turns to the camera and asks the viewers: "What do you think? Do you think they've a chance of winning? You are on their side, aren't you? So who will you bet with?" And when the father of the family asks the criminals to kill them and end it once and for all, the answer he gets is that the film isn't long enough yet.[32] The funny game has to go on a little longer, in order to satisfy the spectators. What should be noted in these - by no means unique - meta-referential moments, is that the film acknowledges the impossibility of an innocent story. The very production, as well as the reception, of a movie already imply a stand, a compromise, a restraint. On one occasion this consciousness is taken one step further. In an unexpected moment the mother of the family manages to grab a gun and kill one of the two intruders. His companion becomes furious (so far in the film, he has only showed a creepy combination of extreme politeness and relentless evilness), and starts rummaging around for the remote control. When he finds it he literally *rewinds the film* - the film in which he himself is a character, the film I am discussing here - a few seconds, whereupon everything continues as before, but this time the overpowering fails, and the victims are by-and-by killed in a slow sadistic play - a funny game.

In this erasing of the attempted overpowering something important happens: the winding back of the film visualizes the immanent violence of the form itself. Suddenly we are made aware of the constraints the narration of every movie implies: that everything is in principle decided from the outset; that every redundant little detail which could possibly break the necessary unity of the story has to be cut off; that everything non-identical has to be sacrificed on the altar of identity. Paradoxically, the film thus presents - negatively - a kind of image of the multiplicity of immanent non-realized possibilities, non-identical protuberances, anomalies and deviations which the unity of the work could not harbor. The point is that they nevertheless become visible, indirectly, in this rupture. This *second image* - as we could call it - which emerges exactly in the breakdown of the *first image* (the story) is what Adorno calls the *Erscheinung* (apparition, appearance, semblance) of the artwork.[33] This is the emphatic moment of the film, its simultaneous destruction and realization: the film virtually explodes, everything stops, the process becomes image, and we experience a reconciled identity between the finished identity and all the non-identical aspects of the work. There is nothing transcendent in this *Erscheinung*, nothing metaphysical in a traditional sense, only a sudden and immanent reconciliation between the necessity for the movie to hold together as a unity, and the need to do justice to the particular in its particularity. The form yields to what is being formed, with the emergence of something else. For a vanishing moment there is a truly non-violent identity.

5. Second Example: Nikanor Teratologen

The Swedish novel *Äldreomsorgen i övre Kågedalen* (*Elder Care in the Upper Valley of Kåge*), written by Nikanor Teratologen, certainly is another attempt at narrating evil", heaving as it is with misogynic violence, sadism, pedophilia, Nazism, torture, cannibalism and contempt for weakness.[34] How it may help us in "weaving a moral understanding of the past", as Lara puts it, is hard to see, however. If it can, it is hardly the moral understanding most of us would *want* anyway: what is characteristic about Teratologen's novel is the lack of any attitude against evil on the level of narrating, or, to use another concept, in the implied author of the book. Or even worse: however odd it may sound, this is a hilarious novel; it presents an unsettling mix of atrocities and laughs, without any intention to keep those sides separate. All in all the novel can be seen as an attempt to leave behind the established notion of good literature as by definition *ethically good*, a decided attempt to write *evil literature*.

But why bother? Even if it really *is* possible to write a piece of evil literature, is it necessarily worthy of our attention? Isn't all criticism with any decency and justification - not only the ethical criticism proposed by Nussbaum - obliged to condemn this kind of racism, sexism and sadism?[35] Isn't Lara right in presupposing that much goodness? One answer would be to defend interest in the novel for scholarly reasons, that is, to analyze it in a disinterested way; another variant would be to praise it for literary reasons, and disregard the ethical implications. I don't find those attitudes very convincing; on the contrary I believe any interest - aesthetic, academic, political, literary, etc. - in the book has to be ethically motivated as well. To read is inevitably to take a stand. The question then is in what way Teratologen's book is justified. A short fragment in Adorno's *Minima Moralia* might point to an answer:

> The comfort that flows from great works of art lies less in what they express than in the fact that they have managed to struggle out of existence. *Hope is soonest found among the comfortless*."[36]

While Lara, Levine, McGinn and Nussbaum implicitly urge literature to take a stand against evil, Adorno questions the very possibility of literature to chose its own ethical content. If there is such a moral stand, it is to be found in the hopeless cases rather than in the hopeful ones.

Äldreomsorgen i övre Kågedalen is certainly a work without hope: there is nothing but meanness, selfishness and sadism in the upper valley of Kåge (which actually exists, in the desolate northern part of Sweden), and nothing really gets better during the novel. To live is to suffer and make others suffer, and the one who suffers the most is the weaker of the two protagonists, the young boy "pyret" (approximately: mite), who is continuously reminded of his awkward worthlessness, when he is not being violated or tortured by "morfar" (grandpa) and his odd companions . But precisely *here*, in the most miserable of all the characters, there persists something else. In pyret's own badly formulated words:

> ja streta... spjärna... dom va int beredda på motstånd... dom hårdna... ja skydda de man aldri få ge upp... hur förnedrad man än ä... de där som fanns före allt börja... den du va innan dom börja förgå sä... själva pyrigheten... de där man kapsla in... de där som gör att man måst härdas å bli morfar... De ä nåt litet å varmt... men när de gäll ä de de starkaste som finns.[37]
>
> (I struggled... resisted... they wasn't prepared for that... they hardened... I protected that which you never should give up... however humiliated you are... that which was there before it all began... the one you was before they started to abuse... the tinyness itself... that thing you enclose... that which force you to harden and become grandpa... It's something small and warm... but when it really comes to the point it's the strongest there is).[38]

What's noteworthy in this passage is that it contends that the power relations aren't the way they appear. In his very weakness pyret (whose name significantly is written without an initial capital letter throughout the book) maintains something that - if he is right - in the end is stronger than the humiliating, hardened powers around him. This strength resides, in short, in the possibility not to harden but to change, to become something other than you're supposed to become, a possibility that has disappeared in the evilness of grandpa. While grandpa is nothing but a static reaction to miserable circumstances, the softness of pyret still contains a possibility of becoming. In the midst of hopelessness, there is something vaguely but strongly comforting.

But pyret's words can be read as a meta-poetical statement about the strength of the non-identities of the novel as well. It is not only pyret's voice we hear in the quote above, but also the voice of the novel. The words about "the tinyness itself" are also a description of the tiny intensities which are forced into the hardened form of the narration - "that which was there before it all began..." Enclosed deep inside the conventions of good literature there remains something else, something that resists the death of completeness, something which will always remain stronger than every ethical demand. If there ever was a goodness of literature, it is in this moment, this rest which resists the reconciliation, and one should look for it there, rather than in the presupposed goodness of the narrative form.

Notes

[1] Michael Ignatieff, "The Terrorist as Auteur", *New York Times*, 14 November 2004, sec. 6, p. 50.
[2] Gonzalo Portocarrero, *Rostros criollos del mal: Cultura y transgresión en la sociedad peruana* (Lima: Red para el Desarollo de las Ciencias Sociales en el Perú, 2004), 20. My translation. Unless otherwise stated, the translations of non-English texts are mine throughout.
[3] Susan Neiman, *Evil in Modern Thought: An Alternative History of Philosophy* (Princeton & Oxford: Princeton University Press, 2002), 8.
[4] *Ibid.*, 325.
[5] Lars Fr. H Svendsen, *Ondskapens filosofi* (Oslo: Universitetsforlaget, 2001), 27.
[6] Rüdiger Safranski, *Das Böse oder Das Drama der Freiheit* (München: Carl Hanser Verlag, 1997), 61, 64, 178.
[7] Slavoj Zizek, *Organs without Bodies: Deleuze and Consequences* (New York & London: Routledge, 2004), 50.
[8] Safranski, 328.
[9] *Ibid.*, 328, 330.
[10] Peter Levine, *Living without Philosophy* (New York: State University of New York Press, 1998), 7.
[11] Colin McGinn, *Ethics, Evil, and Fiction* (Oxford: Clarendon Press, 1997), 3.
[12] Martha Nussbaum, *Love's Knowledge: Essays on Philosophy and Literature* (Oxford: Oxford University Press, 1990), 291, 47.
[13] María Pía Lara, "Narrating Evil: A Postmetaphysical Theory of Reflective Judgement" in *Rethinking Evil: Contemporary Perspectives*, ed. María Pía Lara (Berkeley: University of California Press, 2001), 241.
[14] One well-known attempt to break out of this silent idealism and connect literature with the opposite side (with evil) is Georges Bataille's *Literature and Evil.* While Bataille only inverts the opposed traditional association (literature=good) he remains very dependent on the same idealism. Cf Georges Bataille, *Literature and Evil*, trans. Alastair Hamilton (New York: Urizen Books, 1973).
[15] This is indeed a point that could be made against the ethical turn in its entirety: it presupposes the same preconceived image of a certain goodness of literature, an image that is very seldom acknowledged. When Martha Nussbaum pretends to leave all ideological axioms behind except for the Aristotelian question "How should one live?", she forgets that her view of literature and reading (her way of talking of literature in terms of

friendship and love, for example) isn't natural, but rather part of an idealist tradition whose aesthetical and ethical values she will thus unknowingly reproduce. (Nussbaum, 23-25, 29, 48, 173)

[16] Theodor W. Adorno, *Prisms*, trans. Samuel & Shierry Weber (London: Neville Spearman, 1967), 34.

[17] Theodor W. Adorno, "Commitment," *Notes to Literature* vol. II, trans. Shierry Weber Nicholsen (New York: Columbia University Press, 1992), 88.

[18] Theodor W. Adorno, *Negative Dialectics*, trans. E.B. Ashton (New York: Continuum, 1994), 362.

[19] Theodor W. Adorno, *Minima Moralia: Reflections from Damaged Life* trans. E.F.N Jephcott (London & New York: Verso, 1997), 247.

[20] Nussbaum, 289.

[21] Lara, *passim*.

[22] Theodor W. Adorno, *Aesthetic Theory*, trans. Robert Hullot-Kentor (London: Athlone Press, 1997), 225-228, 252-254. However important, this dialectic is often disregarded, and Adorno's theory mistaken for an aesthetics of *autonomy*, where art and society are understood as absolute opposites. Surprisingly enough, as James Martin Harding points out, this distorted image appears also in more initiated Adorno-studies. (James Martin Harding, *Adorno and 'A Writing of the Ruins': Essays on Modern Aesthetics and Anglo-American Literature and Culture* (Albany: State University of New York Press, 1997), 11-13.)

[23] Adorno 1997, *Aesthetic Theory*, 1.

[24] See *ibid.*, 50, 139.

[25] Georg Wilhelm Friedrich Hegel, *Wissenschaft der Logik. Gesammelte Werke*, vol. 11, ed. Friedrich Hogemann & Walter Jaeschke (Hamburg: Felix Meiner Verlag, 1978), 37.

[26] See Adorno 1994, 6-15.

[27] Behind this view one might sense the Kantian vision of the aesthetic experience as an autonomous judgment. Even though Adorno, in some regards, is highly critical towards Kant (mainly to his idealist disregard of the object), he could be said to defend this notion and the unique possibilities of the aesthetic experience. For Adorno the aesthetic experience is the only place - or rather, the only *moment* - in the totally reified society where the ethical (and political) space Lara points to subsists. (Cf. Immanuel Kant, *Kritik der Urteilskraft. Gesammelte Werke* vol. 5, eds. Der preussischen Akademie der Wissenschaften. Berlin: Georg Riemer Verlag, 1908, chapter III, IV.)

[28] Adorno 1997, *Aesthetic Theory*, 132.

[29] See *ibid.*, 176.
[30] For an exhaustive interpretation of Adorno's aesthetic theory along these lines, see: Christoph Menke-Eggers, *Die Souveränität der Kunst: Ästhetische Erfahrung nach Adorno und Derrida* (Frankfurt a.M.: Athenäum, 1988), 156-169.
[31] Michael Haneke, *Funny Games*, producer Veit Heiduschka (Wien: Wega-Film, 1997), film.
[32] *Ibid.*
[33] Adorno 1997, *Aesthetic Theory*, 84-85, 175-178.
[34] The novel aroused mixed emotions among the critics, but what was more remarkable was the refusal of the renowned editorial Norstedts to publish the sequel, notwithstanding the commercial success and critical acclaims of the first part.
[35] Nussbaum, 233.
[36] Adorno 1997, *Minima Moralia*, 223. (My emphasis, translation modified.)
[37] Nikanor Teratologen, *Äldreomsorgen i övre Kågedalen* (Stockholm & Malmö: Vertigo, 1998), 92.
[38] It should be noted that is very hard to translate *Äldreomsorgen i övre Kågedalen* since it is written in a very specific, almost lost dialect. A lot of connotations are lost in translation. On the other hand, many passages are difficult to understand for Swedes in general as well. In addition to this, the language is often consciously bad (the spelling, the expressions etc.), at the same time as it is extremely rich (in associations, allusions, significations etc.).

Bibliography

Adorno, Theodor W. *Aesthetic Theory*. Translated by Robert Hullot-Kentor. London: Athlone Press, 1997.

Adorno, Theodor W. "Commitment." *Notes to Literature*. Vol. II, translated by Shierry Weber Nicholsen. New York: Columbia University Press, 1992.

Adorno, Theodor W. *Minima Moralia: Reflections from A Damaged Life*. Translated by E.F.N Jephcott. London & New York: Verso, 1997.

Adorno, Theodor W. *Negative Dialectics*. Translated by E.B. Ashton. New York: Continuum, 1994.

Adorno, Theodor W. *Prisms*. Translated by Samuel & Shierry Weber. London: Neville Spearman, 1967.

Bataille, Georges. *Literature and Evil*, trans. Alastair Hamilton. New York: Urizen Books, 1973.

Haneke, Michael. *Funny Games*, produced by Veit Heiduschka. Wien: Wega-Film, 1997. (Film.)

Hegel, Georg Wilhelm Friedrich. *Wissenschaft der Logik. Gesammelte Werke*. Vol. 11, edited by Friedrich Hogemann & Walter Jaeschke. Hamburg: Felix Meiner Verlag, 1978.

Kant, Immanuel. *Kritik der Urteilskraft. Gesammelte Werke.* Vol. 5, edited by Der preussischen Akademie der Wissenschaften. Berlin: Georg Riemer Verlag, 1908.

Lara, María Pía. "Narrating Evil: A Postmetaphysical Theory of Reflective Judgement." In *Rethinking Evil: Contemporary Perspectives*, edited by María Pía Lara. Berkeley: University of California Press, 2001.

Levine, Peter. *Living without Philosophy.* Albany: State University of New York Press, 1998.

McGinn, Colin. *Ethics, Evil, and Fiction.* Oxford: Clarendon Press, 1997.

Menke-Eggers, Christoph. *Die Souveränität der Kunst: Ästhetische Erfahrung nach Adorno und Derrida.* Frankfurt a.M.: Athenäum, 1988.

Neiman, Susan. *Evil in Modern Thought: An Alternative History of Philosophy*. Princeton & Oxford: Princeton University Press, 2002.

Nussbaum, Martha. *Love's Knowledge.* New York & Oxford: Oxford University Press, 1990.

Portocarrero, Gonzalo. *Rostros criollos del mal: Cultura y transgresión en la sociedad peruana.* Lima: Red para el Desarollo de las Ciencias Sociales en el Perú, 2004.

Safranski, Rüdiger. *Das Böse oder Das Drama der Freiheit.* München: Carl Hanser Verlag, 1997.

Svendsen, Lars Fr. H. *Ondskapens filosofi.* Oslo: Universitetsforlaget, 2001.

Teratologen, Nikanor. *Äldreomsorgen i övre Kågedalen.* Stockholm & Malmö: Vertigo, 1998.

Zizek, Slavoj. *Organs without Bodies: Deleuze and Consequences*. New York & London: Routledge, 2004.

As Others See Us:
A Critical Reflection of the Role of Humanitarian Landmine Action Organisations

Graeme R. Goldsworthy

Abstract: This paper primarily seeks to demystify and align the mine clearance industry and demarcate its position in the humanitarian aid arena and to make clear the role of such demining organisations less as saints led by the martyr figure of Diana, and more as sinners, compliant forces deployed to areas of political volatility by western governments to do their bidding, including the routine gathering of military, political and economic information for use by intelligence services of donor countries.

Key Words: demining, landmines, bomb, disposal, HMA, force multiplier.

> *Most informed observers of the aid industry would not raise an eyebrow to hear the simple statement that mine clearance organisations are in fact mercenaries. Most would nod in agreement. Some are blatantly neo-colonialist. One British organisations specialist personnel wore union flag badges on their arms and their EOD[1] disposal badges issued by the military prominently displayed on the other sleeve of their work shirts, which were all the same colour. Actually they looked a bit like the boy scouts. I remember that our base located in NW Cambodia had a Union flag flying over the demining base, reminiscent of an outpost of empire and indeed with probably more financial clout and local influence (if not firepower) than during the heady days of empire, and in a place which wasn't even in the British empire. In Cambodia the local police headquarters relied on us for radio communications, sometimes for transport, sometimes for skilled repair of small arms – all done as favours of course – but naturally we had more security than the citizens of the town, we were more valuable.*
>
> *Author to BBC Radio Leeds, November 1994*

Demining is a prima face example of how since the Cold War, the military has crossed into the world of humanitarian aid and NGOs have become more overtly military political actors and thus that the West ,the developed world and its military-industrial complex (MIC) not only controls and dictates war, but also peace.

HMA (Humanitarian Mine Action) actors in NGO guise have assumed a neutrality that is expected to be taken for granted, yet have any such organisations explained the source of their authority to act as a broker in the issue? Do any reveal their relative power to decide their terms of engagement? The appearance of neutrality serves inadvertently (or intentionally) as a powerful political tool for furthering particular agendas, for the broker appears not to have any agenda of its own, to be value-free and ideologically open, and to remain beyond the capture of competing discourses.

This creates the 'power gap' based on wealth and capacity and ensures control. The well-publicised and much-lauded performance of demining NGOs since the early 1990s has established the necessity for demining in the international aid world, now regarded as a prerequisite for redevelopment in any country affected by war. HMA is visible and quantifiable and it looks good on TV; send the deminers in and something is being seen to be done. It's a popular obsession beloved of politicians like, for example, the new fashion to send helicopters to every natural disaster, whether they are needed or not. But demining in the aid sector now under the description of humanitarian mine action fulfils other roles which one imagines would not have been so popular with the people's princess, Lara Croft and the odd saint-like Irish rock star.

A key NGO role in the aid world is to control aid money for their political masters (via a plethora of donors), often necessary, given the kleptocratic states in which NGOs often find themselves working. In return, they provide information through reporting. HMA organisations, given their expertise, go one step further by providing a rich seam of technical, tactical and strategic information vital to governments and back donors who have no other sources of HUMINT for military purposes in volatile areas of interest.

Ostensibly, HMA organisations are there to save life and restore land, the usual laudable and highly publicised goals of such agencies, and many work very hard in hostile environments to achieve these ends, whilst purporting to create national capacity. So how many national mine action programmes are indigenised today? Possible the Afghans, but heavily dependant on US funding even, ironically during the tenure of the Taliban regime, Ironically, the US even bombed its 'own' demining compound in Kabul, killing two personnel, during the post 9/11 attack against that country. Cambodia? Hardly at all. It is simply not in the interests of donors or the global HMA community to see a complete transfer of skills (read power) South. Too many jobs and too much influence are at stake, not to mention the interest of governments and intelligence agencies that depend on having reliable and compliant informant organisations, their networks and personnel in these volatile areas of interest.

1. "It's not the money, it's the money."

Given that many of the people they employ at wages very much lower than expatriate staff have actually much more experience in handling the very munitions and mines that required clearance, it bears asking the question of how much experience the expatriates have that is relevant to the given local situation. In the world of HMA, many expatriate specialists command salaries of up to 8,000 US Dollars per month tax free, plus benefits. These men work alongside local staff - equally at risk in the field and often more so in the societies they live in - who earn somewhere closer to between 200-400 dollars per month. The fatuous argument much used in the past, especially by a leading British organisation, was that this was very reasonable for expatriate staff, in fact two-thirds of the 'commercial rate'. This begs the obvious question, who set the commercial rate? The answer is: the 'experts' who set up the HMA NGOs[2]. There is certainly no financial incentive to make international staff indigenise programmes and thus make themselves 'redundant'. Turkeys probably wouldn't vote for Christmas.

Prior to the Ottawa anti-landmines treaty being signed in 1997, The ICBL (International Campaign to Ban Landmines) and its constituent HMA organisations made a great fuss over what was termed the 'double dipping' theory, where arms companies that produced and sold landmines were paid exorbitant amounts of money to clear them, such as in Lebanon and Kuwait. An interesting aside to this theory applies also to NGO workers in HMA: you got paid to make war, now you get paid to control the clear-up. Nice deal. Or it may be explained in part, perhaps, that the lure of those high-rolling salaries mentioned previously, paid by many (not all) organisations, may explain the reluctance to hand over the reins to local actors. But size is important in this game, much is required to advance an organisation's political agenda, and this can depend on the number of programmes running, (or, that is to say, the number of countries coloured in red on a map and forming the centrepiece of the annual report). There is also a widespread belief that the more staff and organisation has, the more successful it must therefore be. This is the continued top-down approach that pervades HMA, indeed virtually all organisations and agencies in the aid and development sector. Its ego, and the politicians and generals who need the veneer of respectability for their adventures in intervention abroad, have proved adept at stroking those NGO egos.

2. Force Multipliers

Mine Action organisations in effect compromise the neutrality of the broader NGO community who do not want to be coerced into participation in intervention missions and who wish to retain their neutrality[3]. A bold statement, perhaps sweeping, but as the demarcation line between war and peace becomes further obscured, so too the line between aid worker and soldier, combatant and non-combatant, the 'who's who' in nation building or post-conflict reconstruction, is becoming ever more blurred. MSF withdrew last year from Afghanistan, having been compromised by the 2001 invasion and attempts at coercing them onto 'the team' as 'force multipliers,' as the then-US Secretary of State Colin Powell described NGOs. The alignment of MSF to the occupation forces confirmed the misplaced suspicion of Taliban militants and cost the lives of five MSF staff members. Other NGOs in Afghanistan remain highly concerned at NATO military PRTs mixing civilian dress, carrying weapons, and using 'white' NGO style 4x4 vehicles, deliberately co-opting an NGO style identity. Afghans militants aren't fooled by this ruse; thus all white vehicle are suspect. Those communities dealing with NGOs are thus suspect as collaborators with the infidel. Deminers themselves are often seen as little more than mercenaries by host communities, no mistake. Demining mixes active and former military personnel, uses military language and they are, it would seem, the post-modern mercenaries. They directly benefit from war and from the war-making, war-proliferating, war-preparedness and the very war-anticipatory nature our society has come to hold. Worse, the delivery and maintenance of humanitarian aid is itself becoming a strategic tool, a link which HMA organisations have unwittingly or willingly helped to forge. In the nineties the media and NGO world was up in arms because the UK government was exposed linking 'aid to trade'. Today the continued political military assimilation of humanitarian aid goes notably unremarked. NGOs and their paymasters are less accountable than a decade ago, often supported by supra-national and less accountable donors. HMA organisations have availed themselves of these more complex interdependent relationships than most, and unlike many NGOs, do not rely on a 'community' of support, as, for example, a membership organisation in the mould of, say, Greenpeace. Thus HMA organisations are much easier to manipulate and equally, much more willing to comply, in exchange for the high levels of funding they need to undertake programmes. The temptation to find reasons to remain in countries for years; despite the levels of expertise attained by local agencies, is mutually beneficial. Some commentators argue that using demining organisations from developed countries actually only serves a short-term aim and can actually excuse proliferation in mine warfare, because of the 'benefits' of having compliant actors in continuing conflict or immediate post-conflict situations. One well-known British-based organisation has filled that role almost perfectly in Afghanistan[4] during the Soviet occupation through the Taliban regime, and indeed has been in Chechnya for over six years. The ethical intention in using demining organisations as the post-modern mercenaries, the guns (or detectors) for hire of the 21st century, deserves continued enquiry.

So instead of rushing out to get the deminers on the ground, the question should be, in the interests of effective local solutions and the integrity of the post-conflict development process, how can we avoid employing western demining resources?

3. Research and Development

Another area of the HMA Industry is its burgeoning R and D sector, wherein one finds schemes as fantastic as flora that changes colour when plant roots make contact with a mine body, where bees and rats are trained or genetically altered to locate landmines, where multi-million dollar blimps drone over mined areas, using more multi-million dollar ground- sensing radar equipment to map minefields, where in the past a team with prismatic compasses, maps and pencils could do the job just fine. Throw money at science. This demonstrates a prevailing attitude in the developed North in HMA toward displacement activities to do anything but actually focus upon getting into and clearing redundant minefields and mined areas, whilst empowering local actors and NGOs in mine action for the long term. This attitude remains shamefully unchallenged by the demining organisations themselves who reap side benefits from 'trials' programmes and consultancies to support these activities. Governments and other institutional donors are just too content to see funding diverted to this university department (x), or that research institution (y) which has fulfilled the bureaucratic criteria of coming up with a proposal that is just too sexy for its cover, or a MRE programme, a statistics- and data- gathering programme, just about anything that allows the huge trail of camp followers that the seemingly glamorous and righteous world of the demining industry has attracted, to be seen to be involved. In the sense of 'double dipping ' by arms companies, this R and D-*fest* is just another form of 'double dipping'. While all the time governments and donor institutions in the North can blithely quote the amount of money being allocated to Humanitarian Mine Action each year, the truth is that not much actually gets to the end of a breach lane in the minefield, and how much is actually creating local capacity through training? Again, not much[5]. It is this R and D activity, military research masquerading as humanitarian action, which does much to exemplify the niche that demining/HMA, has carved for itself to become another political-military foreign policy weapon, and a direct part of the MIC of the North. Landmines are low-tech weapons, clearing them requires low-tech solutions, and they already exist. The deminers know this.

4. Iraq. The Cover is Blown.

Iraq was envisaged by the US and UK governments as a showcase for the international community and its 'nation building' efforts in the wake of the 2003 invasion and enforced regime change. Many NGOs, including demining organisations, looked forward to lucrative contracts and publicity accompanying the occupation of Iraq, despite its controversial nature, and many NGOs did do an amount of soul searching before committing to projects in the country. Many NGOs, as well funded allies of the governments of the occupying powers, may of course have had no ultimate choice, as other funding for other programmes worldwide could be at risk. This is the crunch about having your cake and eating it. When you've signed up to be a foreign policy actor for your government, well, sometimes duty calls. Many NGOs fulfilled their 'force multiplier' roles as expected. Unfortunately, the rebuilding of Iraq remains opposed by a lethal and seemingly well-organised armed resistance, which may or may not also be linked to the wider global terror practised by those terrorists under the brand name of 'Al Qaeda'. The viewpoint of such extremists is that there is little difference between a US marine in chocolate chip camouflage riding an armoured personnel carrier smoking a Marlboro Light and an aid worker in a white T-shirt in his or her expensive, Western-built and -paid-for, white 4x4 smoking a Marlboro Light. They are all part of the crusading forces of the West, enemies, as they have been for a thousand years. This viewpoint is held from Afghanistan to Darfur, and is becoming widespread, including into the wider former Soviet Union and SE Asia.

NGOs and IOs have been attacked. We are all now too familiar with the horrific scenes shown by the world broadcast media of the aftermath of the suicide truck bombing of the Baghdad headquarters of the in-country mission of the International Committee of the Red Cross. NGOs have been attacked, or have simply found conditions too hostile in which to operate. One British demining NGO, had an expatriate staff member targeted and killed by militants in Iraq. The organisation had no choice then but to withdraw, although only days before the attack they had affirmed the fact that they would not be withdrawing from the country and were fully committed to assisting the Iraqi people. Noble ideals and brave words; it's an old tactic of hyping up threats against the noble staff toiling tirelessly to help the sick and the poor, which always spun well with the donors and an admiring public back home; but the usual rhetoric of commitment trotted out by NGOs *ad nauseam* in aid projects in the past in other countries just doesn't work in Iraq and is becoming less effective in Afghanistan. The price of taking the occupiers' coin is lethal attack resulting in death and injury, loss of impartiality and an exposure of the hollow meaning of the popular NGO jargon of 'inclusion', 'development', 'civil society building', 'indigenisation', 'dignity' or 'partnership'. The rules today are different.

Iraq stands as a salutatory lesson for those demining organisations that have for so long believed their own propaganda whilst conveniently overlooking who their paymasters truly are and what agenda they are working within. The fact is that the post-Cold War honeymoon is over, and that local populations are resentful, suspicious or simply hostile.

5. "HMA is here for good."

I have previously discussed arms companies and the concepts of 'double dipping' - profiting from manufacture, sale and clearance, whether operationally or through lucrative R and D projects. I want to move on now to consider landmines themselves, where their place is in the food chain of weapons technology and proliferation to the developing world. In effect, where do demining organisations get their lucrative business?

Unlike for example, a furniture company, arms companies never have to take financial risks. The 'national interest' of Western states protects their own MIC from such risk. In effect, the taxpayer underwrites the R and D, production and sale, and the transfer of weapons technology. This includes landmines and their hybrids and derivatives. (Landmines, being so cheap, are often thrown in as part of arms deals). Producing weapons under the MIC system of the West is often done on a one-for-one basis. That is, you make two, issue one to your own forces, and sell the other one to subsidise your own weapons procurement programme and 'save' the taxpayer money. Since many such weapon systems are sold to countries overseas that may at some stage move out of the camp (note Iraq again), you may have to use your weapon system against the one you sold a few years ago to your erstwhile ally[6]. Given that arms sales and associated, often innocuous-seeming technology generate enormous revenue for many Western countries means that in effect, the West has through this cycle actually become economically dependent on arms production and sale, thus keeping the world in a state where we must actually permanently anticipate or prosecute war. Everything from Teflon to the Internet was originally designed for military use. Thus, dismantling the MIC would severely impact the Western economy and way of life, not result in the simple exercise of swords to ploughshares so beloved of the peace movement and that eclectic mix of activists at the vanguard of the anti-mine ban with its wider disarmament agenda. Ironically, the industrialised West needs war, or thinks it needs war, to continue to grow the economy and to spread the free market into other parts of the world.

Because it is true that in the violent South, during and after the Cold War and to this day, the West has prosecuted war in the name of peace. NGOs and HMA NGOs go hand-in-hand with this strategy. Strange,then, that the Ottawa anti-landmines crusaders effectively endorsed the political-military agenda that is the veneer of HMA, when the ink had hardly dried on the treaty. A truly Faustian pact.

The Ottawa treaty is a failure of international law within the sphere of international relations; it is in the interest of many Western nations for it to be precisely such a failure. Heralded with rhetoric as ‘no exceptions, no loopholes’, it has in fact proved to be so worthless that the language of the campaigners has shifted in the past seven years to ‘a step in the right direction’. Key signatory states have caveats appended to their signature, and at least two signatory states have used landmines since ratifying the treaty and accepting vast amounts of mine clearance aid. Let us be clear, the technology and means of production of landmines has already been transferred to states and non-state actors outside the reach of Ottawa. In this sense alone Ottawa failed, because it came years too late and of course, that actually suits HMA organisations who will continue to profit from intra-state wars. It is little wonder they are finding it increasingly difficult to work in ‘anti-Western’ countries, where in fact mine clearance is urgently needed.

What further compounds this great tragedy is that despite the years of immoral behaviour by the North toward states of the South through the prosecution of the Cold War by proxy, that with Ottawa, moral behaviour is somehow expected from the impoverished, traumatized and intransigently warlike South that we helped create.

Despite the support of many development organizations for the ICBL and Ottawa process, many hoary old development hands knew it wasn’t going to work. Decades of experience in conflict situations all over the world demonstrated that people will fight with whatever comes to hand or is given to them. The Rwandan genocide was carried out mainly with farm implements. It is unlikely there be an international campaign to ban farm tools.

The ICBL, as a transnational social movement, should have devoted itself to working with small arms projects to attack the arms transfer process and licensing system, instead of an expensive and emotive charade. Ottawa was designed by the West, with Western 'post-modernist' values, to placate Western liberal consciences, whilst not actually impacting the military capacity of Wetern nations, but severely impacting the defence capacities of many Southern developing states to protect themselves against,for example, Western intervention. At best, it criminalises them. The Ottawa treaty has thus given the highly sophisticated Western military another edge over potential future enemies. This observation has not been lost on many developing states, such as the Sudan. Thomas Jefferson once said that the longbow democratized warfare, it made the humble able to combat and destroy the noble. He would have said the same of the landmine; for its simplicity of use, requiring limited training, means that hi-tech forces can be thwarted and made to suffer by low-tech forces. The concept has morphed in that cradle of warfare the Middle East, to the roadside IED and even to the suicide bomber, the ultimate melding of the victim- or target-operated trap and offensive weapon of terror.

The core of the anti-landmines campaign began and was continually supported by Christian non-conformist religious traditions such as the Mennonites and Quakers; which compounds how sinister this Faustian alliance indeed is, as it actually has served to align the elements of the peace movement, anti-mine campaigners and their organisations with Western governments and their political-military agendas in the developing South and has directly contributed to the massive encroachment of the humanitarian sector by military interests and conspicuously compromised its neutrality. The international system of arms licensing will ensure that existing landmine or victim-operated weapons production remains deeply buried. Enough to make Tom Paine or Hugo Grotius weep.

6. A New Deal

The modern world after the Cold War is shaped by what Hans Holsti has described as the US-UK condominium, that is, an Anglo-centric world. NGOs are a key part of this new *Kulturtrager*, so despised in the developing world. The environments in which NGOs work are becoming increasingly hostile. Over one year after the Indian Ocean Tsunami of Boxing Day 2004, millions of dollars remain unspent, projects have not commenced, and dislodged landmines remained uncleared. In part this is the fault of unwieldy and inefficient NGO hierarchies, but it is also due to the political opposition that NGOs face in host countries. This is due to the suspicion of political manipulation that comes with the NGOs and their money. Mine Action has intractable links to issues of political economy, military security, public health, food security and development. It has an important place in the field of international relations and as a 'low political' issue in international law.

The Western military establishments have been creeping into humanitarian arena for three decades; this accelerated after the Cold War. The Balkan wars in the nineties provided the military a perfect showcase in which to consolidate their position.

The development community reacted with dismay when in April 2004 the foreign ministers of the OSCE member states meeting in Paris decided that in future, military involvement in humanitarian interventions would be paid for from members' development budgets. This significant decision only made column inches in the print media; the reaction of the development organizations was masked by the media prioritisation of the war in Iraq. In the UK, this is called burying bad news. Dutch development NGOs alone estimate this will cost them 10m euros over the next five years[7].

The Western-centric geography of the NGO world, especially the demining NGOs has to be readily shifted from North to South. Why describe being in say Afghanistan or Angola as 'the field'? Is an American academic at a conference in Europe 'in the field'? Policy, agendas and decisions need to be made in Luanda, not in London. Modern means of communication and cheaper travel preclude the need for expensive suites of offices to be maintained in the rent-heavy capitals of Europe or North America. Representative offices should be maintained, but only for dissemination of information and donor liaison where necessary. In effect, the NGOs should see the South as their natural location, their place of work and the North as 'the field' where they obtain resources and human capital where required. The shift in perspective is essential.

What is needed is a new mandate, a new contract with the South. HMA NGOs must break their own cycle of financial and political dependence on government back-donors. A step toward this would be the acknowledgement that in fact, they don't need to be running highly expensive and overtly sophisticated programmes. Training teams and advisory support is in fact all that is really required.

Surely it is acceptable, arguable that local, impacted communities have actually a right to clear their own mines, as I would posit, as a form of resistance to or protest against conflict, and to thus demand exclusion of continued military activity. Further, they can demand that NGOs with a clear military political identity can be excluded from benefiting from contracts to clear mines in their communities. Thus HMA and HMA actors can build specialisation in development activity and one that gives real impetus to building genuine human security in impacted marginalised communities.

They would, in effect, take control, restore dignity and strengthen their civil society through control and implementation of such actions. I emphasise that I do not take issue with the courage and commitment of many who work, as I do, as mine clearance specialists in developing countries. Rather, my quarrel is with the nature of the juggernaut that controls their actions. This can only be achieved if the communities themselves are liberated from the political military actors who claim to act in their name. They can reject the interlocutors of their misery by rejecting political-military 'humanitarian' aid and take control of their own peaceful future.

Notes

[1] Explosive Ordnance Disposal (EOD).

[2] That is not to say that indeed training by expatriates in clearance and neutralisation techniques and the logistics thereof is not important in immediate post-conflict situations, given the generally high standards of Western military forces. But it is clear that day-to-day programme management in Southern programmes now lasts for years on end. After 15 years of HMA, there is genuinely no need for such reliance on the expertise of developed countries.

2. Some do this by limiting by charter the amount of institutional or government funds they will accept every year and tailor their programmes accordingly. Interestingly many that do this receive huge public support precisely because of this policy. For example, Médecins sans Frontières accepts only 40% of funds from government sources every year. See www.msf.org.

[4] This organisation actually evacuated the British Embassy during the crisis during the Soviet withdrawal in 1989.

[5] See www.ICBL.org. Each donor nation quotes figures of annual funds for HMA. Note the amount per country for actual landmine clearance.

[6] The Soviet Union sold 'monkey' (ess sophisticated)versions of their weaponry to clients, in order that they would face inferior weaponry in the event of the client changing sides and having to be fought against.

[7] Newspaper: The Trouw. Netherlands 14th April 2004.

‘Paedophiles’ in Contemporary Culture

Sarah Dalal Goode

Abstract: This chapter explores current understandings of paedophilia and child sexual abuse, particularly in the United Kingdom. The focus of the chapter is on heterosexual paedophilia and child sexual abuse, because statistically it is heterosexual abuse which affects the greatest number of children. The first section reviews three key events in the UK over the last six years which have shaped our understanding and triggered significant public responses. Section Two will then go on to discuss competing understandings of paedophilia and child sexual abuse, as demonstrated through examples including tabloid newspaper stories, the charity campaign Full Stop, television comedy, the multi-lingual pro-paedophile website Puellula and the mainstream Hollywood film *The Woodsman*. The final section explores some implications of these competing understandings and presents an overview of recent public health initiatives which attempt to address these issues. It concludes by providing recommendations for developing our response to this urgent social problem.

Key Words: paedophilia, puellula, child sexual abuse, sex offender.

1. Introduction

This chapter explores current understandings of paedophilia and child sexual abuse, particularly in the United Kingdom. The focus of the chapter is on heterosexual paedophilia and child sexual abuse, because statistically it is heterosexual abuse which affects the greatest number of children.[1] Section Two starts by reviewing three key events in the UK over the last six years which have shaped our understanding and triggered significant public responses. Section Three will then go on to discuss competing understandings of paedophilia and child sexual abuse, as demonstrated through examples including tabloid newspaper stories, the charity campaign Full Stop, television comedy, the multi-lingual pro-paedophile website Puellula and the mainstream Hollywood film *The Woodsman*. The final section explores some implications of these competing understandings and presents an overview of recent public health initiatives which attempt to address these issues. It concludes by providing recommendations for developing our response to this urgent social problem.

---

2. Three Key Events in the UK from 2000

A. 2000, murder of Sarah Payne

The narrative begins on the 1st July 2000, when Sarah Payne, an 8-year-old, was murdered by a man who had served a prison sentence for previously sexually attacking a young girl. The police had known, since his release from prison in 1995, that he was a threat to girls but were unable to do anything about this until he committed another offence. After her death, the parents of Sarah Payne, supported by a national newspaper, *The News of the World*, campaigned for people to have the right to know if there were convicted paedophiles living in their community. This campaign for community notification was known as Sarah's Law, similar to Megan's Law in the United States.

Prior to this, earlier cases of children being sexually attacked and murdered had given rise to the Sex Offenders Act, passed in 1997. This Act had imposed a requirement for the first time on those convicted of sex offences against children and other serious sex offences to register their name and address, and any subsequent changes, with the police. In the debate leading up to the passing of this Act the MP David Mellor, in the House of Commons in 1997, had expressed the view[2]:

> Having decided that it is right that the police should be able to keep tabs on people and that their addresses should be notified, we shall have to confront the problem ...that, if the police have a right to know, why do the public not have the right to know? If someone with a string of convictions for sexual offences against children moves into a house, why should the nice young family living next door not be told about him? Why should the community not be told?
>
> If we believe that paedophiles are in a category entirely on their own, we should consider whether it would be appropriate to take the exceptional step of saying that, when a paedophile lives in a neighbourhood, all those living in the neighbourhood should know. ... I believe that, in the longer run, we shall be hard put to resist the claims, which will undoubtedly come, that something should be done so that the public are let in on the secret about who is living in their street.

Three years after Mellor's speech those claims did come, in the public response to Sarah Payne's murder, with unprecedented anti-paedophile rioting which lasted over two months in areas across England and Wales.

Nevertheless, in contrast to the adoption of community notification in the United States, the UK has so far resisted claims to make details of convicted paedophiles available to members of the public. Although the Government decided against any form of Sarah's Law, it did allow public involvement – in a very diluted form - in the form of membership as a lay adviser of MAPPA (Multi-Agency Public Protection Arrangements) panels. Proposed in the wake of the public outcry for a right to know, this scheme now involves a maximum total of eighty-four members of the public across the country – a far cry from the public knowledge demanded by proponents of Sarah's Law.

There continue to be calls for changes in legislation to allow communities to know if sex offenders are living in their neighbourhoods – the latest example is from Scotland, where a petition of 5000 signatures was presented to the Scottish Parliament on 8th September 2005, calling for 'Mark's Law' after the murder of 8-year-old Mark Cummings, again by a known sex offender.[3]

B. 2002, murders of Holly Wells and Jessica Chapman

The next event in the narrative is the murder of two ten year old girls by a man working as a school caretaker, and known to the police in another part of the country as a possible risk to girls (following a number of allegations). Again, although the evidence of risk was there, it had not been acted on, this time because it was obscured both by non-communication between authorities and also because the man involved had not actually been convicted of any offences, only cautioned.

This double murder of Holly Wells and Jessica Chapman led to the setting up of a formal Inquiry chaired by Sir Michael Bichard. The remit was to inquire into child protection procedures, with a focus on record-keeping, vetting practices and information-sharing. The Report of the Bichard Inquiry was published two years later on 22nd June 2004. It called for a national computer-based intelligence system and a new centralised registration or barring scheme for those working with children, to be delivered by 2007. Progress was made rapidly and less than a year later Bichard commented that "[W]e are on the verge of having in the United Kingdom a coherent set of protective measures unrivalled anywhere."[4]

The main response to the Bichard Report was to establish ViSOR - the Violent Offender and Sex Offender Register, operational across the UK from May 2005. This is a national database which holds information on individuals convicted of sex offences, or jailed for more than twelve months for violence. From August 2005, it has also held information on people not convicted of any offence but suspected of offences and who are assessed as posing a risk.

C. 2006, sex offenders working in schools

The third event in the narrative occurred on 8th January 2006, when disclosure of the case of a sex offender being allowed to work in schools highlighted the existence of a number of separate and incompatible sex-offender lists being used by different departments, and anomalies such as ministers over-ruling police advice.[5] Again, there was a rapid response by Government and a tightening-up of procedures. Just eleven days after the scandal broke, a public statement was issued announcing an overhaul of the current system to make it "immeasurably strengthened and fundamentally rebalanced"[6] by proposed new vetting and barring procedures, providing access for "all employers, including domestic employers such as parents contracting private tutors, to make secure, instant online checks of an applicant's status." [7]

Thus it is evident that, over the last six years, there has been a series of incidents which have prompted a response of increasing information-gathering. However, this is not primarily by or to inform the public (which was the original intention of the public campaign) but primarily by and to inform the authorities, anxious to vet and bar and make clear distinctions between the good, normal, individual and the dangerous, deviant, individual.

3. Conflicting Understandings

This response in the UK relies on a particular understanding of paedophiles and child sexual abusers, an understanding summed up by the MP David Mellor in the phrase "paedophiles are in a category entirely on their own". This view of paedophiles as unique, and uniquely dangerous, allows us to endorse encroachments on fundamental civil rights, including (by keeping a register of those who are suspected but not convicted) overturning the basic principle of English law that suspects are innocent until proven guilty in a court of law. Our demand for "a coherent set of protective measures unrivalled anywhere", as Sir Michael Bichard described it in 2005, has led us now to the brink of having "secure, instant online checks" available for all employers, including householders wanting home tutors, and these measure are likely to be fully in place by the summer of 2006.

Is this what we wanted? Why have we arrived at this point? Would these measures have prevented the murders of Sarah Payne, Holly

Wells, Jessica Chapman or Mark Cummings? Will they prevent future sexual murders and future child sexual abuse?

Every year in the UK, of approximately 12 million children, around eight children will be murdered by strangers.[8] A proportion of these murders will be sexually-motivated. Meanwhile, roughly another seventy will be murdered by someone known to them.[9] Around a third of these - over twenty - will be babies killed by a parent.[10] Altogether over 4000 children aged from birth to fourteen will die of causes other than murder[11], usually from accidental injury.[12] Again, if we compare the murder rate for children (around 80 per 12 million children) with the murder rate for adults (approximately 800 per 48 million[13]), the murder rate for adults is nearly three times as high.

These statistics suggest that responses such as ViSOR are an over-reaction. If we want to prevent agonising and needless deaths of children, then preventing half-a-dozen sadistic murders by paedophiles may, from a utilitarian point of view, be of less merit than, say, stopping stressed-out parents shaking their little babies to death, or enforcing speed-limits, or fitting smoke-detectors.[14]

At the same time, somewhere in the region of one in every six children (around two million children in the UK) will be sexually abused, frequently by someone known to them and often by a member of their own family.[15] This reality is not generally represented in the popular media, where the emphasis on paedophiles and 'stranger danger' tends to encourage a sense that if we can protect ourselves and our children from 'those people out there' then all will be well - if we can only know who those people are who constitute the danger, and if we know where they live and where they work, then the problem of child sexual abuse will be solved. A number of influential organisations in the United Kingdom, including newspapers, national charities and at times the Government, tend to encourage this optimistic view. If only we can add enough names to the ViSOR database, then we will be safe.

This sharply-defined distinction between 'the normal' and 'the paedophile' also encourages the use of a particular language of extreme evil and wickedness. It becomes easier, within this moral dichotomy, to portray paedophiles as ruthless, cunning and devious 'others', more animal than human – like sharks or vultures circling round their prey, like snakes hiding in the grass or, like foxes, fit only to be hunted down. Rather than refer to 'child sexual abuser', national newspapers such as the *Sun* use terms such as 'vile', 'sick', 'perv', 'sex field', 'beast', 'monster' and so forth, [16] all terms which serve both to dehumanise the perpetrator and to essentialise their behaviour.

The concept of essentialism is a well-rehearsed one within sociological discourse. It has been used to explain and define normative behaviour among individuals or types of individuals in a variety of ways. Although it can be used in a positive context, for example the study by Sara Ruddick on valuing the nurturing and peace-loving attributes associated with biological femaleness[17], essentialism is more usually seen as a way of explaining devalued and deviant behaviour. Identifying the cause of evil behaviour as located within the essential nature of particular individuals (rather than within, for example, social structures or interactions) can be seen as serving at least three functions: it absolves the rest of society from guilt or blame (it is not our fault, that person is evil and therefore was always going to behave like that no matter what we did); it marks out the individual as different (that person is utterly other than us, there is nothing about our behaviour which is similar); and it allows blame-free scapegoating and rejection of that individual (if someone is utterly other and evil, then they deserve whatever they get and we don't need to feel sorry for them).

Regarding types of individuals as essentially other and evil allows us to scapegoat them. The anthropologist Mary Douglas, for example, has explored the process of scapegoating as a way of dealing with 'interstitial categories' – groups of people who do not fit into the broad framework of society. She uses the example of the witch in African tribal societies, a woman who typically does not fit neatly into the categories of daughter, wife or mother, but 'falls between the cracks' between these categories[18]. She links the scapegoating process to the use of 'libels'. The dominant group make libellous or slanderous accusations of depraved behaviour (such as the accusation that the scapegoated group eat the wrong sorts of food, engage in the wrong sorts of sex, or kill the wrong sorts of people) in order to mark groups out as sufficiently different and evil for them to then be metaphorically or literally expelled out of society, for example through the social rejection of people with Aids or through murder of Jewish or Gypsy communities.

In a similar way, it would appear that people who are sexually attracted to children are essentialised as depraved and evil. As with homosexuals prior to the 1970s, they are clearly vulnerable to what Douglas terms the sex libel – they have sex with the wrong sorts of people. Perhaps they can also be seen to some extent as fulfilling Douglas' concept of an 'interstitial category' – they may be regarded as neither fully adult nor child, but somewhere in between, adult in development but remaining attracted to an age-group much younger than their current chronological age. Defining paedophiles as essentially evil performs the three functions referred to above. Firstly, it makes it unnecessary for us to examine what it might be about contemporary society which contributes to or constructs a problematic relationship between adults, children, and sex. Secondly, it obviates any necessity for us to examine what it is about human sexuality in general which includes the possibility of sexual attraction to children. Thirdly, it removes any necessity from us of responding empathically, since the only rational responses to an essentially evil individual are rejection or destruction. Thus, when tabloid newspapers use phrases such as 'nasty pervs' or 'evil monsters', they enable us – the mainstream public – to separate off the category of paedophile from the category of 'ordinary person' and thereby remove the possibility that we could understand a paedophile or respond in any way other than disgust and revulsion.

In an interesting twist, this reliance on the category of the 'paedophile' as the essence of evil and depravity now seems to have given rise to its use even in a context where it appears actually irrelevant. For example, a news item in the *News of the World*[19], the British tabloid referred to earlier, uses the language and imagery typical of the coverage usually given to child sexual abuse crimes despite the fact that the offender featured in this particular article, Iorworth Hoare, has apparently been convicted of sexual offences (rape, attempted rape and assault) against adults and not against children:

> "EVERY woman and girl in Britain must today be on her guard—for freed Lotto rapist Iorworth Hoare is on the prowl again.
>
> The News of the World TWICE caught the sex beast leering at unsuspecting schoolgirls out for an innocent lunchtime stroll.
>
> And Hoare is only one of a horde of monsters released from jail to kill, rape or maim again and again. …
>
> Hoare—a lifelong sex offender who was sentenced to life but released after 16 years—walked A MILE out of his way to stroll past three schools, swivelling his head to lech over the giggling girls.
>
> Now his neighbours around the upmarket Darras Hall estate in Ponteland, Northumberland, are terrified. One worried parent said last night: "He's a walking nightmare for us. We all fear he could strike at any time." Our shock pictures show 53-year-old Hoare, who won £7million Lotto cash in jail, watching two sets of girls intently.

> First he fixed them with a menacing stare as they approached him in the tree-lined streets. Then as the oblivious girls passed he turned to ogle them from behind. A neighbour who saw the entire scene told us: "There were three girls aged 14 or 15 in the first group and Hoare couldn't take his eyes off them. When they walked by he actually stopped, turned and glared at them for ages as they moved away.
> "It was so blatant. He was obviously leching after them. A few minutes later he did exactly the same thing as another two girls passed. He stared at them walking off into the distance for about four seconds."
> The most disturbing thing about Leeds-born Hoare's predatory prowl is the roundabout route he took from his luxury £700,000 home—to maximise his opportunities for crossing the path of teenage girls.
> The neighbour told us: "He left his home at lunchtime and walked for about a mile to a cashpoint. Then he went to a baker's, bought a pie and ate it. But all the time he was very furtive as if he was looking out for someone. He then took a much longer route home which took him about a mile out of his way. I thought it was odd—but then I realised it was because he wanted to walk past THREE schools as all the girls were coming out for their midday break.
> "It's an absolute scandal that people like Hoare … are free to put innocent communities like us in terror. … we've all told our children to keep as far away from him as they can."
> The parents of Ponteland are right to be worried. [this comment is followed by a description of attacks against adult women and the article concludes] …Now the families of Ponteland can only keep watch and pray THEIR luck holds out."

Thus, even though in this case the sex offender being described is not known to be a paedophile and has not been convicted of sexual offences against children, the references throughout the article are to the 'sex beast leering at unsuspecting schoolgirls', 'horde of monsters', 'worried parent', 'predatory prowl', 'teenage girls', 'furtive', 'parents of Ponteland' and 'families of Ponteland' – all terms usually associated with an article about a child sexual abuser rather than an adult sexual abuser. The threat to adult women is entirely downplayed, despite the fact that in the article the judge involved in Hoare's most recent case, Judge Richard Rougier, is quoted as saying; "Every moment [he is] at liberty, some woman is at risk … If I were a woman I wouldn't feel safe with him living near me."

Advertising campaigns by national charities have also made use of the dehumanising and essentialising category of 'paedophile', this time in order to raise money. An example of this is the Full Stop campaign run by a major British charity, the National Society for the Prevention of Cruelty to Children (NSPCC), which used a leaflet inserted into a number of targeted newspapers and magazines. The front and back of this leaflet (undated but in circulation in 2005), printed in green and black, showed three statements designed to look like headlines torn from newspapers and taken from actual headlines used by *Daily Mail*, *Daily Mirror* and *Metro* newspapers. The headlines are: 'Scarred for life by child abuse', 'Paedophile groomed boy, 14, for sex ring', and 'Britain's worst paedophile'. Beneath these headlines, the caption reads 'The more of them there are, the more we need you.' Inside the leaflet, the text includes information on the NSPCC Specialist Investigation Service and a Banker's Order form for donations to the charity. The text also includes the following:

> "Every day it seems there is another story about a child suffering terrible abuse at the hands of paedophiles. We read about how paedophiles get jobs where they can be close to children. We hear how they spend weeks 'grooming' their victims, earning their trust and frightening them into silence. You may also have heard of paedophile 'rings' – groups of child abusers sharing photographs of abuse and information about their child victims so others can target them.
>
> It's all true. And worst of all is the fact that these are only the ones who have been caught. *Three quarters of children do not tell anyone they are suffering sexual abuse at the time* [emphases in original]. So we can't tell you exactly how many children are being abused right now, too scared or ashamed to speak up."

The text concludes with the following appeal: 'Because paedophiles are organised, we must be better organised. Because they are cunning, we must be more intelligent. Because they are many, we must have the support of many more – as many people as are willing to help us protect children. Please be one of them.'

Statements such as these feed into the view, as discussed above, that paedophiles are so different as to be essentially evil and 'other', they are not like human beings. They are organised (not like us); they have animal-like cunning (where we, as humans, must be intelligent to counter them); and there are many of them – they are an unknown and unknowable threat around us. Taken together with other information garnered from the media, such statements build into a normative social construction of paedophiles, a taken-for-granted commonsense understanding which is shared by mainstream society. This understanding contains the view that, for example, while paedophiles are almost always men, they are radically different from other men. Paedophiles are different from child molesters, child sexual abusers, incest perpetrators, and other sexually abnormal men. Paedophiles are often homosexual. Paedophiles are likely to murder children. Paedophiles are increasingly common. Paedophiles are a serious and frightening threat. Paedophiles are cunning and devious. Paedophiles 'groom'. Paedophiles lurk on the internet. Paedophiles are evil. Paedophiles suffer from a psychopathology, a chronic psychiatric disorder listed in the Diagnostic and Statistical Manual of Diseases (DSM-IV). Paedophiles are different from us. Paedophiles are strangers.

This view of paedophiles has become so prevalent and powerful that, in Britain, it has triggered a comic backlash, poking fun at our sense of horror. This is evident in the *Brass Eye* spoof documentary on paedophilia[20], for example, which was broadcast twice on British television in July 2001, only a year after the murder of Sarah Payne and the outburst of anti-paedophile rioting across Britain. This programme suggested, among other things, that internet paedophiles can project poison gas through a child's keyboard, using a new system known as HOECS (pronounced 'hoax') and included numerous contributions from celebrities who did not realise that the entire programme was itself a hoax: one of the contributors was the MP for Paulsgrove, the main housing estate where the anti-paedophile rioting had taken place, who pontificated solemnly about dangers such as inflatable trousers used by paedophiles to obscure their erections.

A more recent example of this comic backlash is the character of the Paedofinder-General in the British animated cartoon series *Monkey Dust* [21], an award-winning series shown first on the digital channel BBC3 and later, presumably due to high viewing-figures, shown on the more mainstream channel BBC2. The Paedofinder-General follows on from an earlier character, the Internet Predator, a faceless but physically repellent elderly figure at his computer, attempting unsuccessfully to set up meetings with children from online chat-rooms. The Paedofinder-General is altogether more vigorous and violent, a terrifying hooded character who accosts men seen with children and accuses them of paedophilia. In one episode, for example, his accusation of paedophilia is made on the grounds that the man is wearing swimming-trunks with the logo 'peedo' on them. The man protests that the logo is in fact 'Speedo' (a well-known brand) but this does not save him: he is summarily executed. In another episode, a father playing on the beach with his children is accosted and accused of giving his child a '69'. When he protests that it was in fact a '99' (a type of ice-cream), the Paedofinder-General is horrified at how much worse a '99' must be than a '69' and the man is again summarily executed, by hanging, along with the children, who are also hanged on the basis that abused children grow up to be abusers. A family watching the public execution are delighted at the outcome and the little boy of the family comments happily that this is the best holiday he has had. These and similar episodes clearly draw on events such as the anti-paedophile riots in Bristol and Portsmouth in 2000, and the infamous incident in which a paediatrician had her house daubed with the slogan 'paedo'[22].

What we would appear to have in contemporary Britain, therefore, whether promulgated by the Government, the media or national charities, is a mainstream view of paedophiles as evil in their very essence, dehumanised and other – a view generally unchallenged except by occasional dissonant touches of bleak and quirky dark humour.

While mainstream media is offering this vision of clear moral distinction and unambiguous consensus on evil, one has only to log on to the internet to find significantly different versions of reality. It is clear that the internet hosts a number of sites actively promoting paedophilia as both a sexual activity and as a political identity akin to other oppressed sexual minorities. On these sites, paedophilia is often presented in terms of a romantic appreciation of young children, little girls in particular, where paedophiles talk of being 'in love' with children. Self-defined paedophiles such as Lindsay Ashford, who runs a number of websites on paedophilia, are keen to make a distinction between paedophiles (good) and 'child molesters'(bad), arguing that children should have the right to have sex with adults, and that without this legal right children are unfairly disenfranchised.

For example, one of the websites copyrighted to Ashford, Puellula (www.puellula.com), greets visitors with saccharine invitations to celebrate 'the splendor of little girls', and includes on its home-page a Latin verse from the writings of the mediaeval nun Hildegard von Bingen. The verse, which one assumes was originally written in praise of Jesus, is translated as:

O loveliest form,
O sweetest scent of desired delights;
Always we sigh for you
In this mournful exile;
When shall we see you and abide with you?

We are in the world,
And you are in our minds,
And we embrace you in our hearts
As if we had you present.

The website Puellula, which is hosted in the Netherlands, is available in English, Czech, Polish, Spanish, French and Italian and the purpose of the website, according to Ashford, is to 'explain my ideal of consensual childlove'. Visitors are invited to explore the site with the following exhortation:

> "Welcome to Puellula, a place to celebrate little girls in all of their splendor! Nothing can compare to the beauty of a little girl's smile, to the sound of her laugh, to the smell of her hair or the velvet touch of her hands. This is the place to explore that beauty, to marvel at the exquisite grace of the angels who ceaselessly brighten our days and bring winsome smiles to our lips. Enter into our midst with wonder and expectation. Tarry as long as you please. Depart with joy and elation."

There are a number of sections to the website, some of them perhaps rather surprising. For example, as well as a section entitled 'Anne Frank: Flower in a Crannied Wall', the website also includes a memorial website called 'Taken from our Midst' on girls who have been murdered, including those murdered for sexual gratification. Here we can see photographs of Sarah Payne, Holly Wells and Jessica Chapman, among many others. This may not be what one would expect and visitors to this site may find it startling and unsettling to be confronted with sentimental memorials to 'little angels' murdered by - among others - paedophiles, on a pro-paedophile web-site. Incongruities such as these point to the extreme level of conflicting understandings on paedophilia within contemporary society.

Another, perhaps equally disturbing section of the Puellula website is titled 'Sugar and Spice'. This claims to be 'Just for Girls!' (although - one assumes - written entirely by Ashford) and is described as being:

> "THE place for young girls who want to learn about love and romance. Falling in love is a very exciting thing that every girl experiences at some time in her life. Many times she falls in love with a boy her age, but sometimes she may fall in love with another girl or even with an adult. It is important for her to realize that there is nothing wrong with falling in love with anybody, regardless of their age or gender, as long as she is doing what SHE wants to do."

The site then goes on to discuss questions about 'what is love?', 'how old do I have to be?', kinds of touching, links to sites on 'girl' issues (including a large number on sexual issues), and sections on 'Girllovers' and 'Special Friendships'. There is a great deal of use of the word 'special'. For example, the section on Special Friendships states:

> "When an adult and a young girl discover that they like each other very much, this is the beginning of one of the most special types of relationship anybody can have! A girl and a loving adult can form a very special bond, as the adult provides experience and knowledge, and the girl provides a fresh way of seeing the world and her excitement for life.
>
> Special friendships usually start out as friendly love, but over time they begin to look like a combination of spiritual love and romantic love. This means that the young girl and her special friend begin to understand each other very deeply and to care about each other very much. It also means that they miss each other very much when they don't see each other, and always eagerly look forward to the times when they can be together!
>
> As special friendships develop, a girl and her special friend learn many things about each other, sharing their ideas, thoughts and feelings with each other. This results in each occupying a very special place in the other's heart. Special friendships can be very long-lasting, and special friends usually remain friends even if their romantic feelings for each other eventually fade way [sic]."

Although there is a great deal of use of the word 'special' there is no use in these sections of the words 'sex' or 'sexual'. This is particularly obvious in the section on Girllovers where Ashford attempts to define 'Good people and bad people' without any reference to sexual acts:

> "A long time ago, girllovers were called pedophiles. Back in those days, people understood that pedophiles were simply people who loved children in the same way that girllovers love girls today. Unfortunately, when people hear the word pedophile now, they think it means child molester. A child molester is a very evil person who hurts children. Girllovers do not like child molesters at all, and think that child molesters should go to jail. While a girllover wants to make girls happy and do only things the girl wants to do, child molesters are selfish people and want to force girls to do things that they don't want to do. Unfortunately, even some good people can become bad. Some girllovers lose the ability to exercise self-control, and become selfish, and these things sometimes result in them doing bad things. The main difference between girllovers and child molesters is very simple: girllovers want to love and to give, while child molesters only want to take and are not interested in love."

One wonders what age-range this explanation is aimed at, and what the average 'young girl' would make of phrases about losing 'the ability to exercise self-control' or only wanting 'to take' – how could any child make sense of convoluted euphemisms like these? Such a deliberately coy description seems particularly odd, given that the aim of this site is apparently about helping girls 'learn' and given also that this site links to a number of other more sexually-explicit sites.

Ashford also offers a ten-point covenant that your 'special friend' might want to make with you. The covenant is solely from the perspective of the adult (rather giving the lie to the romantic notion that this is a mutual and equal relationship) and contains ten items that the adult 'will always' do:

> "treat you with dignity and respect; put your wellbeing ahead of my own; give to you first before accepting anything from you; stop when you tell me to stop; avoid the use of force, coercion or manipulation to get my way with you; do my utmost to ensure that no physical or emotional harm comes to you; strive to encourage and contribute to your emotional, intellectual and spiritual development; answer your questions with honesty and sensitivity; respect your opinions, thoughts and wishes; ask rather than assume".

This quasi-chivalrous attitude appears to have some currency on the internet. Lindsay Ashford's websites are linked to many other pro-paedophile sites on 'girl-love', 'boy-love' and 'child-love', although the term which he has coined to use instead of paedophile, 'amarso' (plural, amaros) does not appear to have taken off in popularity - it produces only a small number of hits on Google (distinct from the Zimbabwean place-name of Amarso).

However, despite the efforts of Ashford and his colleagues to promote a positive and updated view of paedophilia as chivalrous, caring and protective of children, there is still a clear disjuncture for many men between their experiences of being sexually attracted to children and their wish to define themselves as paedophile. For example, a police operation conducted in 2002, Operation Ore, picked up 7272 men in Britain who had accessed sites advertising images of little girls (aged from 9 upwards) advertised as looking 'pretty' or 'pretty and sexy'.[23] One user of such internet child porn sites, a man known as Jim Bell, in an article in the *Guardian* newspaper, explains why men using such sites do not identify as paedophiles, even though they are collecting and masturbating to images of young girls, and at least some of whom are likely to be actively sexually abusing children, as well as accessing pornography. In his explanation, using language reminiscent of Ashford's, he states that the men are masturbating not because the images are sexually graphic but because the men see the girls as being innocent and pretty and this fits in with cultural norms of men being attracted to and 'protecting' innocent little girls.[24]

A further example of this is the 2005 movie *The Woodsman*[25], the only mainstream Hollywood movie where the central character is a paedophile. In one scene in the film, we see the central character, Walter, a 45-year-old man played by the actor Kevin Bacon, 'chatting up' an 11-year-old girl, Robin, in the park. Walter wants to hold Robin, sit her on his lap, smell her hair, and rub himself against her. He links this back to his feelings as a small boy for his little sister, whom he still loves and misses. Walter distinguishes in his own mind between himself and a character he calls Candy, who is clearly shown seducing young boys. He also distinguishes himself from men who have violently sexually assaulted girls.

In the film Walter regards himself as gentle and loving, perhaps almost as the Woodsman of the title - in the traditional children's story the Woodsman who rescues Little Red Riding Hood from the Big Bad Wolf. Walter therefore would agree with Lindsay Ashford on the distinction between the 'good' paedophile who wants to cherish and 'celebrate' little girls (by smelling their hair or masturbating against them) and the 'bad' child molester who wants to hurt little girls (by raping them). Walter's attitude, that he is loving and appreciative - and protective - towards young girls, is one which appears to be shared by many of the men picked up by Operation Ore, of whom a significant proportion regularly worked with children. Returning to the article by Jim Bell, he describes the content of much internet child pornography as being not about sex but:

> about innocence: the sexual innocence of the child offered for the pleasure of adults [sic] who have no innocence left. … it was fatally easy for 7000 men to convince themselves that looking at pictures of heartbreakingly pretty little girls was not wrong. It is why I do not find it surprising that men who enjoyed teaching children, or keeping them safe in society, should have enjoyed such pictures. … In prison I met perhaps 100 men who had been convicted of offences against children. None of them admitted that they were paedophiles – none. The social stigma is too appalling. I cannot admit what I am to myself. ... None of us use that word or even admit to ourselves the thought.[26]

In this extract Bell makes two interesting comments. Firstly he refers to men 'looking at' (although perhaps a more accurate description might be 'masturbating to') pictures of 'heartbreakingly pretty' girls. 'Heartbreakingly pretty' is a very romantic, adolescent, even asexual, turn of phrase. It is reminiscent of puppy-love, Valentine's Day, slushy love songs … but it also has an undertone of aggression. If you break my heart, you have wounded me. The wound is to *me*. I, the adult man, am the victim of something this little girl has done to *me*.

The second comment is his description of men 'enjoying' teaching children or keeping them safe (for example as social workers or police officers) and 'enjoying' pornographic pictures of children. This conflation of two meanings of the verb 'to enjoy' - to derive pleasure and satisfaction from caring about others, and to derive arousal and orgasm from sexual fantasies - seems to point to a fundamental confusion about how adults (usually men) relate to children (usually girls). One wonders about the content of the sexual fantasies: are the men fantasising about protecting and caring for little girls as they ejaculate by their computer keyboards? Altogether, Bell's references to 'innocence offered for the pleasure of adults', the breaking of (adult) hearts, and the double meaning of 'enjoy' suggest to the reader an earlier, 18th century, interpretation of the word 'enjoy', containing the meaning of patriarchal entitlement to pleasure.

Men such as these are certainly not rare. Operation Ore identified over 7000 from just one police investigation. But does the current and proposed legislation by the Government provide an effective response to the beliefs and actions of men such as these, and others sexually attracted to children?

4. Alternative Constructions: Implications and Ways Forward

This chapter has traced out a number of issues about child sexual abuse and child protection. It has noted that of the over four thousand children who die each year in the UK, probably fewer than ten will be killed by sex offenders. Nevertheless, a very significant number of children will be sexually abused, typically by a family-member. There are also, as noted, thousands of men in UK society who, while not identifying as paedophiles, believe that 'enjoying' pornographic imagery of girls is not wrong. This chapter has noted that the response of the Government in the last few years has been to increase the capacity of the police to identify and monitor offenders and to 'vet' and 'bar' known offenders from occupations involving children, by using databases such as ViSOR. This is an approach which could be seen as analogous to the War on Terror, an attempt to seek out a hidden but well-defined threat and render it harmless before damage is done. This approach relies on sophisticated and expensive tools of information-gathering, surveillance and registration and it springs from the same simplistic and reductive world-view which sees identity cards as making us safer in the fight against terror. Such an approach is partial and inadequate. Like the War on Terror, the fight is, in reality, not so much against an isolated and extremist few (those who attack and murder) but for the hearts and minds of wider segments of society, including those thousands of men who see themselves as harmlessly 'enjoying' little girls. It will always be only a small minority of sexual abusers who are known to the authorities; therefore any child protection strategy which relies on bureaucratic processes of monitoring, surveillance and registration to vet and bar offenders from working with children will always be largely unsuccessful in its stated aim of protecting children and preventing abuse (although arguably it may be more successful in the unstated aim of softening-up the British population for rapidly-increasing erosions of civil liberties).

Even where those who are merely suspected, as well as those who are actually convicted, are included on offender databases this will continue to represent only a tiny proportion of all the people who have or who are currently sexually abusing children, or who have the desire and intention to sexually abuse in the future.

In conclusion, this chapter endorses a more radical approach to child protection. In distinction to a centralised and formalised top-down reliance on professional intervention and surveillance, there are now approaches being developed which are informal and small-scale. They locate sexual abusers in their everyday environment - their local community.

The first example is the Stop It Now! campaign. This was started by Fran Henry in 1992 in the United States and is now operating in several areas around Britain and Northern Ireland. It is based on three simple principles. The first is to talk openly about sexual abuse, without shame, as we would talk about drink-driving or cancer or any other public health issue. The second is to hold abusers accountable, at the same time as we understand them as human beings. The third is to focus on prevention by strategies such as awareness-raising and sex education for the general public, together with effective treatment including voluntary treatment and work with abusers, their partners and their families.

The second example is more narrowly focused on the treatment of abusers, and in particular relapse prevention, but again adopts a community-based, public health approach which avoids demonising paedophiles and child sexual abusers. Like Stop It Now!, this example shifts the balance of responsibility away from professionals back to the local community. Circles of Support and Accountability (known simply as Circles) is a Canadian initiative which has also now begun to be used in Britain. It is based on the premise of the community taking responsibility for protecting itself. On release from prison, a convicted sex offender is resettled into the community with the help of six trained volunteer supporters, who each commit to spend time with the offender one day per week, and who all get together with him as a group on the seventh day. The goal is to support the offender on a daily basis, and to hold him accountable for his actions. As members of Circles explain:

> It's all about people forming and creating community, and not excluding anyone. It's about looking at people as people. ... The key thing is the acceptance of that individual as a member of society - a contributing member - not as a paedophile, who has only and will only ever have that label. If you don't let them forget that, then that's all they will ever be - a paedophile.[27]

These approaches see paedophilia and child sexual abuse as complex human experiences which take place within relationships and communities, and which are the outcomes of an irreducibly intricate mix of beliefs, understandings, histories, fantasies and desires. The key to child protection lies less with essentialised notions of evil and with formalised bureaucratic processes than with 'forming and creating community, and not excluding anyone'.

If we, in whichever country we live, really want "a coherent set of protective measures unrivalled anywhere" as Sir Michael Bichard for the UK suggested, then we cannot afford the response of demonising paedophiles as evil. Sexual behaviour towards children is profoundly wrong: sexual attraction towards children appears to be part of the continuum of human sexuality. We must have the courage to accept that there are many thousands of men in our societies who see themselves as 'enjoying' and 'celebrating' the 'splendor of little girls' and we must recognise that an integral part of any protective measure needs to include community-based initiatives which reinforce ordinary, everyday, human interactions and individual responsibility - initiatives which do not blame any of us for our thoughts but which hold us all accountable for all our actions. In the final analysis, this may be the most realistic way to keep all our children safe.

Notes

[1] Colin Pritchard, *The Child Abusers: Research and Controversy* (Maidenhead: Open University Press, 2004).
[2] The United Kingdom Parliament, House of Commons, *Sex Offenders Bill: Second Reading*, column 42, David Mellor MP, 27 January 1997, (9 March 2006).
<http://www.publications.parliament.uk/pa/cm199697/cmhansrd/vo970127/debtext/70127-11.htm >.
[3] BBC News online, 'Mother in call for "Mark's Law"', 8 September 2005, (20 February 2006).
<http://news.bbc.co.uk/2/hi/uk_news/scotland/4224334.stm>.
[4] United Kingdom Government, Government News Network, Cabinet Office, *Bichard Report Conclusions*, 15 March 2005, (7 March 2006). <http://www.gnn.gov.uk/Content/Detail.asp?ReleaseID=151850&NewsAreaID=2 >.
[5] BBC News online, 'Sex offender offered teaching job', 8 January 2006, (10 January 2006).
<http://news.bbc.co.uk/2/hi/uk_news/england/norfolk/4591850.stm>.

[6] United Kingdom Government, Government News Network, 'Improving recruitment practices, safeguarding children – Kelly', 19 January 2006, (18 March 2006).
<http://www.gnn.gov.uk/Content/Detail.asp?ReleaseID=184642&NewsAreaID=2 >.
[7] ibid.
[8] Claire Flood-Page and Joanna Taylor (eds) *Crime in England and Wales 2001/2002: Supplementary Volume*, National Statistics, section on homicide, January 2003, (18 April 2006).
<http://www.homeoffice.gov.uk/rds/pdfs2/hosb103.pdf >.
[9] Susan J. Creighton and Gerry Tissier, 'Child killings in England and Wales', NSPCC Inform, January 2003, (18 April 2006). <http://www.nspcc.org.uk/Inform/OnlineResources/InformationBriefings/ChildKillingsInEnglandAndWales_asp_ifega26015.html>.
[10] Fiona Brookman and Mike Maguire, *Reducing Homicide: Summary of a review of the possibilities*, RDS (Research, Development and Statistics Directorate) Occasional Paper No. 84, January 2003, (10 February 2006).
<http://www.homeoffice.gov.uk/rds/pdfs2/occ84homicide.pdf >.
[11] Number of children aged 0 to 14 who died in England and Wales in 2002 was 4503 (3127 of infants aged under one year and 1376 of children aged 1 to 14). Statistic from National Statistics, *News release: childhood and infant deaths in 2002*, 30 March 2004, (18 April 2006). <http://www.statistics.gov.uk/pdfdir/chdeath0304.pdf>.
[12] For most years, accident and injury is the leading cause of death for children in the UK, closely followed by cancer. For details on cancer deaths, see Cancer Research UK, (10 February 2006).
<http://info.cancerresearchuk.org/cancerstats/childhoodcancer/mortality/>. For details on accidental death, see L Millward, A Morgan, M Kelly, *Prevention and reduction of accidental injury in children and older people: evidence briefing summary*, Health Development Agency, NHS, 2003 (18 April 2006).
<http://www.publichealth.nice.org.uk/download.aspx?o=502599 >.
[13] Brookman and Maguire, op. cit.
[14] See Creighton and Tissier, op. cit. For facts on prevention of accidental injury, see Child Accident Prevention Trust, *Factsheet: child accident facts*, revision date 9 January 2006, (18 April 2006).
<http://www.capt.org.uk/index.htm >.
[15] Pat Cawson, Corinne Wattam, Sue Brooker, Graham Kelly, *Child Maltreatment in the United Kingdom: a study of the prevalence of child abuse and neglect: executive summary*, section 8: sexual abuse, NSPCC

Inform, November 2000 (18 April 2006). <http://www.nspcc.org.uk/Inform/Publications/Downloads/ChildMaltreatmentInTheUKExecSummary_pdf_gf25453.pdf >. This study found a prevalence-rate of 19% among respondents reporting experiences of abuse (contact and non-contact) in a sample of 2869 people aged 18-24 in the UK. See also discussions on intra and extra-familiar sexual abuse in Pat Cox, Sheila Kershaw and Joy Trotter (eds), *Child Sexual Assault: Feminist Perspectives* (Basingstoke, Palgrave, 2000), Catherine Itzin (ed) *Home Truths about Child Sexual Abuse: Influencing Policy and Practice: a reader* (London, Routledge, 2000), Colin Pritchard, *The Child Abusers: Research and Controversy* (Maidenhead, Open University Press, 2004).

[16] A search of articles over three months during Spring 2005, covering the *Sun* (www.thesun.co.uk), Britain's biggest-selling daily paper, and its companion paper, the *News of the World* (www.newsoftheworld.co.uk), found only two articles which referred to 'child sexual abuse' but 94 referring to 'paedophiles', in other words an average of just over one article per day in this 90-day period: a period during which there were no particularly high-profile cases, but rather a 'background' of incidents including publicity for the recently-released Hollywood film, *The Woodsman.* Not only were there constant references to paedophiles, but the language was highly emotive, including the terms 'pervert', 'nasty pervs', 'sex attacks', 'sickest', 'vile', 'nauseating', 'outrage', and 'horror'. The film *The Woodsman* was described by readers of the *News of the World* as a 'sick paedo flick' (letters page, 6 March 2005).

[17] Sara Ruddick, *Maternal Thinking: Towards a Politics of Peace*, (London, Women's Press, 1990)

[18] Mary Douglas, *Purity and Danger: An Analysis of Concepts of Pollution and Taboo*, (London, Routledge and Kegan Paul, 1966). See also Mary Douglas, *Risk and Blame*, (London, Routledge, 1992) for a later revision of some of these concepts.

[19] Neville Thurlbeck "Monsters on our streets: all freed early … and they all struck again", *News of the World*, 19 March 2006, (28 May 2006). <http://notwats.blogspot.com/2006_03_01_notwats_archive.html>.

[20] For an unofficial copy of the transcript of this episode see the pro-paedophile site <http://www.glgarden.org/foreverman/brasseye.html> (28 January 2006)

[21] For information on this series, see http://www.bbc.co.uk/bbcthree/tv/monkeydust/about_the_show.shtml>.

[22] Allison, R. "Doctor driven out of home by vigilantes", *Guardian Unlimited*, 30 August 2000

www.guardian.co.uk/child/story/0,7369,361031,00.html > (29 January 2006).

[23] *The Economist* print edition, "Buried by a pile of porn", 16 January 2003, (10 March 2006). <http://www.economist.com/world/europe/displayStory.cfm?story_id=1536429>.

[24] Jim Bell, 'I cannot admit what I am to myself', *Guardian*, G2, 23 January 2003.

[25] Nicole Kassell, *The Woodsman* (Dash Films and Lee Daniels Entertainment, Tartan Video, 2005). Videorecording.

[26] Bell, pp 2-3, and p 8.

[27] Jon Silverman and David Wilson, *Innocence Betrayed: Paedophilia, the Media and Society,* (Cambridge, Polity, 2002), p. 178.

Bibliography

Cox, Pat, Sheila Kershaw and Joy Trotter, eds. *Child Sexual Assault: Feminist Perspectives*. Basingstoke, Palgrave, 2000.

Itzin, Catherine, ed. *Home Truths about Child Sexual Abuse: Influencing Policy and Practice: a reader*. London, Routledge, 2000.

Kassell, Nicole. *The Woodsman*. Dash Films and Lee Daniels Entertainment, Tartan Video, 2005. Videorecording.

Pritchard, Colin. *The Child Abusers: Research and Controversy*. Maidenhead: Open University Press, 2004.

Silverman, Jon and David Wilson. *Innocence Betrayed: Paedophilia, the Media and Society*. Cambridge, Polity, 2002.

Terrorism: Within and Without

Nancy Billias

Abstract: In the preface to Deleuze and Guattari's *Anti-Oedipus - Capitalism and Schizophrenia* (1972), Michel Foucault wrote: "The strategic adversary is fascism... the fascism in us all, in our heads and in our everyday behaviour, the fascism that causes us to love power, to desire the very thing that dominates and exploits us." The proposed paper will address the question not only of the fascist, but of the terrorist within each of us. After the events of the last four years, we should no longer speak of terrorism without recognizing that the key to combating this global pandemic is the recognition that it is, in fact, an auto-immune disease. Following Badiou and Baudrillard, I propose that we look beyond the traditional polarities of Good/Evil and Other/Same; instead, we must look at terrorism through the looking-glass. If we survive terrorism, it will be because we free ourselves from the delusion that terror lies somewhere 'out there', and realize instead that we must take a much more radical approach to the problem, by understanding and coming to terms with our own deep-seated propensities for terrorism. The paper will include a call to a radical form of hope which will attempt to begin a rapprochement between the philosophies of Badiou and Levinas on the subject of evil.

Key Words: Badiou, post-modern, terrorism, subjectivity, psychoanalytic, recognition, ethics, Levinas, event, phenomenology

1. Introduction

> The strategic adversary is fascism... the fascism in us all, in our heads and in our everyday behaviour, the fascism that causes us to love power, to desire the very thing that dominates and exploits us.[1]

After the events of the last four years, we should no longer speak of terrorism without recognizing that the key to combating this global pandemic is the recognition that it is, in fact, an auto-immune disease. Following Badiou and Baudrillard, I propose that we must look beyond the traditional polarities of Good/Evil and Other/Same; instead, we must look at terrorism through the looking-glass. "Philosophy," says Badiou, with a nod to Lacan, "is always the breaking of a mirror." As Baudrillard has said, "terrorist actions are both the magnifying mirror of the system's violence, and the model of a symbolic violence that it cannot access, the only violence it cannot exert: that of its own death."[2] If we do manage to survive terrorism, it will be because we free ourselves from the delusion that terror lies somewhere 'out there', and realize instead that we must take a much more radical approach to the problem, by understanding and coming to terms with our own deep-seated propensities for terrorism, with the fact that we are all terrorists at heart. The difference between those labelled as terrorists and the rest of us, I will argue, is that some of us have integrated our fears in such a way that we are not compelled to act them out. This means that we may need to reconsider the origins and meaning of such action. One way to do so is from a psychoanalytic perspective.

The question of subjectivity - the self in relation to the other - is central to philosophy, and most especially to the study of ethics. While postmodernism seems to throw the question wide open, and give rise to several new problems, it seems to me that the rising tides of terrorism demand that we continue to examine this question.[3]

I propose that we look at the ethical agent *within* the network of social interactions in which it finds itself, but not as *defined by* these interactions. I suggest that we assess the moral worth of an action not in terms of one social construct or contract, but rather phenomenologically, that is, in terms of our ineluctable ongoing engagement with others in the phenomena of everyday life. Breaking down the traditional Western duality between self and other, the aim of this proposal is to draw all parties into a phenomenological understanding of mutuality, privileging neither self nor other, but rather simply pointing to the myriad layers of their interpenetrating actions.

At the same time, I want to offer a new idea of ethics that might be acceptable within the post-modern worldview, an ethics, that is, which does not rely on a metanarrative of meaning, an ethics which is based on and in the events themselves. In the schema I propose, the ethical value of an action lies simply and solely in the *intensification* of the event. This perspective has roots in Hegel and Levinas. Hegel set forth the mediation of self and other on an intersubjective level: a knowing subject reaching through other subjects to realize its own meaning (as a subject). Later, Levinas clarified the ontological significance of this distinction: the essential necessity of this mediation. I would like to rehabilitate the notion of the necessity of the other for the composition of a 'self'.

2. Badiou's Notion of the Event

I have found an (unexpected) ally for this development in the thought of the contemporary French philosopher Alain Badiou, in his theory of the event. Badiou

> takes it as given that in the contemporary world the subject can no longer be theorized as the self-identical substance that underlies change, nor as the product of reflection, nor as the correlate of an object.[4]

Like many others in the French thought currents that flow back and forth between philosophy and psychoanalysis,[5] Badiou is troubled by questions of ethics and ontology, and the relationship between the two. Two basic problems confront him: the question of identity and the question of ethical agency.

Badiou attempts to resolve these questions by an unusual reconfiguration of ontology and subjectivity. Let me quickly sketch out Badiou's theoretical project. Badiou does not equate the two, as Levinas often seems to. Rather, Badiou focuses on the event of a subject's coming-to-be in the development of any given situation. For Badiou, a subject is not understood as pre-existent, but rather as emerging from, as a consequence of the event. As the phenomena of our everyday life flows around us, we must (*nolens volens*) make decisions; as we do, a sort of self is formed. Insofar as we respond to the events in what Badiou calls a "faithful" way, these events transform us into subjects. We are faithful, in Badiou's meaning of the word, if we allow an event to disrupt and change our lives, both in its initial phase and as we discover what we can from it. Not all events are catalytic, and not all humans are so transformed. Only chance determines what occurs. We cannot know for certain if there is any overarching rational structure guaranteeing a planful meaning in the events of our lives. What we can and do know is that events happen. They happen to us - either as objects who are acted upon, or as subjects who react, or both. We *may* develop into a more or less consistent pattern of action, which is what Badiou calls a 'self' or a subject. But this is by no means a sure bet. Neither does someone who has become a subject remain a subject - that is determined by subsequent events in an ongoing process of becoming.[6]

Badiou uses two key examples to illustrate this point, one microcosmic (falling in love) and the other macrocosmic (the Copernican revolution). Philosophers since Plato have been arguing over whether one falls in love with a specific person or rather with a general quality that is 'housed' in the person. That argument aside, when one falls in love, one has the opportunity to react in any number of ways, and continue the interaction with another. In the lover's eyes, no one can substitute for the love object (or is it a love subject?). As the love affair continues, both lovers change and are changed by the experience. It is up to us to respond in ways that are authentic to the structure of the relationship in order to keep it going, but whatever our choices, we cannot help but be affected (and, Badiou would say, effected) by the events of loving and being loved. The event of the Copernican revolution is analogous. After Copernicus' literally earth-shaking discovery, one could not un-know the true state of affairs. Wilful blindness could not undo the knowledge that the earth revolved around the sun, and not the other way around. Whether one had made the discovery for oneself, or was merely reacting to it, one could not help but be changed by the event, which set the Enlightenment in motion. The phenomenon was catalytic.

Thus, for Badiou, to speak of subjectivity one need not predicate the modern notion of a free rational agent, a consistent self. One need only understand a phenomenon in relation or reaction to its circumambient phenomena, an *x* which can be the subject of an equation. *X* performs action *y*. *X,* as he says, 'counts for one.' Phenomenologically, this statement is unarguable. As soon as 'I' act, I count for one. Whatever the meaning(s) of my action, and whether or not I take ethical responsibility for it, no one else performed the action but me. The action takes place in the context of this 'I,' and the action in some way disrupts *X* from its identity with itself.[7]

Rather than argue the subject as some sort of ontological entity, Badiou prefers the term "situation," which he "defines as a 'presented multiplicity,' or as the 'place of taking place.'"[8] Each of us is, as it were, a canvas on which life splashes paint. The decisions we make in response form us into artists, or not. That remains to be seen. Badiou makes no attempt to argue for the self as a unity, nor even for being-as-such as a unity. (He sees no need to equate unity and being.) Yet for the purposes of working out an ethics, he insists very strongly on the notion, following Lacan, that the structure of the self depends on the development of some one(ness), someone who is there, to whom things happen. "*Il y a de l'un.*"

> That is, although unity is not primordial, there is some kind of effect of unity in the presentation of being. Badiou's solution to this problem is to argue that situations – presented multiplicities – do have unity, but such unity is the result of an operation termed the count-for-one…Unity is the effect of structuration – and not a ground, origin, or end.[9]

"Counting-for-one" is what may happen when a situation of disruption occurs, when someone takes up, even for a moment, an identity as an active *element* of some unity. Thus, for Badiou, subjectivity always occurs within relationality (in relation to other elements, other *Xs)*, and in the context of the between - the ontological void within which all being can be said to exist. So being is always belonging, and to not belong is, in a sense, to lose the structure by which one could 'count for one' (because without some structure, one is unrepresentable). As 'I' act, I begin to take shape as a self.

> So, for Badiou, every situation is ultimately founded on a void. This is not Heidegger's Ab-grund, nor is it some theological creation *ex nihilo*. The void of a situation is simply what is not there, but what is necessary for anything to be there.[10]

Each situation, Badiou asserts, can be seen as occurring in the context or against the backdrop of the void. It is representable first by virtue of its distinction from the void, and then, by the various ways in which it 'counts-for-one'. For example, I count-for-one as a woman, as an American, as a philosopher, as a teacher, and so on. I count-for-one not by virtue of my passive membership as an element of a set, but rather only in terms of my active engagement, by taking actions which proclaim or reify my membership. The multiplicities which form my 'self' are constantly shifting as I react to new events. Counting-for-one is the result of an individual choice, a choice to differentiate oneself which, paradoxically, leads to unity. Counting-for-one provides the structure within which the dynamic process of the situation unfolds.

For Badiou, if counting-for-one is to be considered ethical, it must be responsive to the other who presents itself to my situation. The event of otherness becomes the event of my 'self'. But counting-for-one has one other very important defining characteristic, as far as Badiou is concerned, namely: an action which is going to be transformative must be part of a truth-process. Thus, all actions of counting for-one are inherently good in themselves, for in the process of counting-for-one, I stand over against the void, in phenomenological defiance of the void. And I stand for the truth of being over against not-being. Badiou explicitly links the notions of being, goodness, and truth, on the one hand, and not-being, evil, and terror, on the other. "Evil is the process of a simulacrum of truth. And in its essence, under a name of its invention, it is terror directed at everyone."[11]

At the same time, Badiou urges us to move beyond the mere categories of good and evil, towards a wider and more processual understanding of intersubjective unity. He advocates the development of an understanding which has room both for the individual, as a constantly shifting and evolving reality, and for the unified set of which the individual may become a part. Badiou does not set self and other into opposition; both are members of possible sets. In this schema, what is always privileged as 'good' is that which enhances being, either of the individual or the other, since they are not in competition. In that sense, this theory can be thought of as an adaptation of the categorical imperative. So act, such that your action can be taken to be a universal act of nature, on behalf of some self or other whose claims you recognize as equal to your own. Yet Badiou does not make this claim solely on moral grounds, but rather on ontological and phenomenological arguments: as the situation develops, the shape of the acting self changes and is changed by events. The effects of the actions of differentiation and non-identity do not diminish, but rather enhance what emerges. As a manifestation of the principle of differentiation, I *need* the other to remain other and not to be subsumed into the self, for my goal is disruption, to stand over against the undifferentiated of the void, to count-for-one. Thus, intersubjectivity is not a diminution of the self; the other adds to my concept of who I might become. The other is not primarily a source of fear, but of hope. The other holds the key to my future development. Any action which is aimed at the destruction of the other is by definition anti-intersubjective, and thus thwarts my own attempts at becoming. Phenomenologically and ontologically, I cannot get along without the other. The other is my bridge to the truth of being. In this understanding, difference is conceived not as a (necessary) evil, but rather as both a harbinger and the instrument of possibility.

In contrast to this hopeful view of the other, the object relations analyst Otto Kernberg has written at length about the psychoanalytic roots of terrorism. Kernberg maintains that much (or even all) terrorist activity is a result of primitive paranoid process, rooted in the fear of the other as the earliest internalization of a persecutory experience - separation from the mother. Following Melanie Klein, Kernberg proposes that we can link the desire for "the natural love and trust and dependent longing for the good mother" with

> the profound need for affiliation, for 'belonging', for being positively responded to by those around us, who, generally, share our language, accent, skin colour, clothing, behaviour patterns and preferences, [which] becomes contrasted with potential fear and suspicion of those who are different, alien, 'not like us'. From a psychoanalytic perspective, 'maternal' and 'paternal' principles are involved here...the 'maternal' principle here refers to the search for an idealized, symbiotic

> relationship with a mothering image, the ecstatic fusion in an 'all good' relationship that provides total pleasure, security and closeness…[12]

Thus, intolerance is difference perceived as trauma, as wound or lack. The desire for totalization is intolerance of the other **as** other, of the otherness of the other, and the desire to annihilate the other is the desire to annihilate otherness, at whatever cost. It is unreasoning, irrational, beyond good and evil, because it is in the service of the id, of the primitive processing that desires only fulfilment of its primary narcissistic need.

As any student of existentialism knows, the void is terrible. But it is also terribly important, because without the gap of the void, differentiation can never occur. The id strives to wipe out the reality or even the memory of the void. But without the void, nothing can ever emerge. No change can ever occur. The ironic paradox is that we need otherness as much as we fear it, in order to become separate from what surrounds us, to emerge from the background of the void.

According to Badiou, whatever is in the service of the id is in the service of a *simulacrum* of truth – rather than of a truth itself - and thus inherently unethical, or anti-ethical. Before we venture into a discussion of what Badiou might mean by this, a word of clarification from the devil's advocate. If we are taking seriously the post-modern premise that there is no such thing as 'Truth' (in terms of a metanarrative of meaning superimposed on the phenomena), in an attempt to begin to formulate a post-modern ethics, what are we suddenly doing talking about truth or simulacra thereof? Badiou wants to reinsert this term into the discussion, again as a matter both of phenomenology and of ontology. He admits that he is aiming at a re-visioning of contemporary philosophy, and to be looking for a way to bring the term back into some form of meaning, hence the subtitle of his 2003 text ("Truth and the Return to Philosophy"). Badiou contends that unless we are going to give up on language altogether, we must acknowledge a place for truths, for statements that bear common connotation and significance. We may need to redefine the place of these premises in our lives and our philosophies, but neither lives nor philosophies can be conducted without them. Rather than abandoning the term, Badiou recommends that we open both them and ourselves to continual questioning and reflection. Truths and Truth (with a capital T) need not be, should not be collapsed into one category; in fact, doing so produces a simulacrum rather than a truth. Truths are ideas which can be the basis for *X*'s action, or the response developed in reaction, or the building self-understanding of *X*'s non-identity with the void. The truth is in the doing and the becoming, as we shall see further in a moment.

Badiou sees simulacra as dangerous. Simulacra of truths can give rise to political fidelity, to blind faith in a religion or an ideal. "The exercise of fidelity to the simulacrum is necessarily the exercise of terror."[13] A simulacrum of truth reduces the other (and the would-be subject) to counting for less-than-one, in two ways. First, it reduces the one who acts to counting for less-than-one by virtue of being pre-determined by something other than the event in which it finds itself. Second, it reduces the other to less-than-one, by refusing to accept the other as wholly other than itself, as capable of also emerging from an event and being transformed by it. It strives to eliminate the otherness of the other, reducing the other to a nameless, faceless, passive abstraction, rather than an active or interactive reality. Thus a simulacrum of truth strives to undo that primary narcissistic wound. Thus, it is the perfect weapon for the terrorist.

In this struggle, ideology is the enemy of the truth, because ideology does not allow for me to 'count-for-one' except as part of a group: not by an individual choice responding to an other's unique and individual needs or demands, but only from within the framework - or prison - of a pre-figured, pre-determined set of options. It replaces the individual conscience with an 'immoral,' fascistic conscience that demands absolute allegiance to the same, no matter what the cost. The ideologies of radical Islamism are no different, in this respect from the ideologies of capitalism or Marxism. Ideology does not allow situations to flower into events.

As noted earlier, for Badiou an event is the opportunity for action within which transformation may occur. A genuine event brings into being a singular, particular response, the possibility of a truth. A truth is "the real process of a fidelity to an event" – a lived response in a transformed way to the circumstances of a particular phenomenal situation, by means of which a human being becomes someone new. What Badiou calls the "ethic of a truth" is "the principle that enables the continuation of a truth-process…*that which lends consistency to the presence of some-one in the composition of the subject induced by the process of this truth.*[14]

This understanding of the event flows from Badiou's ontology, from the notion that being itself is absolutely neutral.

> What allows a genuine event to be at the origin of a truth…is precisely the fact that it relates to the particularity of a situation only from the bias of its void. The void…neither excludes nor constrains anyone. It is the absolute neutrality of being – such that the fidelity that originates in an event, although it is an imminent

> break within a singular situation, is none the less universally addressed.[15]

Like chance, being is impersonal – it addresses itself equally to all, and all must respond in their own, singular fashion.[16]

Badiou seems to follow Heidegger to some extent (in concept if not in language) in relating the notion of truth to ethics and art alike. What is true, or genuine, is that which is singular and disruptive. To put this in Heideggerian language, one might say that where being discloses itself in a rupture, truth emerges. If one is faithful to the rupture, one allows being to disclose itself and responds to it by striving towards it. To put it in Lacanian terms, one allows a hole (*trouée)* to be made from the realm of the symbolic into the Real. In either case, the activity *may* result in a subject. As Heidegger and Lacan did before him, Badiou acknowledges that this type of disruption necessarily entails violence.[18] But it is the violence of birth, not death. "The process of truth *induces* a subject."[19]

3. Towards a Post-Modern Ethics

Although the idea of a single, unified subject may have been shattered by the advent of post-modernism, Badiou makes a strong argument for the case that each fragment can and does retain an individual value. He would encourage us to see each event in its own light, unobscured by any overarching ideological framework, although it will always be subject (no pun intended) to its capacity to be reacted to severally by each participant. And any hope, such as it is, lies in that event: fidelity to the process of truth, the painful emergence of some subject, no matter how fragmentary, which can maintain itself in the development of a presentation in differentiation to the void.

This, finally, is where my proposal comes in. Suppose we redefine the ethical quality of an interaction. Rather than locating the ethical essence of the action in the agent (subject) or the one acted upon (object), why not locate the essence of the action between the two, in the event of the action itself? In this structure, right and wrong cease to be abstract and absolute. Only one course of action will yield the optimal impact, the greatest amount of intensity that the moment has to yield, the greatest potential for mutually interactive unfolding and fulfilment. Thus the event itself will disclose to me what is right and wrong, in terms of what is most fruitful of potentiality.

One could, of course, argue that intensity is a poor standard by which to measure ethical action; for example, murder is the most intense impact one person can have on another. (Witness the spectacular intensity of the events of 9/11, so movingly and thoughtfully contemplated in other papers at this conference.) But according to my proposal, such an action would be unethical precisely because it would foreclose any further activity on the part of the other.[20] Such an action would be merely an action, not an interaction, and would preclude any further interaction. Therefore, such an action would intensify the moment only *in actu*, and not also *in potentia*. It would preclude the other's ever again counting-for-one, or the possibility that they could act in fidelity to that event. It would be the simulacrum of an event, rather than an event, and a simulacrum of a truth, rather than ever approaching truth.

An action which could intensify the moment in both activity and potentiality would clearly be more ethical. I want to argue that the event of life is utterly and unquestionably ethical: life has everything to do with me, and everything to do with the other. Badiou has shown us how this is perspective is ontologically and phenomenologically plausible. Through the intensification of the moment, I can get a clearer, brighter picture of thie 'self' of mine. I rely on the other to provide the greatest possible intensification of that experience of myself - yet it is also my doing, my responsibility to pack the moment with as much intensity, as much mutuality as possible, to extend myself out against the other who is all around me. Locating the ethical value within the event itself frees me to experience this otherness and to experience myself more fully. It therefore becomes my ethical responsibility to intensify the moment for the other whom I encounter, as far as I am able. The ethical thing to do is that which sees the other as 'counting-for-one' and facilitating the progression and potentiality of that movement.

In this interpretation, the traditional Western understanding of the ego disappears into the community of those who respond to one another. The agent and the one acted upon are constantly exchanging roles, both with one another, and within the community of otherness. This is a true liberation: if the self is undefined, with permeable boundaries, there is no limit on the scope of 'my' activity or the sphere of 'my' influence. Constantly acting and being acted upon, I am a member of the infinite set of a community of responsive others.[21]

In fact, the notion of a fragmented and undetermined self makes possible the freedom inherent in the concept of autonomy in a new way, and perhaps for the first time. For in this view autonomy arises organically from the interaction with and intermediation of the world around me. In this theory, autonomy can be found in living without being categorized or otherwise determined. Whatever determination I have (if necessary or even possible at all) comes about through my interaction with the others, but is not determined by *them*, but rather by the events in which I participate. From this perspective, I accept autonomy as an inescapable ontological condition: all that I am is what I am right now, the self that is acting and being acted upon, in the company of those with whom I move through time. This is not only a condition to be achieved, but an event to be celebrated: the event of life itself.

Notes

[1]Michel Foucault, in the preface to Deleuze and Guattari, *Anti-Oedipus - Capitalism and Schizophrenia* (1972).
[2] Jean Baudrillard, *The Spirit of Terrorism* (London: Verso, 2002), 14.
[3] Any new ethical theory must consider seriously the hold that postmodern thinking has taken on the Western world, and attempt to present an ethical framework that can both incorporate postmodern 'truth' and allay the postmodern fear of the loss of personal meaning 'Truth' in scare quotes since, of course, according to the postmodern perspective there is no such thing as objective or absolute truth.
[4] Oliver Feltham and Justin Clemens, "An Introduction to the Philosophy of Alain Badiou," in *Infinite Thought: Truth and the Return to Philosophy* (New York: Continuum, 2003), 3.
[5] I am thinking primarily of Miller, Foucault, Lacan, and the Strasbourg school of post-structuralism.
[6] Of course, this schema does not solve the problem of how something new ever comes into being, of why events happen at all, and then of how or why certain events lead to the development of a subject. But I am not here to argue Badiou's ontology. I merely mention it in passing. I would refer the reader back to *Infinite Thought* for a full discussion of Badiou's theory.
[7] This movement is reminiscent of the movement in Schelling between the ground and the unground which brings being into manifestation.
[8] Feltham and Clemens, *op.cit,* 9.
[9] Ibid., *10ff.*
[10] Ibid., *16.*
[11] Alain Badiou, *Ethics: An Essay on the Understanding of Evil* (New York: Verso, 2001), 77.
[12] Otto F. Kernberg, "Sanctioned social violence: A psychoanalytic view, part II", International Journal of Psychoanalysis, 2003; 84, 960. (953 – 968)
[13] *Loc.cit.*
[14] Badiou, *Ethics*, 44.

[15]Ibid, 73.
[16] The imperative arises phenomenologically, not in any moral sense.
[18] In *The Anaximander Fragment*, Heidegger spoke even of the violence that occurs in translation, the violence of wrenching ideas from one language into another.
[19] Badiou, *Ethic*s, 43.
[20] Thus, in one sense, I am back where Hegel and Levinas started: with the recognition of the other as the primal and primary ethical moment.
[21] Much of Badiou's ontology is based on set theory. See *Infinite Thought*, especially the introduction.

Bibliography

Badiou, Alain. *Ethics: An Essay on the Understanding of Evil.* New York: Verso Books, 2001.

——— *Infinite Thought: Philosophy and the Return to Truth*. Trans. and with an introduction by Justin Clemens and Oliver Feltham. New York: Continuum, 2003.

——— *L'Etre et l'Evénement.* Paris: Seuil, L'ordre philosophique, 1988.

Baudrillard, Jean. *The Spirit of Terrorism*. Translated by Chris Turner. New York: Verso Books, 2003.

Debord, Guy. *The Society of the Spectacle*. Translated by Donald Nicholson-Smith. New York: Zone, 1995.

Deleuze, Gilles and Guattari, Felix. *Anti-Oedipus: Capitalism and Schizophrenia.* Minneapolis: University of Minnesota Press, 1983.

Heidegger, Martin. *Early Greek Thinking.* Translated by David F. Krell and Frank A. Capuzzi. New York: HarperCollins, 1985.

Kernberg, Otto. "Sanctioned social violence: A psychoanalytic view, part II", *International Journal of Psychoanalysis*, 2003; 84, 953 – 968.

Born to be Bad or Born to Die? Evil and Finitude in Freud's Death Drive

Havi Hannah Carel

Abstract: Freud's death drive hypothesis postulates an inherent drive towards destructiveness and aggression. His theory of the death drive has been conceived by many as the height of Freud's pessimism, as an admission that we are indeed born evil. But, as I argue below, this is not the only moral position that can be derived from the death drive hypothesis. Even if we accept (albeit in reconstructed form) Freud's hypothesis that we are born with an inherent aggressive drive, the problem of innate aggression does not have to be viewed pessimistically. In this paper I develop a different notion of an ethics of finitude, and show how this view can arise from the death drive and the terminality of human life.

Key Words: Death drive, Freud, ethics of finitude, evil, Eros, Thanatos, transience, mortality.

1. Introduction

In 1933 Sigmund Freud and Albert Einstein, both Jews and the greatest living intellectuals of their time, were invited to exchange letters on the question 'why war?'. Freud's letter reveals a surprising view: not only is it understandably bleak, given the political circumstances, but it seems as though he actually justifies the existence of violence and cruelty through an instinctual-biological hypothesis of innate aggression, which he named the death drive. These are his remarks in the closing pages of *Why War?*:

> [The death drive] would serve as a biological justification for all the ugly and dangerous impulses against which we are struggling. It must be admitted that they stand nearer to Nature than does our resistance to them for which an explanation also needs to be found… there is no use in trying to get rid of men's aggressive inclinations.[1]

In order to understand why Freud took this view, and moreover why he regarded the death drive as a necessary component of the human mind, we must step back to examine his model of the psyche. Freud's late model described the psyche as composed of two opposing forces, the life drives,

Eros, and the death drives, Thanatos. Their conflicting aims and processes create an internal dynamic of the mind. Whereas Eros aims to promote unity and cohesiveness, procreation and creativity, Thanatos aims to destruct and destroy. The tension between the two drives is the source of ambivalence, duality and strife, which permeate human behaviour through and through. For example, Freud comments in *The Ego and the Id* that "love is with unexpected regularity accompanied by hate (ambivalence), and in human relationships hate is frequently a forerunner of love."[2] When we love someone, we also, in part, hate them; the human psyche contains love and hate, ambivalence and duality, not because we are fickle creatures, but because we are structured that way. We are constructed of dualistic sets of opposite aims and drives, and the struggle between them results in the ambivalence that characterizes human thought and behaviour.

By structuring the psyche as containing conflicting forces, Freud brings ambivalence and duality to the fore. These, in turn, produce conflict and frustration both internally and externally. Internally we find conflict between the different psychic agencies. Externally we find conflict between people with clashing aims, and between each person and external reality, which is always more harsh and disappointing than we would like it to be. With his plural model of the mind, Freud has brought conflict closer than ever to the human mind. So close, in fact, that it is now internalized; a part of the psyche, and a product of the clashes and duality that characterize it. Not only are conflict and frustration part of the psyche, they actually structure and motivate psychic processes, permeating the psyche with violence and discontent.

Conflict and frustration are built into Freud's model of psychic agencies. This is a pluralistic model of the psyche, regarding it as containing different agencies – id, ego and superego – opposing in aim and action. Freud describes the ego as desperately trying to mediate between the greedy demands of the id, the severe criticism of the superego and the cruel lack and insufficiency of reality. In *Dissection of the Personality* Freud describes the ego as serving three "tyrannical masters," running between them in a failed attempt to reach a compromise, but never satisfying anyone: "The poor ego has things even worse: it serves three severe masters and does what it can to bring their claims and demands into harmony with one another. These claims are always divergent and often seem incompatible. No wonder that the ego so often fails in its task."[3] Conflict is inherent and internal to human existence, which is therefore condemned to frustration and discontent. This pessimistic view of psychic reality as governed by conflict and frustration lead Freud to suggest that evil, the tendency to aggression and destruction, is innate and as such finds its source in the death drive.

2. The Death Drive

Before turning to the death drive, a caveat is in order. Freud's general drive theory and his later speculations on the life and death drives were stringently criticized, and moreover met with hostility and suspicion, from their inception until the present day. The reasons for rejection are manifold. Some argue that Freud's general drive theory is based on dated neurophysiologic assumptions, some resist the speculative and anti-scientific status of Freud's life and death drives, others point to internal inconsistencies in Freud's formulations and others yet reject the death drive on ethical grounds. I discuss these objections and present a detailed reassessment of the death drive elsewhere.[4] What I should like to do here is argue that despite these problems, there is still much to be gleaned from Freud's notion of the death drive. But in order to see this, the death drive has to be released from the erroneous assumptions grounding Freud's drive theory and made coherent and independent of dated scientific grounding. I therefore propose a metaphysical and philosophical focus, rather than a psychoanalytic or neurophysiologic one. My question in this essay therefore is: in what ways can Freud's death drive illuminate our understanding of the notion of evil? Within this metaphysical context, I claim that Freud's notion of the death drive contains useful insights and can shed substantial light on the concepts of evil and human aggression.

A major source of confusion about the death drive is Freud's metaphysical vagueness about the relationship between life and death. Is death a negation of life? Is it an active counter-force resisting life, or a simple lack of all positive attributes? Is it a part of life or an external border? Freud's formulation of the death drive is problematic partly because he was shifting between several views on these issues, not all of which were compatible with one another. From 1920 onwards Freud repeatedly attempts to put forth a dualistic and dialectical model of the drives, but his model collapses time and again. The dualistic view fails, I argue, because it presupposes the life and death drives are separate and opposing, whereas I believe that strictly speaking no such separation exists. What I suggest is a metaphysical view of life and death as interlinked, rather than as discrete and contrasting forces, as Freud claimed.

Finally, by postulating the death drive Freud attempted to unify contradicting aspects, namely, aggression and the drive towards complete rest, the Nirvana principle. As such, the death drive was an attempt to bring together in an explanatorily effective way a wide range of tendencies. Therefore the death drive has different objects and modes of action, diverse manifestations, and is used by Freud to explain several psychic functions. These caveats make it clear that the death drive has to be treated with caution. Nonetheless, in what follows I excavate this notion for hidden treasures, namely, a lesson in human finitude, while bearing in mind the problems and limitations of the concept. As I hope to show, the death drive has a more positive ethical significance than the usual pessimism it is taken to yield.

What is the death drive? Freud postulates a force governing psychic life, an active, non-pathological component of the psyche. In order to explain why Freud postulates a death drive, we need to understand Freud's general drive theory. On this view, drives are psychical expressions of somatic stimulation, pushing the psychic system to achieve some aim. As long as the aim has not been fulfilled, the drive will continue to excite the psychic system. This excitation Freud takes to be unpleasurable. We therefore seek to avoid unpleasure by filling the need underlying the excitation. Pleasure, therefore, corresponds with the lowest possible level of excitation within a system, while unpleasure signifies a raised level. Freud postulates the Nirvana principle as the principle pushing us towards lowering tension, where the logical endpoint of this pressure would be zero tension, or in other words, death. It is important to note that the economic model of excitation as unpleasurable and of the mind as a closed system has long been discredited.[5] But hopefully this brief account of Freud's drive theory makes the death drive more understandable.

The death drive bridges the metaphysical and biological domains. It is Freud's attempt to understand life and death on the most general, speculative, metaphysical level. As a drive it is an instinctual element linking soma to psyche and thus providing an account of how psychic phenomena arise from somatic origins. As an amalgam of these two levels – the metaphysical and the biological – the death drive is conceptually fraught. Freud's account is a baffling attempt to express a metaphysical speculation about life and death in a quasi-empirical manner. It is the product of Freud's effort to incorporate a broad metaphysical view of life and death into his scientific drive theory.

Although the death drive is a fundamental concept in Freud's later work it is based on extraordinarily speculative hypotheses and its clinical application is highly contentious. Hence the circumstances of its appearance and its credibility have been much discussed. These discussions culminated, by and large, in complete rejection of the death drive. Eissler, for example, remarks that "Freud's final systematization of drives is still being rejected by the vast majority of psychoanalysts."[6] In his biography of Freud Jones writes: "The book [*Beyond the Pleasure Principle*] is further noteworthy in being the only one of Freud's which has received little acceptance on the part of his followers."[7] Friedman holds that "the same situation exists today; there is no support for Freud's notion of the death instinct."[8] Freud explains the rejection of the death drive and its lack of clinical application as expressing a cultural tendency to repress death and reject views of the human psyche as inherently aggressive. The idea of an opaque, dark force of negativity and destruction is difficult to swallow, claims Freud, for "'little children do not like it' when there is talk of the inborn inclination to 'badness', to aggressiveness and destructiveness, and so to cruelty as well."[9]

Given that the basic human attitude towards death is not one of acceptance and acknowledgment, Freud's formulation of the death drive cannot be taken at face value. It itself is subject to denial and repression both on a personal-psychical and on a socio-cultural level. Freud writes at the end of Civilization *and its Discontents*:

> The assumption of the existence of an instinct of death or destruction has met with resistance even in analytic circles [...] it was only tentatively that I put forward the views I have developed here, but in the course of time they have gained such a hold upon me that I can no longer think in any other way. To my mind they are far more serviceable from a theoretical standpoint than any other possible ones; they provide that simplification, without either ignoring or doing violence to the facts, for which we strive in scientific work [...] I can no longer understand how we can have overlooked the ubiquity of non-erotic aggressivity and destructiveness and can have failed to give it its due place in our interpretation of life.[10]

Freud goes on to articulate several central principles he uses to formulate his notion of the death drive: the explanatory contribution of the death drive to psychoanalytic theory (accounting for unpleasurable repetition and explaining the origin of sadism and masochism); the question to what extent the death drive fits into his existing theory of the drives and how it improves it; and how close a match exists between the theoretical concept and the clinical data.[11] His introduction of the death drive into his drive theory can be seen as motivated by these considerations.

But even if there was a theoretical and clinical need to postulate a death drive, a central problem remains. In his formulation of the death drive Freud is attempting to validate two contradicting notions: the first describes death as the Nirvana principle, and is formulated in *Beyond the Pleasure Principle* and in *The Economic Problem of Masochism.*[12] This position regards death as the discharge of all excitations, as the zero point of all tension and the complete halt of all life processes. The second position regards the death drive as aggression, destructive energy generating violence and tension. This position is prevalent in *Civilisation and Its Discontents* and in *The Ego and the Id*, where antagonism and dualism become dominant psychic features.[13]

The existence of these two contradictory tendencies in texts written and published in chronological proximity is not accidental; the tension and swift changes in Freud's theoretical formulations are a result of the fact that Freud was trying to explain more than one set of phenomena with the death drive, and therefore could not develop a coherent and stable concept. I argue that the death drive as formulated by Freud is not a single concept, but an umbrella term covering several tendencies and forces, which are contradictory on economic and dynamic levels. If we approach this term with the demand for a single unified concept, contradiction is inevitable. Rather, what is required is a prising apart of the different elements and a close examination of each. This will enable us to determine which parts of the concept are anachronistic, and which are illuminating and deserve reconstruction.

3. Beyond the Pleasure Principle

Freud first posited the death drive hypothesis in *Beyond the Pleasure Principle* (1920). He opens the essay by positing the pleasure principle as regulating mental processes. Organisms in general, including humans, seek pleasure, and seek to avoid unpleasure. Pleasure corresponds to a diminution in the quantity of unbound excitation while unpleasure is its increase in a given period of time. But in his clinical work Freud came across many examples of behaviour that cannot be explained by the pleasure principle, such as the urge to return to painful memories and experiences displayed by war-neurosis patients or other forms of post-traumatic behaviour. These behaviours seek to raise the level of unpleasurable excitation and therefore seem to be operating beyond the pleasure principle. Freud claims that these clinical phenomena are empirical evidence pointing towards the existence of a negative and destructive force, undermining the basic assumption that human beings strive towards pleasure. The dreams in traumatic neuroses repeatedly reproduce the traumatic moment, contradicting the principle set in *The Interpretation of Dreams*, according to which dreams are a wish-fulfilment.[14] The *Fort-Da* game played by Freud's grandson recapitulates the painful separation from the mother; and transference itself is re-experiencing painful memories that have been repressed by the patient. He concludes that a compulsion to repeat painful experiences must exist, which is powerful enough to overcome the pleasure principle:

> If we take into account observations such as these, based upon behaviour in the transference and upon the life histories of men and women, we shall find the courage to assume that there really does exist in the mind a compulsion to repeat which over-rides the pleasure principle.[15]

This compulsion to repeat transforms our view of the drives: from a source of progress and change, they are now viewed as agents of conservation and repetition. "A drive is an urge inherent in organic life to restore an earlier state of things which the living entity has been obliged to abandon under the pressure of external disturbing forces."[16] Freud concludes that the aim of the drives is to promote "the expression of the inertia inherent in organic life" and the only reason for change is the pressure of external circumstances disturbing this inertia. If this claim is followed to its logical end, it must be concluded that the most fundamental aim of every living creature is to return to an inanimate form, which is the earliest state of things in organic terms, or in other words, to die. In this sense – a restricted instinctual sense that comprises only half of the instinctual domain (the other half being Eros) – "the aim of all life is death."[17] This leads Freud to the paradoxical conclusion that life is a detour on the way to death, based on "the drive to return to the inanimate state."[18] . Thus death becomes an organizing principle in life. "Death itself, as 'the aim of life', does not appear as some brute fact, but rather as the (silent) defining and de-limiting force of life itself. It appears, in Freud's reflection, as the *fundamentum inconcussum*, a necessary precondition for the advent of any life at all", writes Friedman.[19]

Although this is not stated explicitly, the entire struggle for life, and so also the Erotic drives, is placed in the service of the death drive and as subordinate to it. The preservation of life is nothing but a conservative persistence to die in the same fashion as all other organisms belonging to the same species. The pleasure principle, we now learn, harbours death in it, and a simple striving for pleasure hides behind it a powerful destructive force.

> The emergence of life would thus be the cause of the continuance of life and also at the same time of the striving towards death; and life itself would be a conflict and compromise between these two trends. The problem of the origin of life would remain a cosmological one; and the problem of the goal and purpose of life would be answered *dualistically.*[20]

As the source of negativity and destructiveness the death drive operates in two ways. It can be directed outwards, externalized as sadistic aggression, or it can be masochistically internalized, as aggression directed towards the ego. These two paths form a zero sum system, so any unused portions of the death drive must be externalized in order to protect the organism from its own destructiveness. "The organism preserves its own life, so to say, by destroying an extraneous one," writes Freud.[21] Directing aggression outwards is essential to the survival of the organism, otherwise this same aggression would be directed against the organism itself as self-destruction. So it is in the interest of each organism to behave in a sadistic way, and try to rid itself from as much aggression as possible.

Where does this account leave us? Freud seems to be saying that aggression, as a given and inherent tendency, must be, expelled or expressed somehow. This grim assumption might even be used to justify aggression, since according to Freud's view, if it is not expended outwards, it will be turned against the ego. And so, Freud's hypothesis of the death drive explains the existence of aggression and destructiveness, and moreover naturalizes its existence, which is postulated as a central component of the human psyche.

Freud's first conclusion is that whether directed inwards or outwards, aggression is a fundamental phenomenon that affects our thoughts, actions and emotions to a considerable extent. As Laplanche and Pontalis note:

> […] Indeed there is no kind of behaviour that may not have an aggressive function […] Psychoanalysis had gradually come to give great importance to aggressiveness, showing it to be at work in the early stage of the subject's development and bringing out the complicated ebb and flow of its fusion with and diffusion from, sexuality. The culmination of this increasing stress on aggressiveness is the attempt to find a single and basic instinctual underpinning for it in the idea of the death instinct.[22]

Freud goes on to say: "Some portion of the death instinct, however, remains operative *within* the organism" and is expressed in "a number of normal and pathological phenomena."[23] This naturalizes not only sadism, i.e. aggression directed outwards, but also masochism – in a move that is even less intuitive. Repetition of painful situations, self-destructiveness, death wishes and self-inflicted suffering are all expressions of the internally directed death drive. By positing the death drive as a general constituent of the psyche Freud normalizes aggression, and weakens the distinction between normal and pathological (since all human beings contain a death drive as part of their instinctual makeup). We all contain the kernel of destructiveness in us, whether categorized as healthy or sick, normal or perverse. Moreover, the death drive necessitates and entails aggression, pure and simple, whether that aggression is directed inwards or outwards. The death drive is not the individual disturbance or abnormality of any particular person; it is rather a postulate at the basis of Freud's conception of humans. We all contain a dimension of destructiveness in us; we all have the innate capacity for aggression and evil-doing. That is Freud's working hypothesis in his late work: evil is here to stay, as close as it can get: it is within us. What moral lesson can we draw from this apparently pessimistic postulate?

4. Moral Meaning of the Death Drive

Postulating the death drive as the source of aggression raises the question of its moral implications: how should we treat the death drive? What would be possible ways of re-directing the destructive urge? Is it possible to control aggression? This theory of the death drive has been conceived by many as the height of Freud's pessimism, as an admission that we are indeed born evil. But, as I argue below, this is not the only moral position that can be derived from the death drive hypothesis. Even if we accept Freud's hypothesis that we are born with an inherent aggressive drive and destructiveness, the problem of innate aggression can be viewed in a less pessimistic way. In fact, a further lesson about the ethics of finitude can arise from the death drive and the terminality of human life.

Some have suggested viewing aggression as neutral energy. On this view aggression is a force whose objects can be changed and direction reversed. This flexibility in direction and aim means that aggression is not necessarily harmful, nor inherently evil. Aggression can serve as neutral energy, as a resource that can be applied to ethically diverse aims. The death drive is an inherent tendency, which cannot be eliminated, but can be diverted or sublimated. So although "there is no question of getting rid entirely of human aggressive impulses," we can control aggression via sublimation and a strengthening of the superego, resulting in a tame but unhappy social order.[24]

It must also be remembered that the death drive is countered by Eros, the life drive. A more correct view of human nature, on Freud's model, is a dialectic picture of ongoing struggle between Eros and Thanatos. In *Civilization and its Discontents* Freud employs the dualistic model of the life and death drives to explain civilization. Civilization is an evolutionary process that develops through the action of Eros, striving to unite people, families and nations into one human unity. Against this synthetic drive stands the opposite destructive force, attempting to disintegrate biological, psychological, and social unities. Human development evolved out of this dialectic struggle between Eros and destruction, between affirmation and negation:

> And now, I think, the meaning of the evolution of civilization is no longer obscure to us. It must present the struggle between Eros and Death, between the instinct of life and the instinct of destruction as it works itself out in the human species. This struggle is what all life essentially consists of [...].[25]

Within the broader, dualistic picture the death drive can be seen as productive, perhaps even necessary to the development of human culture and society. But the civilizatory process does not go hand in hand with the achievement of happiness. Freud has already concluded that violence and aggression cannot be extirpated from human existence, surely not without a price. The idea that people can be totally satisfied and thus released from the need for violence is a naïve illusion for Freud. So human aggression is innate, but nonetheless not necessarily negative and definitely not uncontrollable. The first step is to acknowledge its presence in life, in human behaviour and psychic processes, and then to see whether the destructive outlet of the death drive can be sublimated or transformed into a neutral or even a positive outlet. So, for example, masochism could be externalized and turned into aggression directed at an external object, which could in turn promote the survival or enjoyment of the organism. Freud's crucial step is to try and overcome the resistance to acknowledging the fact that we contain aggressive tendencies. The interpretation of this assumption is what will actually give content to Freud's claims, as the question of how to handle our aggression is the one that has practical implications, on both a clinical and a social-political level. In this sense the ethical question is not whether aggression can be abolished from the human psyche, but rather how this aggression can be channelled to non-destructive activities and turned into a positive energy source. On this reading, the thesis of inherent aggression does not necessarily lead to ethical determinism.

But this view has several severe flaws. Firstly, it overlooks the deeply negative nature of the death drive, as well as the high toll taken by sublimation. Secondly, the idea of neutral energy is already captured in Freud's notion of libido, which is very different from the death drive, and this view does not explain how two, very different, concepts could be applied to the same idea. Finally, the description of aggression as negative energy fails to account fully for the idea of the death drive *qua* death drive. It is a drive towards annihilation, death, zero excitation and self-destruction. It is not simply an aggressive tendency, or an instinctual source of excitation. It is a force that is diametrically opposed to life, albeit active within it. Recall that Freud was trying to explain two tendencies in his notion of the death drive: aggression and Nirvana, striving towards complete rest. The view described above completely overlooks the Nirvana principle, so central to Freud's drive theory. For these reasons I believe that viewing the death drive simply as negative energy, or aggression, is a partial, and therefore inappropriate, understanding of the death drive. In what follows I should like to provide a more complete account of the death drive, emphasizing death and finitude, rather than aggression.

The Ethics of Finitude

Given the full meaning of the death drive as both aggression and striving towards complete rest, I suggest re-interpreting its ethical dimension as expressing the finiteness of life. The death drive marks the essentially finite nature of human life. I believe that Freud gave the death drive its name not merely to express the idea of innate aggression. Deeper significance lies in the name: the *death* drive. Ultimately it captures the idea of a force negating life, of the terminality of life. The death drive expresses the essential trajectory of life, leading it towards its end. We all owe nature a death, Freud wrote. The death drive offers an understanding of this succinct statement. By seeking a fuller meaning for the death drive, a fuller meaning of life will arise. By thinking through the meaning of our finitude we can find within it an ethical imperative, which, in turn, provides an ethical reading of the death drive.[26] In this reading, supported by the arguments of *Beyond the Pleasure Principle* discussed above, life and death are not symmetrical and opposing forces, but rather life is subjected to death, finitude and mortality. Life is death-bound, and this predicament is captured by the prominent role of death in life. Understanding life demands first and foremost an understanding of death or of life as bound by death.

The ethical significance Freud gave death is stated in his 1915 essay *Thoughts for the Times on War and Death*: "If you want to endure life, prepare yourself for death."[27] How should we understand this statement? What death should we prepare for? And how will preparing for death help us endure life? Laplanche reads Freud here as calling us to prepare for the death of another. He bases this claim on Freud's treatment of death in *Negation*, where he says that the only death our unconscious can acknowledge is the death of another person. The unconscious is structurally barred from knowing its own death, annihilation or negation. So any unconscious attitude towards death must be an attitude towards the death of another.[28] As Deleuze says: "Freud supposes the unconscious to be ignorant of three important things: Death, Time and No".[29] Thus Laplanche reads Freud's call to prepare for death as the call to prepare for the death of another, or in other words, to be ready for the possibility of loss and mourning, for disappointment and failure. The death drive is not only the final fact of our mortality, our ceasing to exist, but the many forms of loss and transience experienced *within* life. Laplanche reads a pessimistic message in Freud:

> If a certain ethic in relation to death might be evolved from the Freudian attitude, it would be in the sense of a distrust concerning every form of enthusiasm, be that of *Amor Fati*, and of a lucidity that does not hide the irreducible meshing of my death with that of the other.[30]

I take the 'irreducible meshing' of my death with the death of another to mean that the only way we can grasp our own mortality is through an ambivalent identification with a loved person, whose death we both fear and desire. This ambivalence is most prominent in mourning, where the loss is taken to be both a punishment and a secret wish fulfilled. Our only unconscious experience of death is the experience of the death of another, manifesting itself in loss and mourning. Laplanche thinks that we can only prepare for our own death (denied by the unconscious) by preparing for the death of another. In other words, preparing for death is acknowledging that all things in life are transient and susceptible to loss.

This account is no doubt interesting and faithful to Freudian thought. But I think Laplanche places too much weight on our inability to understand our own death. Let us bracket the Freudian ideas about the unconscious lacking negation, and specifically the concept of its own annihilation, and look at the Freudian imperative from a broader point of view. Do we really live as if we were immortal? Are we really incapable of understanding ourselves as temporally finite? What I would like to suggest is that in particular situations, namely ones of serious illness, the general rule Freud stipulates does not apply and we become acutely sensitive to our finitude, attuned to our impending mortality. While healthy we may be able to repress the thought of our mortality and put our finitude out of our minds. But when we become ill, the legitimating power of the rationalisation process ('everyone dies at the end, but not now, not me') disappears and we are called upon to confront our own unique dying. Evidence for the depth and sincerity of this confrontation can be found in accounts of the terminally ill, as well as in the denial with which these accounts are often met.

What does it mean to have an existence confined and constricted by nature and drives, but which also acknowledges the ethical sphere as contained within nature, and as open to many possible interpretations? This brings forth what Adam Phillips calls 'the death of immortality', or in other words, the death of the fantasy of permanence and eternity, giving up the idea of an absolute. The Freudian world view of secular immanence acknowledges the death of immortality and works within the confines of that knowledge: "We are not merely trapped in what they call nature: we are also released into it".[31] And once released, it is up to us to decide in which way to shape our life, how to live and tell it. What seems like the confinement of the human by nature does not arrest our existence, but rather provides us with a necessary basis from which we can choose how to live.

Embracing this position means realising the limitation of the fantasy of transcendence and immortality. Only when we are "happily convinced that there is nowhere else to go," can we begin to live. "When transience is not merely an occasion for mourning, we will have inherited the earth," writes Phillips, who wishes to extract from Freud a lesson about acceptance and the realization of human limitation.[32] In this sense Freud's project involves making sense of our lives as *bound by mortality* and not as seduced by transcendence and promises of an after-life. Mortality is what makes life intelligible, as it provides us with a key to decipher the way we live. For Freud this is the starting point of life, and therefore of an ethical relation to others and to ourselves.

Freud postulates the death drive because death marks life with finitude, operates as the ultimate signifier of loss, limitation, and inability.

Death is what makes life into a constant work of mourning for all things that are transient. But this double bind of life and death does not leave life simply shadowed by death, imprinted with loss and grief. The dismay and disappointment that are a part of life do not ultimately designate it as a sad parade of loss and irony. Rather, life is ruled by nature as the source of the laws and limitations constituting our lives, the first and foremost being death. Like the rules of chess, which not only regulate the game but also constitute it, nature can be viewed as the welcome constraint that makes up the conditions of possibility for having a life at all.

In his short essay *On Transience* Freud describes the impasse between himself and his companion, a young poet, taking place during a stroll in the Dolomite Mountains. The young poet is saddened by the transient nature of all things beautiful, and experiences the worthlessness of "all that he would otherwise have loved and admired," but which he now sees as "shorn of its worth by the transience which was its doom." Freud, on the other hand, claims that "Transience value is scarcity value in time. Limitation in the possibility of an enjoyment raises the value of the enjoyment."[33] As Phillips puts it, for Freud "it is impermanence that confers value; it is the fact of death, of the prodigal forms of transience, that creates pleasure." Moreover, death as the extreme and ultimate form of loss and transience is what "makes life loveable; it is the passing of things that is the source of our happiness."[34]

This attitude is clearest in the case of mourning, a process of coming to terms with loss, in which mourning the death of a loved one is the epitome of irrevocable loss. Freud uses mourning to make a broader point about loss and disappointment. He suggests incorporating loss and mourning into our lives in a way that will help us understand life as a holistic experience that is not burdened with disappointment and grief, but rather takes these as a starting point. But mourning is not just mourning for our loss of others. We can also mourn for ourselves. Again, the experience of illness seems to be a case in point. When health, physical and mental abilities and expectations are lost, a process of grieving ensues which is most similar to other types of mourning. The loss of health and ability, the loss of a future and the loss of opportunities are as big a loss as the paradigmatic case of mourning, the loss of a loved one. More attention should be paid to these types of loss and mourning, as they are more significant as preparation for our own death and as teaching us a lesson about our finitude, both temporal finitude and finitude of possibility.

But is not seeing existence as confined by disappointment and grief simply pessimism? With the notion of the death drive, and in his discussions of mourning and melancholia, of transience and loss, Freud defines human existence as mortal and fragile. He describes it thus not because of his pessimism but because he thinks that overlooking these experiences is a mis-description of human psychology and life. What is painful, he says, is nonetheless true. This worldview works within the immanent confines of the human, while finding a positive meaning to this confinement. "A flower that blossoms only for a single night does not seem to us on that account less lovely."[35]

Through the death drive Freud expresses a sentiment both sober and deeply sympathetic to the hardship of enduring modern life, disenchanted and free from the idols of permanence and eternity. We must acknowledge that everything we achieve may be lost; everything gained may be taken away. In our refusal to acknowledge this we are, as Freud says, "living psychologically beyond our means," i.e. demanding more out of life than it could possibly offer.[36] Understanding life as transient and fallible is not necessarily pessimistic, nor need it stop at that. Rather, says Freud, acknowledging finitude can actually have a positive function on life by making life more bearable, and "to tolerate life remains, after all, the first duty of all living beings."[37]

Tolerance here does not denote mere bare endurance, but the art of adjusting, of affirming the total complexity of life, of accepting the easy and the pleasant with the difficult and the dark. The ethical imperative inscribed in the death drive is one of tolerance, patience, and acceptance. These are not to be confused with resignation, cynicism or despair. The ethical imperative is to learn the lesson of ambivalence, that life consists of fulfilment and disappointment, and that the two are inseparable. Striving towards absolute happiness creates only frustration, as it cannot be achieved within this ambivalent worldview. But nor should we give up the idea of happiness; rather we should use the ethical imperative to delimit what is achievable within a human life.

According to Freud, once we make room for death, loss and contingency, we can start shaping our lives from a realistic, modest, achievable standpoint. Phillips adds that if we give up the ideals we measure our failures against, if we give up the idea of perfect happiness, we need no longer deem ourselves constant and necessary failures. That with which we must live – mortality, suffering and death – can be a point of departure for a self-conception that is not burdened *a priori* with guilt, shame and sin. Relinquishing the ideal of perfection opens up a creative space for human attempts and errors, for play and imagination, for quaint forms of satisfaction, and therefore gives us hope. Exchanging our perfectionist ideals for ideas of attainability means pursuing life in a way that is no less hopeful.[38]

The notion of the death drive is usually read as an affirmation of a thesis of innate evil. But it can be read not as a simple message of despair, but as a new way to formulate the ethics of finitude. Instead of taking death as a limitation, we can use it productively to understand life as a source of limitation but also of joy. Freud saw the way in which love and hate, life and death, Eros and Thanatos, link together making love, joy and beauty, contain transience. Positive emotions and experiences can be seen as intimating mortality, revealing a truth about life that is also a truth about death.

The superego, or conscience, is an internalized death drive, resulting in guilt and self-persecution (masochism) on the one hand, but serving as the source of ethics on the other:

> Ethics is thus to be regarded as a therapeutic attempt – as an endeavour to achieve, by means of a command of the superego, something which has so far not been achieved by any other cultural activities.[39]

Ethics, according to Freud, is an attempt to conquer human destructiveness and aggression by attaining control of the superego. This turns ethics into a work of sublimation and self-control, but moreover into a therapeutic attempt to heal humanity of one form of suffering. Once we understand the death drive as creating and enabling such an ethical dimension of human existence, rather than simply crippling and limiting it, we can begin to see how it connects desire and restraint, instinct and reason, nature and moral law. In response to the question 'why war?' Freud was correct in saying that war arises as a result of the death drive, which makes human nature cruel and aggressive. But if we stop here we miss the crucial link between ethics and the death drive, or in other words, the productive dimension of death.

Notes

[1] Sigmund Freud, *The Standard Edition of Sigmund Freud's Complete Works*, translated under the general editorship of James Strachey, London, 1953-1974, vol. 22:211; *Freud Studienausgabe*, Frankfurt am Main, S. Fischer Verlag, 1972, vol. 9:282-283 (hereafter SE and FS, followed by volume and page numbers).
[2] SE 19:42-43; FS 3:309.

[3] SE 22:77.
[4] Havi Carel, *Life and Death in Freud and Heidegger*, New York, Rodopi, 2006.
[5] Ibid.
[6] K.R. Eissler "Death Drive, Ambivalence, and Narcissism", *The Psychoanalytic Study of the Child*, vol.26, p.26, 1971.
[7] Ernest Jones, *Sigmund Freud, Life and Work*, vol. 3, London, Hogarth Press, 1957, p.287.
[8] John Friedman, "Freud's Todestrieb: An Introduction, Part I", *International Review of Psychoanalysis*, vol.19, 1992, p.189.
[9] SE 21:119-120; FS 9:247-248.
[10] SE 21:119-120; FS 9:247-248.
[11] SE 21:119-20; FS 9:247-8.
[12] SE 18:7, FS 3:215 and SE 19:159, FS 3:341.
[13] SE 21:64, FS 9:193 and SE 19:12, FS 3:275.
[14] SE 4:122.
[15] SE 18:23; FS 3:232.
[16] SE 18:36; FS 3:246.
[17] SE 18:38; FS 3:248.
[18] SE 18:38; FS 3:248.
[19] John Friedman, "Freud's Todestrieb: An Introduction, Part I", *International Review of Psychoanalysis*, vol.19, 1992, p.194.
[20] SE 19:40-41; FS 3:308.
[21] SE 22:211; FS 9:282.
[22] Jean Laplanche and JB Pontalis, *The Language of Psychoanalysis*, trans. D. Nicholson-Smith, New York, W.W. Norton, 1973, p.17.
[23] Ibid.
[24] SE 22:212; FS 9:283.
[25] SE 21:122; FS 9:249.
[26] Jean Laplanche, *Life and Death in Psychoanalysis*, trans. J. Mehlman, Baltimore, Johns Hopkins University Press, 1976, p.6.
[27] SE 14:300; FS 9:60.
[28] Freud made this point in his short essay *Negation*, SE 19:233-239; *Die Verneinung* FS III:371-378.
[29] Gilles Deleuze, *Difference and Repetition*, trans. Patton Paul, Columbia University Press, New York, 1994, p.114.
[30] Laplanche, Life and Death in Psychoanalysis, p.6.
[31] Adam Phillips, *Darwin's Worms*, Faber and Faber, London, 1999, p.12.
[32] Ibid.
[33] SE 14:306; GS 11:292.

[34] Phillips, *Darwin's Worms*, p.26.
[35] SE 14:306; GS 11:292.
[36] SE 14:299; FS 9:59.
[37] SE 14:300; FS 9:60.
[38] Phillips, *Darwin's Worms*, p.115ff.
[39] SE 21:142; FS 9:267.

Notes on Contributors

Christopher T. Burris and John K. Rempel are Associate Professors of Psychology at St. Jerome's University, Waterloo, Ontario, Canada. Thanks to Amber-Dawn Scott for her assistance with data coding, and to Katrina Moore, Armand Munteanu, and Geoff Navara for their comments and/or technical assistance.

Havi Hannah Carel is a Senior Lecturer in Philosophy at the Faculty of Humanities, Languages and Social Science, UWE Bristol. She is the author of *Life and Death in Freud and Heidegger* (Rodopi, NY: 2006) and the co-editor of *What Philosophy Is* (Continuum, London: 2003). Her current research focuses on the phenomenology of illness and disability. Email: havi.carel@uwe.ac.uk

Alejandro Cervantes-Carson is Associate Professor of Sociology at the University of Mary Washington. He is currently working in becoming an independent scholar. His research and writing are situated at the intersection of Political Sociology, the Sociology of Intimacy, and Cultural Sociology. Involved in two long term research projects ("The Embodiment of the Political" and "Sexuality, Human Rights, and Citizenship"), he is currently writing a book on sexual rights and the decentring of heterosexuality, and designing a book project based on the work presented here.

Wayne Cristaudo is Associate Professor of European Studies at the University of Hong Kong. Since 2005 he has served as Coordinator of the University's European Studies Programme. Professor Cristaudo can be contacted at: cristaud@hkucc.hku.hk

Roger Davis is an instructor in English Literature at Grant MacEwan College in Edmonton, Alberta, Canada. His literary interests include Contemporary Poetics and Poetry, Literary Theory, Canadian Literature and Popular Culture.

Graeme Goldsworthy is a former British Army Officer who has been mine clearing and co-ordinating mine action programmes in Southeast Asia, Africa and Central America since 1993. He is a graduate of the Department of Peace Studies at the University of Bradford in the United Kingdom and currently a Senior Research Fellow at Harvard University.

Sarah Dalal Goode is a lecturer in Social Care and Convener of the Research and Policy Centre for the Study of Faith and Wellbeing in Communities at the University of Winchester, Hampshire, United Kingdom. Sarah is an occupational therapist and a sociologist of health and wellbeing. Her doctoral research at the University of Warwick was on the everyday experiences of drug and alcohol-dependent mothers. She has published in the areas of substance misuse, research methodology, the social construction of adult-child sexual contact and child protection issues.

Anders Johansson is a researcher and editor in the faculty of Literature at the University of Goteburg, Sweden. His research interests include Adorno, Deleuze, Borges, the notion of the essay as theoretical strategy, and the future of the humanities.

Nancy Billias is Assistant Professor, Chair of the Department of Philosophy, and Co-ordinator of Leadership Studies at Saint Joseph College, West Hartford, Connecticut, USA. She is also a psychoanalytic psychotherapist. Her primary research interest is the intersection of psychoanalytic theory and Continental philosophy in the area of ethics.

Stephen Morris is an independent scholar living in New York. He holds degrees from Yale, St. Vladimirs Seminary (Crestwood, New York), and Hunter (New York City) and has studied with J. Pelican, J. Meyendorff, A. Schmemann, and J. Boswell. He is on the Executive Advisory Board for Inter-Disciplinary.Net and is a former Eastern Orthodox Chaplain at Columbia University. Specializing in early-medieval religious history and thought, his work includes the oft ignored Byzantine and Slavic worlds.

Charles Nuckolls is associate professor of anthropology at Emory University. The author of *The Cultural Dialectics of Knowledge and Desire*, published by the University of Wisconsin Press, he is also the editor of The Cultural Construction of Diagnostic Categories: The Case of American Psychiatry and Siblings in South Asia: Brothers and Sisters in Cultural Context.

William Andrew Myers is professor of philosophy at the College of St. Catherine in St. Paul, Minnesota, USA. He may be reached at wamyers@stkate.edu.

Scott M. Powers is assistant professor of French at the University of Mary Washington, in Fredericksburg Virginia, USA.

Lee Quinby is the author of three books, editor of two collections, and holds the Zicklin Chair in the Honors Academy at Brooklyn College and the Harter Chair in Humanities at Hobart and William Smith Colleges.